# Jeep, Da Chrysler Differentials

## How to Rebuild & Upgrade the Chrysler 8¼, 8¾, Dana 44 & 60, & AMC 20

### Larry Shepard

**CarTech®**

# CarTech®

CarTech®, Inc.
39966 Grand Avenue
North Branch, MN 55056
Phone: 651-277-1200 or 800-551-4754
Fax: 651-277-1203
www.cartechbooks.com

Edit by Paul Johnson
Layout by Monica Seiberlich

ISBN 978-1-61325-049-5
Item No. SA253

Library of Congress Cataloging-in-Publication Data

Shepard, Larry.
  Jeep, Dana & Chrysler differentials : how to rebuild the 8¼, 8¾, Dana 44 & 60 & AMC 20 / by Larry Shepard.
    p. cm.
  ISBN 978-1-61325-049-5
  1. Jeep automobile–Differentials–Maintenance and repair–Handbooks, manuals, etc. 2. Dana Corporation. 3. Chrysler automobile–Differentials–Maintenance and repair–Handbooks, manuals, etc. 4. Automobiles–Differentials–Maintenance and repair–Handbooks, manuals, etc. I. Title.

  TL215.J44S54 2013
  629.2'45–dc23

  2012045775

Printed in China
10 9 8 7 6 5 4 3 2 1

## Title Page:

*Many carrier-tube axle designs use C-clips to retain the axles into the housing. The C-clip fits over a groove cut in the end of each axle and fits inside a recess cut in the side gear. You can see the C-clip just above the cross-shaft in the center of this photo.*

## Back Cover Photos

### Top Left:

*The casting number on the Chrysler 8¾-inch axle is located on the left side, below the pinion centerline. Here, the yoke is to the far left and the 7-digit casting number is at the bottom left. Typically only the last three digits are used for identification, 489 in this case. This is also a 742 case and a 741 small-stem case. The 741 case is the weakest and parts for it are very limited so you should generally upgrade to one of the other two assemblies.*

### Top Right:

*Attach a dial indicator to the carrier flange so the pointer of the indicator is squarely contacting one ring-gear tooth face on the drive side. A gear tooth has a top and bottom, which are along for the ride. The drive side is the front face of the tooth and the coast side is the back side of the tooth. Most wear occurs on the drive side. Use a dial indicator with a magnetic base before checking the ring gear wear pattern.*

### Middle Left:

*Once the rear cover has been removed, you can check the differential to see if it is an open or limited-slip style. This is an open differential; there are no C-clips. The main cap is loose in preparation for removing the ring gear and differential assembly.*

### Middle Right:

*Use a wrench or socket and ratchet to remove both differential bearing adjuster lock screws and locks (one per cap) and center between the two main cap bolts (top and bottom).*

### Bottom Left:

*Many limited-slip differentials use a spring-and-plate mechanism to apply the frictional pressure in the unit. These springs and plate can be seen in the window and the case is a one-piece unit. A Yukon unit is shown.*

### Bottom Right:

*Remove the pinion shafts and the pinion gears. Be careful that the four pinions mounted on the pinion shafts do not fall off.*

OVERSEAS DISTRIBUTION BY:

PGUK
63 Hatton Garden
London EC1N 8LE, England
Phone: 020 7061 1980 • Fax: 020 7242 3725

Renniks Publications Ltd.
3/37-39 Green Street
Banksmeadow, NSW 2109, Australia
Phone: 2 9695 7055 • Fax: 2 9695 7355

# CONTENTS

# ACKNOWLEDGMENTS

The photography and writing required to create a book is a big project and not something that happens overnight. This rear axle book project was even more difficult because of the complexity of four completely different axles to discuss. The research led in many directions, some related and some independent. This book has its roots in the Chrysler Institute of Engineering (CIE), the Chrysler Drag Racing seminars, and the various tech support lines that have helped customers solve problems. There are many racers and chassis shops that have contributed to these organizations over the past forty-five years.

On rear axles, the biggest help came from the many manufacturers that participate at race track events and shows such as SEMA and PRI. Representatives are always willing to answer questions and show the latest hardware. Manufacturers at custom shows, such as Autorama, and car events like the Woodward Cruise, were also very helpful. I thank all of these people for their time and patience.

I extend a very special thanks to John Ziejka of Warren Gear and Axle for all the effort and assistance that he has given me on this project.

Perhaps most of all, I all owe a great deal of thanks to my editor, Paul Johnson, who made all of this stuff fit into a book and be readable.

Finally, a special thanks to my wife, Linda, for keeping our household going and her patience with the ever-mounting piles of research material, special tools, and tons of photographs.

# INTRODUCTION

Axles and differentials are often discussed as just axles, or rear ends. However, axles are more than just rear axles because the same basic axle is often used in the front of four-wheel-drive (4WD) vehicles. And then there are the other axle-related acronyms like AWD (all-wheel-drive), 2WD (two-wheel-drive), RWD (rear-wheel-drive), and FWD (front-wheel-drive). Note that RWD can also be 2WD.

Passenger cars are generally pretty straightforward and use either FWD or RWD. Pickup trucks generally fall into two general categories: RWD and 4WD. Jeeps tend to have the most options such as RWD, 4WD, and AWD.

In this book I focus on the basic RWD axle package, which you might call the traditional layout. These RWD axles are often used in the front of 4WD Jeeps and trucks.

In the basic automotive application, the transmission is attached to the engine and the axle is located at the rear. If the transmission is pushed rearward, it merges into the rear axle. These units are called transaxles. They combine the functions of the transmission and axle. They are commonly used in mid-engine cars and also cars that have a rear-engine position. Transaxles are also used in all FWD cars. In this book, I focus on RWD axles, realizing that some versions are also used in the front location on 4WD models. If this were an engine rebuild book, you would expect wear or breakage to be the main reasons you need to rebuild your engine. Rear axles do wear out and can be broken but the most common reason for changing the rear axle is to change the axle ratio. You aren't likely to change the engine because of the axle ratio but you may change the axle ratio because of the engine.

Engine performance improvements are a major reason to change the axle ratio. Some other reasons for axle rebuilds are on-road increased acceleration, more torque for off-road applications, bigger tires, and noisy, worn-out, and broken differentials. Today you have to add on-road-improved fuel economy. In the past, torque and acceleration selection went in the opposite direction from better fuel economy but today there are more options, such as 4- and 8-speed automatic transmissions or 6-speed manual transmissions with more speeds and overdrive ratios that allow both acceleration and fuel economy in the same vehicle.

Engine performance improvements can be related to engine displacement, horsepower output, RPM range and peaking speeds, and torque. But automatic or manual transmissions and torque converter/clutch selections should also be considered. More engine performance usually means that you want more gear. "More gear" means a bigger axle ratio and this means that the ratio is a larger number (4.0 versus 3.0). In commonly used axle ratio terms, the axle ratio is like the transmission ratio: The high gear is a low number, such as 1.00, and low gear is a large number, such as a 2.50 to 3.00.

In axle ratios, it has always been popular to swap a 3.0 ratio for a 4.0 ratio. The reverse approach, replacing a 4.0 with a 3.0, is for improved fuel economy. While this hasn't caught on yet, installing some form of overdrive, such as a .7 ratio, is becoming more popular. Note that a 4.10 rear axle ratio used with a .7 overdrive ratio yields a final drive ratio of 2.87 (4.10 x .7 = 2.87).

In the past, performance enthusiasts have tended to over-recommend one axle, whether it was a generic 9- or a 9¾-inch. In the late 1960s and through most of the 1970s, the 9¾-inch Dana 60 was the answer for everything. Aftermarket manufacturers have slowly introduced improved technology and a vast array of axle parts that offer upgrades over the basic hardware, which allows for many solutions to problems; not just a 9¾-inch axle swap, but that is still an option.

This book focuses on axle selection, not the how-to design aspects and the high-powered math that goes with it. Axle selection math is easy but the number of options available is making it much more difficult.

Rear axle rebuilds can be done in the car. If the axle is removed for rebuilding, it can cause some confusion relating to orienation (left and right). To solve this problem, I define the left side of the axle as the driver's side (as installed in the vehicle) and the right side as the passenger's side.

As with an engine project, it is a very good idea to use an assembly notebook for your axle rebuild. Use this notebook to record everything: casting numbers (if used), part numbers, suppliers, measurements, and model build dates if available. Also record all shim sizes, thicknesses, locations, and conditions (color) of origi-nals. This is the digital age so storing digital photos in the notebook keeps all your important information in one spot. Digital photos are helpful if there are worn or damaged parts but they can also be used for recording the final contact pattern on the gear teeth.

Not all manufacturers make parts for all axles but all axles are currently covered. For example, Chrysler production axles (the 8¾-inch in this case) used ratios of 3.55 and 3.91 but did not offer a 3.73, while several aftermarket manufac-turers offer all three ratios.

# REAR AXLE BASICS

Like the transmission and driveshaft, the rear axle is a key part of the vehicle's drivetrain. It has the basic job of using engine's output to move the vehicle. The rear axle is the rearmost part of the drivetrain. The main parts of the rear axle are the housing, two axle shafts, ring and pinion, yoke, and differential.

Many different rear axles have been used in various production cars and trucks. This book covers the axles used in

Chrysler, American Motors (AMC), and Jeep vehicles. This isn't as easy as it may sound because of the amount of overlap in the actual usage of specific axles in production vehicles. Chrysler bought AMC/Jeep in 1986, so there are Jeep vehicles with basic Chrysler axles, and both Chrysler and Jeep vehicles used Dana/Spicer rear axles in many applications.

The main focus of this book is rear-wheel-drive (RWD) cars and trucks.

Both Jeeps and Dodge trucks have four-wheel-drive (4WD) drivetrains that use special axles in the front, but these units are closely related to similar versions at the rear and can be rebuilt using the same steps.

A few years ago, the aftermarket began making special axle ratios—ratios with larger numbers used in applications such as drag racing. In production vehicles, only a few ratios were offered, and differential options were very limited. The aftermarket responded by offering many different ratios and several differential options. The aftermarket now makes all major components for most of the rear axles in this book, including actual housings.

## Rear Axle Operation

In the typical RWD vehicle, the rear axle is considered a solid axle. Only a few American-made cars use an independent rear based on an independent rear suspension (IRS). There are also cars, such as the Prowler, that use a rear transaxle, which combines the transmission and axle functions. The typical front-wheel-drive (FWD) vehicle also uses a transaxle. This book focuses on the basic solid rear axle.

*The typical rear-wheel-drive rear axle installation is crowded in the area with the fuel system and exhaust system, so there is little spare room. This 9¾-inch Dana 60 is a carrier-tube design, so the pinion comes out the back. The axle cover has 10 bolts and a unique shape. The left and right tubes are pressed into the center carrier. On the far side here you can see the leaf-spring rear suspension and its two U-bolts holding the axle to the suspension. The wheel and drum brake assembly are outboard of the suspension.*

*The ring gear is bolted to the differential and typically has about 40 teeth. The pinion is inside the case (to the right) and has around 12 teeth. The yoke (far right) is splined onto the end of the pinion. This carrier housing assembly for an 8¾-inch unit (or out-the-front) design bolts to the front of the banjo-design axle housing.*

### Torque Direction

The basic function of the rear axle is to change the direction of the engine/ transmission output. The typical engine produces torque and it rotates around the front-to-rear centerline of the vehicle. The rear axle changes the direction of this torque rotation by 90 degrees and sends this torque to both drive wheels of the vehicle, so it can be used to move the vehicle. It also provides a speed change or gear reduction, so that the engine speed, in RPM can be matched to the designed or usable vehicle speed in MPH.

### Gear Ratio

The basic definition of the gear ratio is the number of times the driveshaft turns for one full revolution of the wheel/tire. Production ratios range from 2.71 to 3.91:1 (as high as 2.20), while performance ratios often are 3.55 to 4.86:1, or higher (5.12 and up) in some cases.

The gear ratio can also be calculated by dividing the number of teeth on the ring gear by the number of teeth on the drive pinion. Highway vehicles prefer low numerical ratios such as 2.76 or 2.91:1, while performance vehicles prefer lower numerical ratios such 3.91 or 4.10:1, and racing vehicles like even lower ratios such as 4.56 or 4.86:1.

### Differential

The differential is located in the center of the rear axle housing. The ring gear bolts to the differential flange and mounts inside the housing. The ends of the axle shafts are splined into side gears located inside the differential. Early in automobile development, engineers found that the two rear wheels had to be allowed to rotate at different speeds so the vehicle could turn, resulting in the open differential. In a turn, the outside wheel rotates faster than the inside wheel. The open differential is by far the most common type of differential used in production cars and trucks. Open differentials allow power to be applied to one wheel and the other to spin freely (in poor traction conditions).

This isn't the most effective manner to apply torque to the pavement, particularly for high-performance applications. Therefore, manufacturers developed limited-slip differentials. Chrysler labeled its version as the Sure-Grip. General Motors called its version the Posi-Traction. Ford named its version Traction-Lok. AMC and Dana used Trac-Loc. These limited-slip differentials allow cornering but divide the engine torque to both wheels.

In typical RWD vehicles, the width of the rear axle defines where the rear wheels are located. The actual wheel location is dictated by the wheel and rear

*The limited-slip differential for Dana axles holds the ring gear on the flange at the rear. Inside the case are the springs and plates that can be seen through the side window, along with the plates, discs, and gears that can't be seen. All the parts inside are assembled through the side window.*

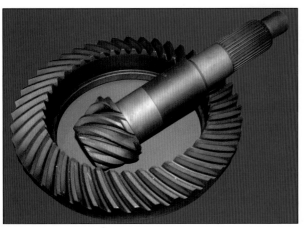

*This is a basic ring-and-pinion. The long shaft on the top is the pinion (or pinion gear) and the round part on the bottom is the ring gear.*

*A large nut (not shown) holds the splined yoke onto the rear axle's pinion. The rear universal joint fits in the machined saddles; one bearing to the right and one to the left. Two straps and bolts or two small U-bolts (not shown) retain the U-joint.*

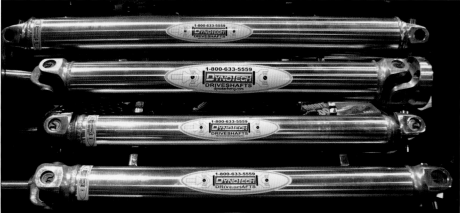

*The four driveshafts shown here are all made of aluminum. They are commonly made in 3-inch-, and 3½-inch-, and (sometimes) 4-inch-diameter tubing.*

axle specifications, such as wheel offset and axle width. The rear axle width, rear track, and other widths are related.

The manufacturer, such as AMC, Chrysler, or Dana makes up the first part of a differential's name. The number part of the name indicates diameter of the ring gear. Chrysler axle names are a direct reference to the sizes of 7¼-, 8¼-, and 8¾-inch differentials. Dana axle names are not so simple, such as Dana 44 (8½ inches) and Dana 60 (9¾ inches).

The basic theory is that the larger the ring gear, the more load capacity the axle has. While most of us might think this capacity is horsepower, it is actually torque. Therefore, big-cubic-inch engines that produce more torque put greater demands on differentials than high-horsepower outputs.

### Driveshaft

The driveshaft sends the engine torque through the yoke to the rear axle pinion. The yoke is splined onto the pinion and held on by a large nut.

The rear universal joint fits into the saddle machined into the yoke. Two

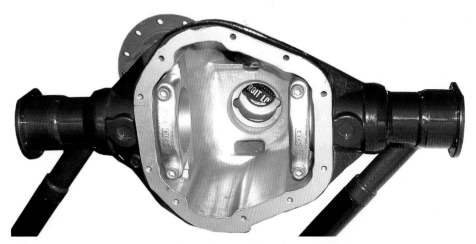

*This is a rear view of a bare carrier-tube axle. Note the number of cover-attaching bolts (10 are shown) and the shape of the cover gasket surface (non-symmetrical). These two items might indicate a Dana 44 or Dana 60 axle. Although typical tubes are between 1 and 2 feet long, this axle has very short tubes, perhaps 6 inches. Aftermarket suppliers, such as Strange, Moser, or Mark Williams, make these narrowed axle housings. In the 1970s, Chrysler's Performance Parts (then Direct Connection) sold 52½- and 44½-inch Dana 60 assemblies designed for drag racing, but those units haven't been available since the early 1980s.*

*The pinion has been removed from this typical bare carrier-tube center axle housing. You must remove the pinion out the back. The end of the pinion sticks out of the center hole, and the yoke installs from the front. Here, the axle tube to the right has been installed but not the one to the left.*

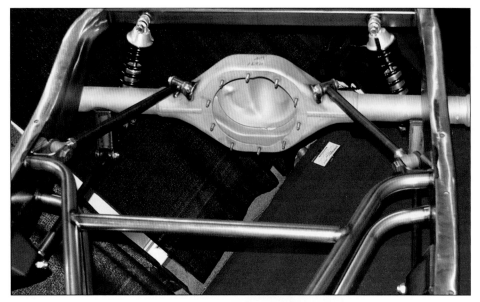

The out-the-front style of rear axles takes the complete ring-and-pinion assembly out the front, leaving the big axle housing in the vehicle. The large axle housing looks something like a banjo, which gives this group of axles its common name: banjo axle. This housing has been modified for coil-over-shock suspension behind the axle and a modified four-link rear suspension, which requires special brackets welded to the housing itself.

The end of the axle has the spring seat for the rear suspension (leaf spring in this case) and the axle shaft flange. The brake assembly bolts to the end of the axle housing but is not shown. The spring seat is welded to the axle tube or housing. If it is to be moved, cut if off and discard and use a new spring seat at the new location. Your welder will thank you. New spring seats are readily available in the aftermarket.

Fabricated axle housings have a unique look. Moser makes this version for the Chrysler 8¾-inch banjo axle. This is the rear view, since the center section goes out the front. This housing has the rear stiffener brace already incorporated.

The typical carrier-tube axle has a removable rear cover and 9, 10, or 12 attaching bolts. The tubes from the left and right sides are pressed into the center carrier and then welded. The differential is in the center and has four small gears inside (you can see three of them here).

straps retain the U-joint in the yoke and bolts on by two U-bolts with nuts on the underside.

## Rear Axle Identification

Before you start buying parts to rebuild your rear axle, identify all aspects of the axle. You obviously know your brand of vehicle, but an AMC vehicle may not have been built with an AMC 20 axle in it. It may have a Chrysler or Dana axle, or possibly another version of one of these axles. Perhaps the original axle has been modified. One of the more common Chrysler drag race modifications is changing the 4-inch bolt-circle axles/wheels to 4½-inch units on the early (1967–1973) A-Body (Dart/Valiant/Barracuda).

Once you have identified the particular axle, you can then plan your rebuild project—repair if necessary, modify if desired, or swap-in an upgrade if that is the only way to meet your requirements.

Although not previously available, the aftermarket now supports upgrading most heavy-duty axles, and you don't have to rely on finding special used parts at salvage yards.

### Pinion Removal Direction

There are two directions of pinion removal: out-the-front (OTF) and out-the-back (OTB).

In a rear axle, the front direction is toward the engine. The driveshaft connects the engine-transmission assembly to the rear axle, so the driveshaft

attaches to the axle on its front side. Axles removed toward the front have the attaching bolts on the front side. OTB axles are called drop-out axles or banjo-style axles.

Axles removed toward the rear have the bolts on the rear face that hold on a cover. OTB axles are much more common and are called carrier-tube axles.

### Rear Axle Features and Equipment

You can identify a differential by the number of bolts used to hold the center section in (or the cover on) the rear. The

most common number of bolts is 9, 10, or 12. While helpful, this is not the final answer. The shape that the bolts form or the gasket shape can also be helpful and is detailed in the chapter pertaining to each differential manufacturer. (See Chapters 4, 5, and 6.)

The most common passenger-car bolt circle is 5-on-4½ inches, or five bolts/studs equally spaced and mounted in a 4½-inch bolt circle. There are also 4- and 5-inch bolt circles, plus with four, six, and eight bolts. The wheel bolt-circle may indicate if the axle has been changed or a limited-production option was added to your vehicle. The bolt circle can help you learn whether the ends of the axles have been modified.

Determine if the location of your axle is in the rear (common) or in the front. Front axles have unique ends in order to accept steering requirements. Some service parts are unique to front-axle applications.

### Rear Axle Widths

| Category | Year/Model | Rear Track or Width (inches) |
|---|---|---|
| Small Cars | 1966 Dodge Dart | 55.6 |
| | 1967 Plymouth Valiant, Barracuda | 55.6 |
| | 1977 Jeep CJ5, CJ7 | 50.0 |
| | 1985 Jeep CJ, Scrambler | 55.1 |
| | 1967 Jeep Wrangler, Jeepster | 48.4 |
| | 1966 AMC Rambler | 55.0 |
| Mid-Size Cars | 1966–1967 Dodge Coronet | 58.5 |
| | 1967 Plymouth Belvedere, Satellite | 58.5 |
| | 1977 Dodge Aspen | 58.5 |
| | 1977 Plymouth Volare | 58.5 |
| | 1966 AMC Rebel, Marlin | 58.5 |
| | 1977 Jeep Cherokee, Wagoneer | 57.8 |
| | 1985 Jeep Cherokee | 57.0 |
| | 1966–1967 Jeep Wagoneer | 57.0 |
| | 1977 AMC Hornet, Gremlin | 57.1 |
| | 1985 AMC Eagle | 57.6 |
| | 1985 Dodge Diplomat | 59.6 |
| | 1985 Plymouth Gran Fury | 59.6 |
| | 1985 Jeep Grand Wagoneer | 57.8 |
| Large Cars | 1966–1967 Chrysler Newport | 60.7 |
| | 1977 Chrysler Newport | 63.4 |
| | 1967 Dodge Monaco | 60.7 |
| | 1967 Plymouth Fury | 60.7 |
| | 1977 Dodge Monaco, Charger | 62.0 |
| | 1977 Plymouth Fury | 62.0 |
| | 1977 AMC Matador | 60.6 |

*If you assume that the production car wheel has an offset of 1/2 inch, which is typical, then the axle width, flange-to-flange, is 1 inch greater than the rear track. For example, for a 1967 Coronet with a 58½-inch rear track, the axle assembly width would be 59½ inches. (While not listed separately, the high-performance 15 x 7.0-inch wheel had a 1/4-inch offset, so it would have had a 59-inch rear track and the axle would have been 1/2 inch wider or 59½ inches.)*

*A differential is most commonly open, which means that one wheel can spin. A Sure-Grip differential has clutches and springs inside the case, which helps divide the engine torque between the wheels. The ring gear attaches to the flange (at the left). The two side gears are just to the left and right of center. The clutches are located behind each side gear and are squeezed between the side gear and the differential housing. The springs in the center provide the pressure.*

The width of the rear axle dictates the width of the back end of the vehicle. The only published specification for rear axle width is the rear track. Although related, the track is actually not the width of the axle housing.

The chart on page 11 lists the published rear track widths on selected models. Several random model years and body sizes were chosen for reference.

### Casting Number

The casting number has seven digits. On 8¾ axles, it is located on the left side of the center housing, parallel to the pinion. On the 8¼- and 9¼-inch carrier-tube axles, it is located on the bottom of the carrier. The Dana axles use a stamped number on the rear-machined face, toward the right side.

*Never trust an add-on tag. Rotate the yoke or driveshaft enough times for one full revolution of the wheel(s). For cars equipped with Sure-Grip, both wheels must be off the ground. Use chalk to mark both wheel/tire and driveshaft so you can see the rotation of the wheel/tire. Once you start to disassemble the rear axle and have access to the actual ring-and-pinion, count the number of teeth so you can find the exact ratio. Here, there are around 40 on the ring gear and 12 on the pinion. Using the formula (40 ÷ 12), you get a ratio of 3.33:1.*

### Ratio Tag

Most production axles are fitted with a ratio tag on one of the attaching bolts when first manufactured. This tag is typically made of aluminum or steel and has the actual gear ratio, such as 3.55:1, stamped into it. These tags tend to get lost over time, usually removed and discarded during a rebuild. In some cases, the ratio is changed and the same tag is left on. Always check to see if you have one and record the number.

*The casting number on the Chrysler 8¾-inch axle is located on the driver's side, below the pinion centerline. Here, the yoke is to the far left and the seven-digit casting number is on the bottom left side.*

*Typically only the last three digits are used for identification, 489 in this example. This is also a 742 case and a 741 small-stem case. The 741 case is the weakest and parts for it are very limited so you should generally upgrade to one of the other two assemblies.*

## Limited-Slip

The type of differential is only spelled out on the ratio tag or separate tag if a Sure-Grip is used. The letters "SG" are also on a tag and is also easily lost.

## Length

The length of the axle housing is not a consideration unless you are swapping axles. The axle's yoke distance ahead of the axle/wheel centerline factors directly into the length of the driveshaft. While it is not important for identification, it is very important in planning driveshaft selection.

## Rear Axle Specifications and Selection

When rebuilding any axle, the biggest decision is to determine the actual gear ratio, and then select the best gear ratio for your application and vehicle. Once you know the current ratio, you can select to move up or down in gear ratio, or just replace or re-use your existing gear set. The chart "General Axle Specifications" on page 14 is very general and relates to the axles discussed in other chapters.

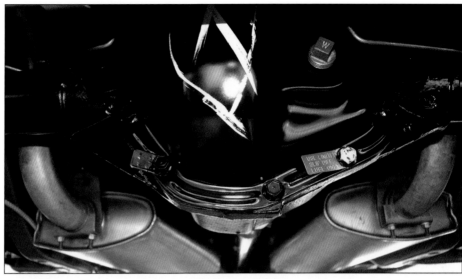

*This carrier-tube axle, 9¾-inch Dana 60 has a 10-bolt rear cover. The ratio tag is attached to one of the lower cover attaching bolts, at about the 7 o'clock position. The other tag, at the 4 o'clock position, specifies Sure-Grip oil only. In contrast, the 8¾-inch units are bolted in from the front side and typically have the tag on one of the upper bolts.*

### Axle Length in Side View

| Axle | Length (inches) |
| --- | --- |
| Chrysler 7¼ | 10.09 |
| Chrysler 8¼ | 11.69 |
| Chrysler 9¼ | 11.69 |
| Chrysler 8¾ | 12.35 |
| Dana 60 or 9¾ | 13.47 |

*Axle lengths are listed in this chart and graphically in the drawing (below left). It's shown as dimension "A" and measured from the centerline of the yoke to the centerline of the axle shafts.*

### Gear Ratio

The bottom chart on page 14 uses tire diameter and gear ratio variables to estimate vehicle speed in MPH based on 3,000 rpm.

### Overdrive Add-on

Gear Vendors offers another option: add-on overdrive units. These units replace the stock extension housing and add another gear set that yields a .78:1 overdrive ratio. These units make the length of the transmission longer, so the existing driveshaft must be shortened.

## Rear Suspension

The vehicle's rear suspension bolts to the rear axle and is used to locate the axle in the vehicle. Two main types of rear suspensions are typically used—leaf spring and coil spring.

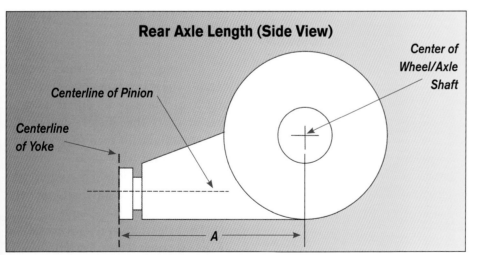

**Rear Axle Length (Side View)**

*The driveshaft is not part of the rear axle, but it bolts directly to the axle yoke. Many changes to the axle can affect the driveshaft. The length of the rear axle (dimension A) in this side view is one of those things that can cause problems if parts are being swapped. It is not a concern in the typical rebuild.*

## General Axle Specifications

| Axle | Ring Gear Diameter (inches) | Axle Type | Style | Lube Capacity (ounces) | Ratios (:1) |
|------|------|------|------|------|------|
| 8¼ | 8.250, 8.375 | Semi-floating hypoid | OTB | 70 | 2.71 to 4.56 |
| 9¼ | 9.250 | Semi-floating hypoid | OTB | 76 | 2.76 to 4.88 |
| 8¾ | 8.750 | Semi-floating hypoid | OTF | 64 | 3.55 to 5.57 |
| Dana 44 | 8.500 | Semi-floating hypoid | OTB | 60 | 3.08 to 5.89 |
| Dana 60 | 9.750 | Semi-floating hypoid | OTB | 88 | 3.54 to 5.38 |
| AMC 20 | 8.800 | Semi-floating hypoid | OTB | 76 | 3.08 to 4.88 |

*OTB = out-the-back   OTF = out-the-front*

## Rear Tire Outside Diameter (inches)

| Gear Ratio | 24 | 26 | 28 | 30 | 32 |
|------|------|------|------|------|------|
| 2.76 | 76.7 | 83.1 | 89.5 | 95.9 | 102.3 |
| 3.55 | 59.6 | 64.6 | 69.6 | 74.6 | 79.5 |
| 3.91 | 54.1 | 58.7 | 63.2 | 67.7 | 72.2 |
| 4.10 | 51.6 | 55.9 | 60.2 | 64.5 | 68.9 |
| 4.30 | 49.2 | 53.3 | 57.4 | 61.5 | 65.6 |
| 4.56 | 46.4 | 50.3 | 54.2 | 58.0 | 61.9 |
| 4.86 | 43.6 | 47.2 | 50.8 | 54.5 | 58.1 |

The equation for calculating the gear ratio based on the other parameters is:

$$GR = (RPM \times OD) \div (MPH \times 336)$$

## Rear Tire Outside Diameter (inches)

| Engine RPM | 24 | 26 | 28 | 30 | 32 |
|------|------|------|------|------|------|
| 3,000 | 1.98 | 2.15 | 2.31 | 2.48 | 2.64 |
| 4,000 | 2.64 | 2.86 | 3.08 | 3.30 | 3.52 |
| 5,000 | 3.30 | 3.58 | 3.85 | 4.13 | 4.40 |
| 6,000 | 3.98 | 4.31 | 4.64 | 4.97 | 5.30 |
| 7,000 | 4.64 | 5.02 | 5.41 | 5.79 | 6.18 |

I selected 3,000 rpm and 60 mph for these charts because these speeds are realistic for almost all street vehicles.

Very few 1950s, 1960s, 1970s, or 1980s cars used an overdrive transmission. However, today several manual and automatic transmissions do offer the overdrive feature. An overdrive gear basically changes the vehicle's final drive ratio from 1:1 to numbers such as .69:1 and .75:1. This slows the engine RPM relative to any given vehicle speed and provides better fuel economy at highway speeds.

## Effect of Overdrive Ratios on Final Drive Ratio

| Rear Axle Ratio (1:1) | .75 Overdrive Ratio | .69 Overdrive Ratio |
|------|------|------|
| 5.12 | 3.84 | 3.53 |
| 4.89 | 3.67 | 3.37 |
| 4.56 | 3.42 | 3.15 |
| 4.30 | 3.22 | 2.97 |
| 3.91 | 2.93 | 2.70 |
| 3.55 | 2.66 | 2.45 |
| 3.23 | 2.42 | 2.23 |
| 3.00 | 2.25 | 2.07 |

*This general specifications chart lists the axles being discussed and the generally available axle ratios and the amount of fluid that will be required after the axle rebuild. Note: there is only one axle shown as an OTF axle, more commonly called a banjo, which is the 8¾-inch Chrysler.*

*Lower chart: These ratios are not production ratios, but gear sets that are currently listed as available in the aftermarket. Several axles used production gear ratios of about 2.4:1. Additionally, lower gear sets (larger numbers) have been offered in the past, but do not seem to be offered currently, so they are not included.*

*Balancing the vehicle's speed against the engine's speed in revolutions per minute determines the actual gear ratio selection. The outside diameter of the tire is also part of the equation.*

*The equation for calculating the vehicle speed based on the other parameters is:*

*MPH = (RPM x OD) ÷ (GR x 336)*
*Where:*
*MPH = miles per hour, vehicle speed*
*RPM = engine revolutions per minute*
*OD = rear tire outside diameter*
*GR = rear axle gear ratio (or final drive ratio)*
*336 = constant, but assumes a manual transmission*

I have included this section because these two types of suspensions attach to the axle in different ways. The brackets that are welded to the axle are unique for each style and may vary from one body style to another. This makes the housings unique and the appearance is different, but the rebuild procedure is the same.

The axle width and track are related to the axle itself. The axle width directly correlates to the rear track since axle width is defined as the distance from axle flange to axle flange with the axle shafts installed, measuring to the wheel mounting face of each axle. Another way to view the rear track is the wheel's offset or backspacing of the wheel.

Wheel offset is defined as the distance from the center of the wheel to the mounting face. Typical production wheel offsets are 1/4, 1/2, and 0 inch. The mounting face is at the center of the wheel, halfway between each edge. For example, if you have a wheel with a 6-inch-width 0 offset, the mounting face is 3 inches from one edge and 3 inches from the other. If the offset is .500 inch,

the mounting face is 3½ inches from one edge and 2½ inches from the other. If the wheel is offset to the outside, the track is increased by 1.00 inch (2 x .500 inch) over the zero-offset number.

Another reason to be aware of width, rear track, and wheel offset is the affect that they have on tire clearance. Tire clearance issues arise from many different causes and occur in many different directions, front, back, inside, outside, and top. In some cases, wheel offset can be used to solve tire clearance problems,

and in some cases, a selected wheel and its offset can create problems. However, I do not have the space to discuss how offset and other wheel features affect handling dynamics.

Two bolts hold the pinion snubber to the top-front of the axle assembly. The assembly consists of a steel bracket with a rubber bumper on top. It is actually part of the rear suspension. It is an important part of the back end of the car in high-performance applications, especially with manual transmissions.

*The pinion snubber is bolted to the top of the axle assembly, just above the yoke (at lower right). This makes the Chrysler Dana 60 axle, as used in HP passenger cars, somewhat unique from other applications which don't use a pinion snubber (most trucks and Jeeps). Note that the square block to the right is the rubber bumper which is inserted into the bracket.*

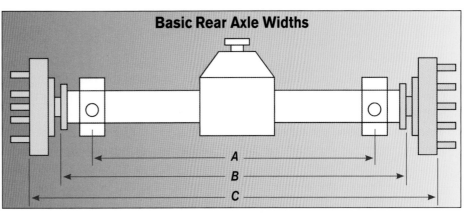

**Basic Rear Axle Widths**

*There are several important widths relative to the rear axle. Production data for axle width is very limited but the aftermarket can make almost any width. If it is a leaf-spring vehicle, dimension A is the center-to-center distance between the two spring seats or mounting pads. For performance purposes, these spring seats can be moved and new ones welded on. The small round hole in the spring seat actually locates the axle on the spring.*

*Dimension B is the actual width of the axle from flange to flange. Outside of the aftermarket, this data is rarely published. Only an axle manufacturer can change it. If it is changed, new axle shafts are required.*

*Dimension C is the width of the axle assembly from the wheel mounting face on the left to the mounting face on the right. If dimension includes the axle flange overhang and the brake assembly width. Disc brakes and drum brakes do not all have the same thickness.*

*The add-on overdrive unit is added to the rear of the standard transmission. This one (made by Gear Vendors) is added to a 3-speed Torqueflite A727 automatic transmission. Note that the speedo-cable output has been moved to the rear overdrive unit so it can read correctly. The long extension holds the overdrive unit and replaces the stock extension housing. Some newer units use shorter adapters or have less overall length.*

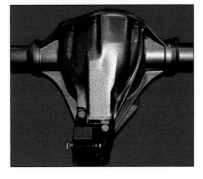

*The pinion snubber is bolted to the top of the axle assembly, just above the yoke (toward the bottom of the photo). This makes the Chrysler Dana 60 axle, as used in HP passenger cars, somewhat unique from other applications.*

# GENERAL PREPARATION

You are probably more familiar with engine-related terminology and hardware than with rear axle items. Dress-up items on an engine can be changed quickly and easily, but a rear axle rebuild is much more complicated. Similar to major engine work, the vehicle isn't going anywhere during the rebuild process. Therefore, some effort must be put into the preparation process. Many of the required tools are unique and most of the terms and technology are not used in other areas of the vehicle.

## Inspection

Perhaps the most important question in a rear axle project is: Why change it? If it's broken and/or worn-out, it must be rebuilt. But on the other hand, it is more likely that you want to change the ratio. Rear axle ratio is very important to the vehicle's overall performance, so you could be looking for increased torque or acceleration. On the other side of the performance curve is trying to gain fuel economy, lessen noise during normal driving cycles, or even lessen wear on the engine at highway speeds. These are all good reasons to change the ratio. However, if you are rebuilding the rear axle

and not changing the ratio or ring-and-pinion, you should not remove the ring from the differential.

Chapter 1 discussed general steps involved in identifying the rear axle. Even when you know what you have, the actual ratio can be tricky. The common approach is to find the ratio tag on one of the cover/housing bolts. In many cases, this tag is missing. If the ratio was ever changed at an earlier time, the tag

is probably incorrect. It is always a good idea to measure what you have by rotating the driveshaft.

If you plan on rebuilding the axle and swapping it into another vehicle or swapping a different axle into your vehicle, more checks must be made. All of the following, including widths, brackets (bolt-on, weld-on), leaf or coil spring suspension, and flanges, are very important in swaps.

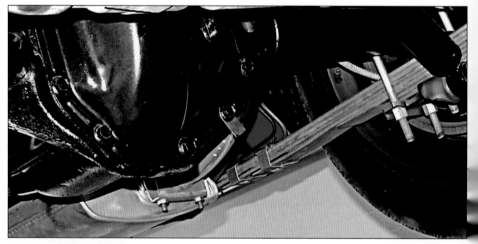

*While the car is raised, you can examine the basic hardware. The bolts that hold the cover on the rear of the center section indicates that this is a carrier-tube design. On the right side, you can see the rear leaf spring and the two U-bolts that hold it onto the axle. The lower shock mount on the far right and the rear drum brakes can be seen. A somewhat closer inspection shows the ratio tag on the cover bolt at about 4 o'clock. You can also check for a lower drain (none here) and the fill hole.*

### Tapered Axle Shafts

Only two Chrysler/Dana/AMC/Jeep differentials used tapered axle shafts—most of the AMC 20 axles used in Jeeps and AMC vehicles and the early Chrysler 8¾-inch (1957–1964). In both cases, the ends of the axle shafts have a large nut and a cotter pin. This style of axle shaft requires a special axle puller. You may not be able to see the nut and cotter pin with the wheels installed. Each is described in more detail in the specific chapter on that axle.

### Gear Ratio

The first step in nailing down your actual gear ratio is to find the small metal tag that is attached to one of the attaching bolts of the cover or housing. Original equipment manufacturer (OEM) factories are the only ones to use these tags at the time of production. They are often lost or left off during a rebuild. If you find the tag, the stamped number on it does not read directly as the axle ratio, such as 3.91:1. The numbers on the tag are the number of teeth on the pinion and the ring gear, such as 11 and 43. (Note that 43 ÷ 11 equals 3.91, which is the actual ratio.)

### Gasket Dimensions

The chart "Rear Axle Cover/Gasket Dimensions" on page 18 shows the basic gasket dimensions for the axles discussed in this book. Note that the Dana 44 and the Dana 60 both use 10 attaching bolts on the cover and have the same shape for the gasket surface. This means that the width of the gasket can be used to differentiate between them, roughly 9½ inches for the 44 compared to 11 inches for the 60.

### Shop Approach

You can rebuild the axle yourself, or you can take it to an axle shop. If you plan to take it to a shop, talk to the shop before you start the project and discuss whether they prefer the whole car or just the axle assembly.

If you do the work yourself, you still need to determine if you're going to remove the whole axle assembly or rebuild the unit in the vehicle. Remember that the complete axle assembly is very heavy and hard to handle, and requires a second person to remove it. This complete axle removal process requires much more work, so rear axles are usually rebuilt in the vehicle. This means that you must have an appropriate work area under the rear of the vehicle.

The exception to this rebuild-in-the-car approach is the Chrysler 8¾-inch axle. This axle has a removable center section, called a pig. This center section removes toward the front of the vehicle

The ring or ring gear is bolted to the differential at left of center. One differential bearing is visible at the lower left (the second differential bearing is not visible). The side gears and the pinion gears are located inside the differential and therefore not visible. Slightly to the left of center, the end of the pinion shaft is visible.

*For this cutaway only, the axle cover is bolted to the center housing on the left (rear of unit) making this a carrier-tube design. The pinion is toward the lower right.*

*If you are lucky, the original production rear axle ratio tag will be located on one of the cover or carrier attaching bolts. Older cars that have been used in typical street use for years often do not have clean bolts. So you have to locate the tag and then clean it so you can read it. The tag typically does not give the actual ratio but tells you the number of teeth on the ring and pinion individually, such as 43 and 11. This means that there are 43 teeth on the ring and 11 teeth on the pinion for a 3.91 ratio (43 ÷ 11 = 3.91).*

*Tapered axle shafts use a castle nut and cotter pin on end of axle shaft in the center of the wheel's bolt circle. Generally these nuts are covered with a dust cap. Tapered axle shafts are commonly used on the AMC 20 but the very early Chrysler 8¾-inch axles (1963 and older) were the only other model to use a similar tapered axle with the nut in the center.*

## Rear Axle Cover/Gasket Dimensions

| Axle | Design | Dimensions (inches) |
|---|---|---|
| AMC 20 | All | 10$\frac{1}{32}$ x 10$\frac{25}{64}$ |
| Chrysler 7¼ | 9-bolt | 8 x 9$\frac{1}{8}$ |
|  | 10-bolt | 9¾ x 9$\frac{3}{8}$ |
| Chrysler 8¼, 8$\frac{3}{8}$ | All | 11$\frac{3}{8}$ round |
| Chrysler 9¼ | All | 12$\frac{3}{8}$ x 11½ |
| Dana 30 | All | 9$\frac{3}{16}$ x 8¾ |
| Dana 35 | All | 9¼ x 10$\frac{3}{8}$ |
| Dana 44 | All | 9$\frac{3}{8}$ x 10¼ |
| Dana 60 | All | 11$\frac{1}{8}$ x 12¾ |

A rear axle assembly is a large and heavy part, which probably needs at least two people to move it. If removed, you have to have a place to put it. This one sits on a steel, double A-frame (designed by Warren Gear and Axle) with a cross-brace and a V-notch at the top.

This rear view of an 8¾-inch pig shows the ring gear bolted to the differential housing. The main bearing caps are to the right and left (two bolts per cap). Not as easily visible are the two-piece differential (bolts are to the right, next to the right main cap) and the Sure-Grip differential (an open differential has large windows in the housing).

One-piece limited-slip differentials are also open (windows) and you can see the springs, discs, etc. inside the housing.

and can easily be taken to your workbench to be rebuilt.

### Removing the Ring-and-Pinion

You can remove the ring-and-pinion from the main axle housing in one basic direction: OTF or OTB. Of the axles being discussed only the Chrysler 8¾-inch removes toward the front. These OTF axles are called banjo axles because the main axle housing looks like a banjo with the center section removed, and they are also called Hotchkis.

All other axles are classified as carrier-tube axles, and this means that the ring-and-pinion go OTB individually. All these axles have a cover bolted on the rear face of the center carrier or housing. The number of bolts and the shape of the attaching bolt pattern help identify this group of axles. These axles are also called Salisbury designs.

Additional information is stamped on the rear side of the right axle tube, several inches to the right of where the tube is pressed into the carrier. This stamped information is typically the build date and the manufacturer's part number (on Dana and AMC axles). On AMC 20

This is a carrier-tube axle design, which is sometimes called a Salisbury. The number of cover-attaching bolts and the shape of the gasket surface help identify them. The Dana 44 and the Dana 60 share the same shape and bolt count. The ring-and-pinion are removed toward the rear, out-the-back (OTB).

*Typically, an open differential has only four gears inside. There are two side gears: one to the left (barely visible) and one to the right. There are two pinion gears; one is at the top (barely visible) while the other is at the bottom. The pin or cross-shaft where the two pinion gears are generally mounted has been removed here. The ring gear mounts on the differential vertical face toward the left side.*

axles, a letter code (one or two letters) is stamped on a small pad on the right side of the rear of the carrier, just outboard of the cover gasket surface. Note that letters, such as BB or M, can tell you that ratio. (See the chart "AMC 20 Identification" on page 35.)

### Differential

The differential is the center part of the rear axle. The ring bolts to the differential case, but the differential has more to do than just hold the ring gear. While most production rear axles use open differentials, the high-performance market demands limited-slip or Sure-Grip differentials to achieve maximum traction when transmitting high-horsepower loads. (See Chapter 7 for more details on the many forms of limited-slip differentials.)

The open differential consists of two side gears, two pinion gears, washers, cross shaft (or pinion shaft), cross-shaft lock, and two bearings that press onto the case.

The open differential case is made in one piece while the limited-slip differential cases can be a one- or a two-piece design, and the two-piece units bolt together.

Independent of the limited-slip aspect, most of the axle designs have two different differential cases. The change is dictated by the axle ratio. (See Chapter 7 for more details.) For example, on the 9¾-inch Dana 60 the case changes between the 4.10 ratio and the 4.56 ratio.

### Brackets

Axles use one of two types of brackets—bolt-on or weld-on—to attach the axle to the suspension. Many vehicles use some form of leaf-spring suspension. Two large U-bolts are present where the leaf spring

*Many styles of limited-slip differential, sometimes called Sure-Grips or posi (Posi-Traction) units, were made in the muscle car era. They were based on clutch discs; discs are behind each side gear. The side of this unit has been cut away for display purposes.*

*The limiting forces are provided in two general methods. One is by small coil springs (shown) the other by Belleville washers. Another method of limiting the relative movement between the two axle shafts is a tapered seat on the back of the side gear and an angled seat in the housing.*

*These are the basic parts of an open differential. The cross-shaft is in the center. The lock pin is to the top-right of the shaft. The two side gears are to the center-left and center-right (the two larger ones). The two pinion gears are to the lower-left and upper-right. The thrust block is on the right below the side gear.*

*While there may be some exceptions, the main suspension bracket that controls the connection between the rear axle and the rear suspension is welded to the axle tubes. This rear shock mount bracket appears to be bolted to the axle by two large U-bolts. The key is the spring seat that is welded to the axle tube but not visible.*

Street cars, trucks, and off-road vehicles typically have dirty rear universal joints. The driveshaft (left) connects to the rear axle through the rear U-joint. Two bolts on each side hold the U-joint cross to the yoke of the rear axle.

There are two basic types of driveshaft attachment to the yoke on production cars. The most common is two bolts and a strap (above). The second type of attachment is two small U-joints without the universal joint (right). The yoke has to be designed for this style of attachment. The U-bolt goes across the U-joint and slips into the yoke. Two nuts are threaded onto the back side.

meets the axle, so you would think that these brackets are bolt-on. In fact, the key to the leaf-spring suspension is the spring seat, which is a small bracket welded to the axle tube. This spring seat goes between the spring and the axle tube, and is hard to see once the axle is assembled.

While bolt-on brackets can be adjusted along the length of the tube, the weld-on type must be mounted precisely the first time. This is an important aspect to consider when swapping an axle into another vehicle or if you are swapping a new one into your vehicle. Most aftermarket axle manufacturers mount the brackets for you, so you don't have to bolt-on or weld-on brackets yourself.

### Suspension

The two basic kinds of suspension are coil-spring and leaf-spring. A coil-over-shock suspension is commonly used in high-performance and racing applications.

The weld-on spring seat used in the leaf-spring suspension is pretty easy to install, but the weld-on brackets required for most coil-spring suspensions are much more difficult to fabricate and align. Note that with a leaf spring the spring seat is the only part requires welding onto the axle while the coil spring design has a spring seat plus side strut brackets or locators and a track bar bracket.

### Axle Width

The width of the axle housing is very important to any vehicle project. It affects the vehicle's handling and controls where the wheel-and-tire combination sits inside the wheel well, which directly affects the tire's clearances.

### Axle Flange

The flange is used to hold the driveshaft's rear U-joint to the axle's yoke. The yoke is splined onto the pinion and held on by a large nut. The pinion splines are slightly different for each axle, so the yokes tend to be unique for each style of axle. Additionally, the driveshaft's rear U-joint affects the yoke because of its size (width across the U-joint and cup diameter) and basic style (threaded or not)—a strap and two bolts (most common), or a small U-bolt and two nuts.

### Bolt Circle

The rear wheels and brakes have a bolt pattern that is defined by the axle shaft's flange. While the axle shaft flange's bolt pattern does dictate the wheels, it is generally less expensive to do it the other way around, to let the wheel define the bolt circle. Special bolt circle wheels are much harder to find, and more expensive if you can, than custom axle shafts.

### Design Strength

The strength of an axle correlates to its ring gear diameter, and bigger is stronger. The troublemaker is large amounts of torque from the engine. Large amounts of torque are related to larger engine

### Axle Bolt Circles

| | | |
|---|---|---|
| **Jeep/AMC** | 5 bolts on 5.0 inch | |
| | 5 bolts on 4.5 inch | |
| | | |
| **Chrysler** | 5 bolts on 4.0 inch | Passenger Car |
| | 5 bolts on 4.5 inch | Passenger Car and Truck |
| | 6 bolts on 4.5 inch | Truck |

*Although the bolt circle doesn't actually affect the axle's rebuild, it is a big player in two key items at the rear: brakes and wheels.*

displacements, which are very easy to build today. The aftermarket offers a variety of hardware for these axles, such as limited-slip differentials, better steels, stronger cases, etc. All of this hardware can allow a smaller axle design to last in an application that the factory engineers may not have approved.

## Vehicle Supports

If you work on the rear end of the vehicle, the back must be raised. There are many ways to lift the vehicle, such as floor jacks or a shop hoist. Once up in the air at the desired height, place jack stands under the frame or rear longitudinals in unibody cars.

For rear axle work, both wheels should be off the ground. While not required, raising the front end to the same height as the rear gives you more room to work. If the front end is raised, use jack stands there also.

Place the rear jack stands on the frame, rather than under the axle or suspension component. The main reason for this is so the rear axle hangs down, allowing the wheels to be removed more easily. This is more of a concern on cars than on Jeeps or trucks.

The first step is to drain the axle fluid. Remember to recycle the oil that is removed.

## Terms and Setup

There are a lot of terms that are unique to rear axles like toe and heel, root and top land, coast and drive side. To run the basic contact pattern of the pinion with the ring gear, these terms are used frequently. The contact pattern shows whether the axle has been

**Gear Tooth Features**

*The gear tooth is complicated. You generally look at a ring gear with the outside edge of the ring closest to you. The root is the bottom section between the teeth. The top of the tooth is called the top land or crown. Here, the drive side of the gear is toward the right side and the coast side of the gear is toward the left. The heel is the side of the tooth toward the outside edge of the ring and the toe is the side of the gear toward the inside edge of the ring. While the profile of the tooth could be a straight line, it is generally curved with a specific shape to match the pinion teeth.*

*The gear tooth contact pattern shows you whether the correct gear pinion bearing mounting shim has been installed and whether the drive gear backlash has been set properly.*

*To obtain this desired contact pattern, apply a thin film of Hydrated Ferric Oxide (known as Yellow Oxide of Iron) on the drive and coast sides of the ring gear teeth. Using a round bar, apply a load against the back of the drive gear. Then rotate the pinion several full revolutions in both directions. This movement leaves a distinct contact pattern on both the drive and coast sides of the drive gear teeth.*

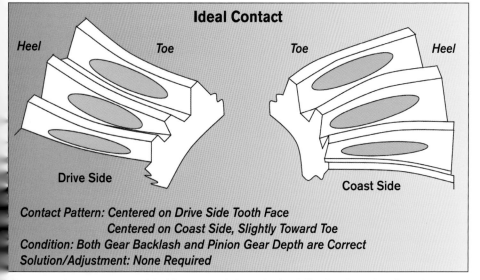

**Ideal Contact**

Contact Pattern: Centered on Drive Side Tooth Face
Centered on Coast Side, Slightly Toward Toe
Condition: Both Gear Backlash and Pinion Gear Depth are Correct
Solution/Adjustment: None Required

*Compare these patterns with this one and those in the following four drawings because each has a unique pattern and you need to properly set up the contact pattern for your differential. The proper tooth contact pattern results when the adjustments are made correctly. Notice that the correct contact pattern is well centered on both the drive and coast sides of the teeth.*

*When the tooth contact patterns are obtained by hand, they are apt to be rather small. Under the actual rear axle operating load, the contact area increases. If an improper tooth contact pattern is observed, increase or decrease the thickness of the rear pinion bearing shim to adjust the pinion depth.*

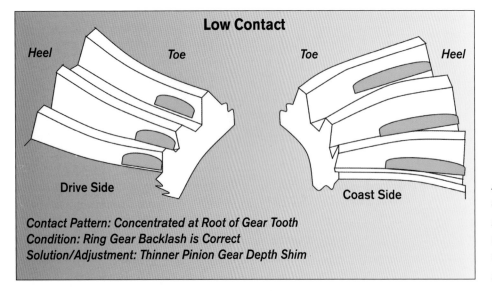

**Low Contact**

Heel    Toe    Toe    Heel

Drive Side    Coast Side

Contact Pattern: Concentrated at Root of Gear Tooth
Condition: Ring Gear Backlash is Correct
Solution/Adjustment: Thinner Pinion Gear Depth Shim

*A low-contact pattern is narrow and concentrated at the root of the gear tooth. If left as is, this contact pattern scores the teeth and results in noise. Installing a thinner shim behind the rear pinion bearing corrects this condition.*

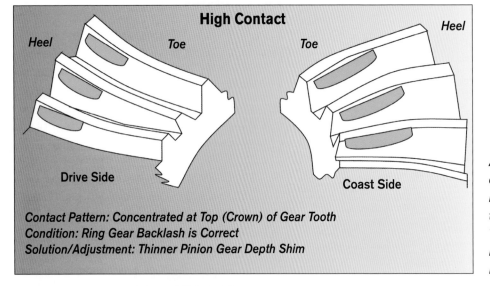

**High Contact**

Heel    Toe    Toe    Heel

Drive Side    Coast Side

Contact Pattern: Concentrated at Top (Crown) of Gear Tooth
Condition: Ring Gear Backlash is Correct
Solution/Adjustment: Thinner Pinion Gear Depth Shim

*A high-contact pattern is narrow and concentrated at the top (crown) of the teeth. If left as is, this contact pattern causes the teeth to wear thin and roll over (score). The result is excessive gear lash and noise. Installing a thicker shim behind the rear pinion bearing corrects this condition.*

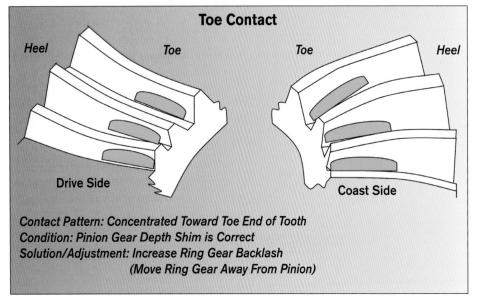

**Toe Contact**

Heel    Toe    Toe    Heel

Drive Side    Coast Side

Contact Pattern: Concentrated Toward Toe End of Tooth
Condition: Pinion Gear Depth Shim is Correct
Solution/Adjustment: Increase Ring Gear Backlash
            (Move Ring Gear Away From Pinion)

*A heavy toe contact pattern is concentrated on the toe (inside) part of the tooth. If left in this configuration, the edges of the teeth may chip resulting in excessive damage to the entire assembly. Moving the drive gear away from the pinion corrects this condition and changes the backlash, which makes it necessary to insert a thinner shim behind the rear pinion bearing.*

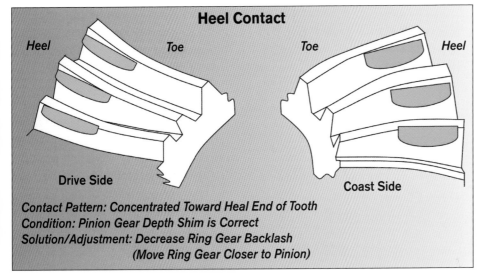

**Heel Contact**

Heel    Toe    Toe    Heel

Drive Side    Coast Side

Contact Pattern: Concentrated Toward Heal End of Tooth
Condition: Pinion Gear Depth Shim is Correct
Solution/Adjustment: Decrease Ring Gear Backlash
(Move Ring Gear Closer to Pinion)

A heavy heel contact pattern concentrates contact on the outside part of the tooth. If left in this configuration, the edges of the teeth may chip, resulting in excessive damage to the entire assembly. Moving the drive gear toward the pinion corrects this condition. This change decreases the backlash, which makes it necessary to insert a thinner shim behind the rear pinion bearing.

properly set up, so it is very important. Adjust the depth of the pinion and the left-to-right location of the differential case. You do this by using shims to set the ideal contact pattern between the pinion and ring gear. The shape and general location of the contact pattern tells you which way to adjust these items. You must use to white lead or blue machinist dye to determine the contact pattern. You use the lead or dye to verify that you've attained the ideal contact pattern when adjusting the ring-and-pinion.

## Tools and Equipment

With any automotive project, many tools are required. Basic hand tools are common, but the rear axle has many special requirements that take special

# Dial Indicator Use

The dial indicator is a precision measuring tool. They generally measure to .001-inch increments. They basically have a round face (or dial) and a point (or indicator) the sticks out the bottom. The rear face has a boss for mounting on a stand.

For measuring axles, a magnetic base is the most common stand. There are many others. The magnetic base has an on-off switch, which allows you to easily attach it to iron objects such as the carrier or center section, both of which are generally made of cast iron. A flat surface for the stand, usually a machined surface, is best. The dial indicator is mounted to the machined outer gasket surface on an 8¾ center section. Once the stand is in position on a flat, smooth surface, you turn on the magnetic switch (the base is not attached to the axle). Generally there is an arm that connects the indicator to the stand. This arm allows you to get the indicator closer to your work and over obstacles.

The key to the dial indicator's use and accurate measurements is to have the pointer/indicator mounted parallel to the centerline of your work or perpendicular to the surface being measured. For example, if you want to measure axle endplay, the stand can be mounted to the hosing and set up so that the indicator is touching the axle flange and perpendicular to the flange.

It is also parallel to the centerline of the axle shaft because of the flange/axle shaft relationship.

Next you compress the pointer/indicator enough to exceed the expected amount of travel, say, .200 inch. Then you zero the indicator face so the the pointer reads zero. This way the dial reads directly. Then you push the axle flange in and then pull it out noting the readings on the dial in each position. For example, the indicator says end play is .006 inch.

On things that rotate, you need a smooth, machined, flat surface. On the differential, that could be the back of the ring gear or the differential flange. In this case, the pointer needs to be parallel to the centerline of rotation, which is between the two main caps. Then it must be mounted perpendicular to the face being measured. In some cases, there isn't much room for the pointer.

Next you zero the indicator face and rotate the differential, while you watch the dial. It may go .002 inch to the right (or plus side) and then .001 inch to the left (or minus side). This means that the total indicator reading (TIR) is .003 inch. You could re-zero the dial at the minus .001-inch location and then rotate it again. It would then go from 0 to .003 inch.

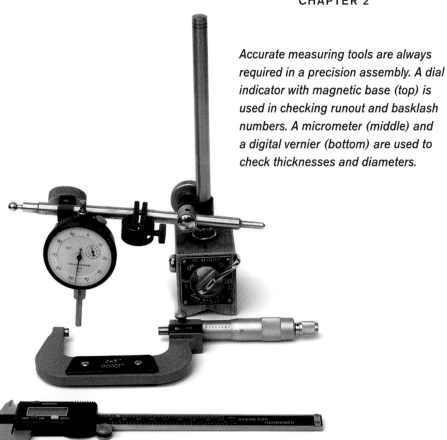

*Accurate measuring tools are always required in a precision assembly. A dial indicator with magnetic base (top) is used in checking runout and basklash numbers. A micrometer (middle) and a digital vernier (bottom) are used to check thicknesses and diameters.*

tools not always common in a standard home shop. This is a general list and some axles do not use all of these tools. Because the center housing comes OTF, the 8¾-inch Chrysler axle does not use a spreader. Most carrier-tube axles use a spreader to slightly widen the rear opening to allow removal of the ring gear and differential assembly. Also, you will note that many special tools used throughout the text are not listed or named here. Some are home-made and don't really have a name, but I will provide a description of them so you can make your own.

### C-Clips

Many carrier-tube axles use C-clips on the inner ends of the axle shafts to retain the axle shafts in the housing. They are visible once the rear cover of the axle has been removed and the differential is rotated so that the differential window is visible. If your

*A large oil drain pan (upper left) is required to drain oil from the axles. A rear axle lube (right) is used to fill the axles once it is reassembled. A two-piece syringe (bottom) can be used to as least partially remove oil from the axle but is more important when you have to re-fill the axle at the end of the rebuild process.*

*This work stand for rebuilding axles was made by Warren Gear & Axle. The two A-frames are connected by a cross-brace. There is a V-notch in the top of each A-section.*

axle is a C-clip design, one of the first steps in the disassembly process is to remove the two C-clips.

C-clips are not used to retain the 8¾-inch axle to the axle shafts.

*This is a yoke holder made by Yukon Gear. The multiple holes allow it to be bolted to several sizes of yokes. Only two bolts are used to hold it. The large hole in the center allows the large socket to be installed on the pinion nut. The somewhat short handle allows you to add some bars for more length and leverage.*

*The basic slider hammer has a long center rod, a sliding weight, and a bolt-on bracket on one end, which attaches to the axle flange with three bolts.*

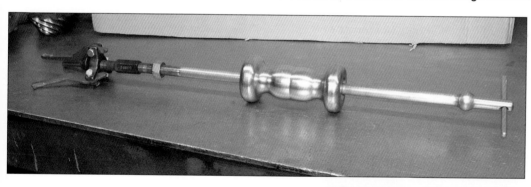

*This slider hammer has a three-finger, seal-puller adapter. It replaces the bracket that bolts to the axle flange.*

*Spanner wrenches are a forked wrench except that each side of the fork has a stud that sticks up to fit into a drill wheel for adjustment.*

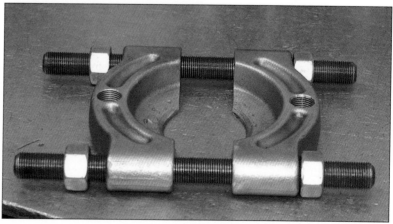

*This bearing puller unthreads so the two jaws fit over the pinion bearing. It is then screwed together and the bearing is pressed off in the arbor press.*

The yoke remover is a two-fingered puller sized to fit the width of the yoke. The threaded adjuster pushes against the center of the pinion stem.

This multi-piece tool is used to pull the differential bearings. The tool is attached to the end of the differential case, then the half-sleeve is slid over the two pieces. The other half is added and then a sleeve is dropped over the outside, which keeps the two pieces from coming apart. The threaded adjuster at the top is then turned and the bearing is pulled off.

Bearing installers can also be used to remove certain bearings. They are selected based on the size of the bearing.

## Rear Axle Tool List

**TECH TIP**

- Slider hammer
- Axle shaft and bearing puller (only with tapered axles shafts)
- Axle bearing installer
- Differential bearing remover
- Axle bearing seal installer and handle
- Axle seal remover (with slide hammer)
- Torque wrench in foot-pound and inch-pound increments
- Dial indicator
- Precision calipers, or micrometer
- Pinion depth gauge
- Large screwdriver or pinch-bar (pry bar)

- Drive pinion flange holder (yoke holder)
- Heavy-duty drive pinion nut socket
- Threaded pinion bearing installer
- Housing spreader or pry bars
- Gear marking compound and a clean brush
- Bearing pullers/removers (differential and pinion)
- Arbor press
- Spanner wrench, 10- or 12-inch
- Breaker bar, 3-foot long
- Axle hub puller (only with tapered axles)
- Pilot studs (8¼- and 9¼-inch

axles only)
- Gear rotating tool (Dana and AMC 20 axles with one-piece limited-slip differentials only)
- Syringe
- Plastic caps to seal transmission
- Brake line wrench
- Ball-peen hammer, 24-ounce
- Sledge hammer, 48-ounce
- Plastic-face dead-blow hammer, 48-ounce
- Brass drifts
- Center punch and chisel selection
- Oil drain pan, large and round
- Jack stands (3) or axle stand

# FIRST STEPS OF DISASSEMBLY

The axle assembly can usually be left in the vehicle during an axle ratio change or basic rebuild. This is also true if you want to add a limited-slip differential at the same time. The rear axle is a large part and affects many of the components in the vehicle, and these aspects need to be planned for before any money is spent.

Before you start the disassembly process, decide how to remove the rear end and have any swapping concerns covered. There are many more choices today than just a few years ago, so cover all the possibilities. For example, a typical add-on overdrive unit or the top-gear ratio in an overdrive transmission is around .70. The resulting final drive ratio of a .70 overdrive unit and a 4.10 axle axle is 2.87.

Another example relates to tire diameters. A 26.0-inch outside-diameter tire was a common production size and 32.0-inch outside-diameter tires are now available. This tire change has the same affect as an .80 overdrive unit.

Today there are also many choices for limited-slip differentials to replace an original-equipment open or non-locking differential.

Twenty or thirty years ago, choices for a rear-axle rebuild were limited to the axle ratio itself and a limited-slip differential. Each axle design had per- haps five to ten different ratios from which to choose, and there were only a couple different limited-slip differentials. While the number of ratios hasn't changed much, many more types of axles are available. In fact, there are more types of differentials than there are ratios, along with several housings and an almost unlimited number of axles, flanges, bolt circles, brakes, and bracket options.

*Removing the rear cover on the center housing of a carrier-tube axle allows you to drain the oil. It also allows you to inspect the existing hardware. You can also check the axle shaft ends to see if there are C-clips holding the axle in place. If present, removing the C-clips is the next step.*

*An early decision to make during a rear axle project is whether to remove the whole axle or rebuild it in the vehicle. These are brand-new, complete Dana assemblies.*

## Axle Assembly Removal

While most rebuilds do not require the complete axle assembly to be removed, if you want to change the basic design, make the assembly stronger, make the width narrower to gain tire clearance, or some similar goal, the complete assembly must be removed. A lot more work is involved when removing the axle, so removing the assembly is only the start of the process. If you do plan on removing the assembly, I strongly recommend getting some additional help.

### Axle Shaft Removal

The axle shafts must be removed for axle rebuilds. This is true even if you do not plan on changing the axle shafts themselves. To remove the axle shafts, you must remove both wheels and the brake drum or disc. Some drum brake systems allow the shaft to be removed without removing the brake shoe assembly once the drum has been removed.

On disc brake systems, the caliper has to be removed first to allow the rotor to be removed. Then the rotor must be removed. On most AMC 20 axles and early (up through 1964) Chrysler 8¾-inch axles, the brake hub must be removed using a hub puller.

### Axle Cover or Pig Removal

Draining the oil from the housing is one of the first steps for an axle rebuild and probably the messiest part. Most rear axles do not have an actual drain plug;

*The open-style (shown) rear axle differential is the most common. Open means that there is no connection between the two axle shafts; it does not refer to the large window in the side of the case. Open and limited-slip differentials look the same on the outside. Inside the differential assembly, the open and limited-slip are different, which is difficult to see. The clutch packs of the limited-slip differential reside inside the differential assembly. The connection usually takes the form of springs in the center between the two side gears (here, bottom center and top center inside the housing).*

*Generally, you don't have to remove the complete rear axle assembly to rebuild the axle or change the ratio. This Dana 60 has the pinion snubber (bottom center) that bolts to the top of the carrier nose. Passenger cars built from about 1965 through the early 1970s use this feature. All complete axle assemblies are large and heavy, so two or three people should take on the task of handling and moving them.*

*A banjo axle disassembles toward the front. The ring and pinion remove as a complete unit or center section (often called a pig). Once removed from the axle housing, it can be taken to your workbench, which makes it more convenient to rebuild. Of the axles discussed in this book, only the Chrysler 8¾-inch axle is a banjo style.*

*A limited-slip differential tries to limit the amount of movement of one axle versus the other. The variations come in when you try to define how the limited-slip functions. Most standard ones use small springs to push on a small clutch pack, including discs and plates. This unit pushes the tapered side gear into a tapered housing. The side is cut out for display purposes. (See Chapter 7 for details on other styles of limited-slips.)*

the center section (the pig) on the banjo-style axles (the 8¾-inch) or the rear cover on all carrier-tube axles must be partially removed. The seal must be broken at the bottom so the oil can drain into a catch-can. Once empty, the center section or rear cover can be removed.

With banjo axles, place the pig on a workbench to finish the disassembly process.

On carrier-tube axles with the cover on the rear, the next step is to determine if your axle has C-clips holding the axle shafts in the housing. This can only be done with the cover removed. The differential may have to be rotated to see in the side opening in the case and check for C-clips on the axle-shaft ends. They must be removed before you can remove the axle shafts from the housing.

## Rebuild Kits

Before you start turning any wrenches, confirm you have the appropriate axle rebuild kit for your axle then lay out all the various parts. The typical kit includes bearings and races, pinion shims and nuts, pinion seal, crush sleeve, marking compound, and a case/cover gasket.

Any parts not included in the rebuild kit should be handled with care, as they must be reused.

Several aspects of the rear axle can be important but do not fit in any of the categories discussed up to this point. They can be important to the hardware that's purchased, but don't tend to affect the actual steps in the rebuild process.

## Swedged Axle Tubes

Early versions of the Chrysler 7¼-inch axle (a carrier-tube design) used smaller 2½-inch axle tubes, while all the other, larger, Chrysler axles used the more common 3-inch tubes. In later model years, Chrysler changed the design to use swedged axle tubes. (Swedging is a process of reducing the diameter on one end while not cutting away any material.) This means that the tube has a 3-inch diameter at the brake end, and it is swedged down to 2½-inch diameter as it is pressed into the center housing/carrier. This means that these axles can use the same spring seat hardware as the larger units.

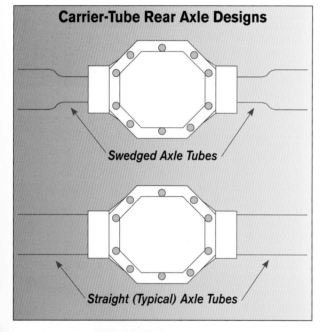

### Carrier-Tube Rear Axle Designs

*Swedged Axle Tubes*

*Straight (Typical) Axle Tubes*

*Most carrier-tube rear axles use straight tubes, which are pressed and welded into the center carrier. Generally these tubes are 3 inches in outside diameter. Some of the older and smaller axle designs use 2½-inch tubes. This change can cause problems in certain axle-swapping and replacement situations. In some newer designs, the small axle used swedged axle tubes, so that the axle tubes on the brake-drum end were 3 inches and they entered the center housing at 2½ inches.*

## Rebuild Kit Sources

Today many different types of rebuild kits are offered. For example Jegs offers four levels of rebuild kits: the half kit, the complete kit (defined as the half kit plus pinion and differential bearings, new ring gear bolts, and marking compound), the mega kit (defined as the complete kit plus axle bearings and seals), and the ring-and-pinion plus the complete kit.

The two big catalog centers, Jegs and Summit, have similar kits but do not offer all kits for all axles and all ratios.

The large distributors are drivetrain specialists, which include DTS (Drive Train Specialists) Randy's Ring and Pinion, Mancini Racing (specializes in Chrysler axles), Precision Gear, and the Ring and Pinion Shop. Most of these distributors put together rebuild kits to meet their customers' needs, which may vary from the approach by catalog centers.

An obvious source for rebuild kits are the ring-and-pinion manufacturers themselves. The most common are Auburn Gear, Richmond Gear, Yukon, Spicer/Dana, US Gear, and Motive Gear. Also, Moser (the biggest performance axle manufacturer) and Timken (a bearing manufacturer) also offer rebuild kits.

## FWD Differentials

In many cases, the Jeeps and trucks that use FWD, which is part of an all-wheel-drive or 4WD system, use the same basic axle as the rear axles. The Chrysler 8¾-inch, the Chrysler 7¼-inch, and the AMC 20 axles were not used in the front of 4WD systems.

Dana axles are the most common axles used in the front, but the Chrysler 8¼- and 9¼-inch axles have also been used up front. Typically, these front axles are different than the axle design used in the rear. Front axles use reverse-cut gears. Most of the axle-ratio manufacturers offer reverse-cut front gears. Front axles rebuild basically the same way as the rear versions.

The more common usage of the acronym FWD is for front-wheel drive. In this context the rear wheels are not driven. These cars use unique front axles that are called transaxles because the transmission and axle functions are in the same unit. These units are unique in size and basic design compared to a RWD axle even if it is installed in the front location. These actual FWD transaxles are not discussed further in this book.

## Disconnecting the Driveshaft

Once you have the vehicle raised and supported on jack stands, and the work area set-up, the first step is to disconnect the driveshaft. The hardware (two straps and four screws, or two small U-bolts and four nuts) hold the typical driveshaft onto the rear axle's yoke. Once loose from the rear yoke, the driveshaft can be pushed forward 1 inch or so into the transmission's tailshaft housing. The driveshaft can now be safely stored for reassembly.

It's probably a good idea to put some tape around the U-joint caps so they do not fall off. A large rubber band can also be used. Some vehicles allow you to move the driveshaft out of the way and to tie it up. If that is not possible or it's too difficult, consider pulling the driveshaft and its slip-yoke out of the rear of the transmission.

Caution: To avoid leaking transmission oil onto your work area, insert a plastic cup seal into the rear of the transmission. Each transmission output shaft has its own splines and size and the plastic cup should be selected by the specific transmission.

## General Disassembly

After the driveshaft has been removed, the general disassembly steps for axles are very similar, except for the Chrysler 8¾-inch design. The Chrysler 8¾-inch is a banjo design, and therefore the center housing comes OTF and you can take the housing to your workbench.

*Disconnecting the driveshaft from the axle yoke is one of the first steps in rebuilding a rear axle. Before actually turning any wrenches, be sure to mark the driveshaft tube and the yoke. Scribe or mark with a crayon. This allows you to reassemble the drivetrain and maintain its dynamic balance.*

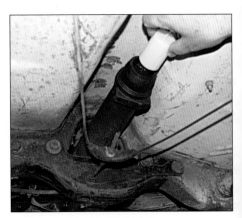

*Once the driveshaft has been disconnected, find a place to safely store it so it's handy when you reinstall the axle. If you slide the driveshaft out of the end of the transmission, the transmission case is open and will leak onto the garage floor. Insert a plastic cap into the end of the transmission to solve this problem. Caps are available for most transmissions.*

*The axles used in front-wheel-drive applications are special, even though the basic design is the same, such as on a Dana 44. Obviously the axle shafts and steering mechanism are different, but in many cases, the axle installs upside-down, and the pinion comes in high. Most manufacturers tend to reverse-cut the actual gears for FWD applications and service them as reverse-cut gears—same axle and same ratio, just designed for the FWD axles.*

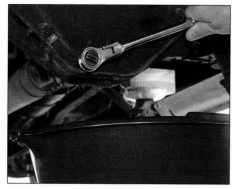

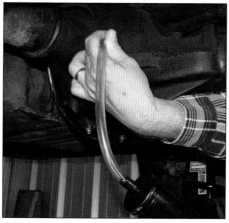

*Before you start loosening any bolts, be sure to position a large drain pan below the housing. For the rear covers, use a socket and ratchet to remove all the screws except the top one or two. Start at the bottom for this procedure. Loosen the top two but leave it attached by a few threads. Pry the cover loose and drain the oil. Then remove the last two screws and the cover.*

*On banjo axles, leave one at the top and two at the bottom. Loosen the two at the bottom but leave a few threads attached. Loosen the top one a couple turns, pry the carrier loose, and drain the oil.*

All other axles discussed in this book are carrier-tube designs and the ring-and-pinion go OTB individually. This difference between OTF and OTB makes the basic disassembly steps somewhat unique.

### Banjo with OTF Design

With the driveshaft removed and both rear wheels raised, the next step is to remove both axle shafts. The 8¾-inch axle does not use C-clips, so you can use the stand and axle-shaft removal tool and the slide hammer to remove the axle shafts. But first the wheels and brake drum (or disc) must be removed. The early 8¾-inch axles with tapered axle shafts are rare today and not very popular, but require a special, heavy-duty axle puller to pull the hub off the axle shaft.

Once the axle shafts have been removed, drain the oil. Place a large drain

*While not required, I recommend you find the oil fill hole, which is sometimes a threaded plug (shown) or a press-in plastic/rubber seal plug. Remove the plug.*

pan under the rear axle gasket surface. The center housing (pig) is heavy, so use caution. Ten studs with nuts hold the pig. Locate the bottom two nuts and back them out to the end of the two studs. Leave at least two or three full threads engaged. Now locate one of the two nuts at the top of the housing, and back it out one or two full revolutions but not to the end of the stud. Remove the rest of the nuts and set aside.

The special arrangement of the nuts allows the pig to be loosened but not fall or drop; the gap at the bottom should be much bigger than at the top. Once drained, remove the drain pan and push the pig back into place. Finish removing the bottom two nuts. Once you are ready to receive the pig, remove the last nut at the top and remove the pig.

Move the pig to a workbench. (See Chapter 5 for further disassembly steps.)

### Carrier-Tube with OTB Design

Once the driveshaft is disconnected, the next step for carrier-tube designs is to drain the oil. This requires the cover on the rear of the axle to be removed. Select one screw at the bottom of the cover and back it out halfway. Select one screw at the top and back it out two full turns.

*You can use a syringe to remove some of the oil. Generally clearance under the vehicle is limited, so using the syringe becomes important at reassembly time when you have to re-fill the axle.*

Remove the rest of the screws. Pry the cover loose against the bottom screw and drain the oil. Once drained, remove the final two screws and remove the cover.

Rotate the differential until you can see the ends of the axle shafts. If there are C-clips on the ends of the axles, remove them now. Then remove the brake drum (or disc) and the axle shafts. If there are no C-clips, use an axle puller to remove the axle shafts.

The next step is to remove the differential. In carrier-tube axles, a spreader

*Banjo (or OTB) axles are a complete center section with the ring-and-pinion that can be taken to your workbench. It is much heavier than it looks, so use caution as you remove it from the housing. There is a gasket between the center section and the banjo housing. Once the center section has been removed, you then remove the gasket.*

is used to spread the opening slightly to allow the differential and ring gear to be removed. Install the spreader. See Chapter 4, 5, or 6 for further steps pertaining to your specific axle.

### Brake Lines

Only disconnect the brakes to the axle if a new axle is to be installed. In some cases, only one brake line runs from the body to the axle, splitting to each side along the axle housing. In other cases, two brake lines drop from the body—one on each side.

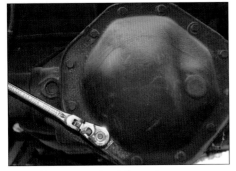

*If you have a carrier-tube axle, remove the cover from the rear of the unit to drain the oil. Be sure to position your drain pan below the axle before you start loosening the screws.*

*The flexible rear brake lines run from the body to the axle. In most cases, one line runs to the axle and then splits off to each side on the axle housing. However, in some cases, there are two lines from each side of the body to the axle. Brake lines on older cars can be rusty, so spray with penetrating oil before trying to loosen them. If the axle is staying in the vehicle, it can be left as is.*

On most production vehicles, a parking brake cable runs to each side of the axle. This must also be disconnected if you plan on removing the complete axle assembly.

### Electric Wires

Any electric wires running from the body to the axle must be disconnected if the axle is to be removed. I recommend taping each one to the chassis and clearly marking where it goes on the axle. On newer vehicles, check the top of the housing, slightly toward the driver's side, for a sensor, which is called the rear wheel anti-lock (RWAL) brake speed sensor. This sensor is typically used with anti-lock brakes. Rear-only anti-lock brakes are common on many newer model trucks, which were built after 1985–1990.

While not OEM or production, there may also be either wires or air

*Always inspect your hardware before you start turning any wrenches. Note the cover shape and number of bolts. Also note that one of the cover-attaching bolts has a small tag on it (lower right). This tag gives you the axle ratio, which is the number of teeth on the ring gear and the number of teeth on the pinion, such as 10 and 41 for a 4.11:1 ratio or 11 and 43 for a 3.91:1 ratio. Also note the large holes on each side of the center carrier that are used with a spreader tool to help remove the differential. Be sure you know where the fill plug is (upper center, slightly to the right).*

lines for air-operated electric limited-slip differentials or Sure-Grip differentials. These are readily available in the aftermarket and may have been installed on your axle.

### C-Clips

C-clips are used to hold certain axle shafts into the housing. They are not used on the 8¾-inch banjo axle. The C-clips must be removed before the axle can be removed.

### Differential Case Change

With many of the axles discussed in this book, the actual differential case changes if the ratio becomes larger than some specific number. This is directly related to the size (diameter) of the pinion gear. (See Chapter 7 for more detail.)

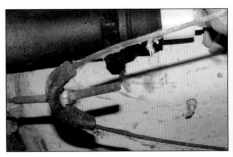

*If the axle is being removed, the parking brakes must also be disconnected. The connections and adjusters tend to get rusty, so spray with penetrating oil first.*

*The parking brake cable is split at the front and runs back to each side. Disconnect the front end and then disconnect the cable from each side of the vehicle in the rear.*

For example, the Dana 60 uses a different differential case between the ratios of 4.10 and 4.56. With the Dana 44 the change occurs in the 3s and on the 8¼- and 9¼-inch Chrysler axles it occurs between the 2.45 and 2.76 ratios.

## Aftermarket Hardware Sources

Years ago, rear axle aftermarket manufacturers made unique axle ratios. These ratios were usually higher numbers, such as 3.91, 4.10, or 4.56:1 rather than production numbers, such as 3.55, 3.23, or 2.91:1. The aftermarket also made limited-slip assemblies. If you wanted a special axle, you selected a production one that was closest to your requirements.

As tires grew larger, demand for narrow axle assemblies became less than for any production axle. This started with the Dana 60 because it was the axle of choice for many racers. Dana first built these special narrower axles, but aftermarket companies eventually took this niche business over by offering narrowed axles for the performance market and expanded upon the axle varieties. In particular, Strange Engineering coordinated with Dana to sell axles through Direct Connection. Strange received basic standard axles from Dana, then finished them to the length desired by the customer. Now Strange makes its own improved 60.

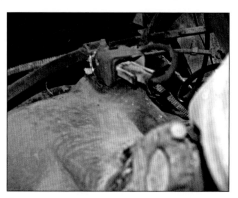

*On later-model cars, especially those with anti-lock brakes, the rear axle housing has a plug-in speed sensor, usually at the top of the housing, slightly to the driver's side of the vehicle. A wire runs from the sensor up into the body and should be disconnected if the axle is to be removed. You can use some tape to mark where it goes for reassembly.*

The NHRA began allowing spools or solid differentials in drag racing, leading to the creation of heavy-duty axle shafts. Many aftermarket manufacturers made housings for the Dana 60, and many were custom fabrications. In the early 2000s, Moser began making a fabricated 8¾-inch unit and in 2011 Moser introduced a new, stamped-banjo, 8¾-inch housing.

*Many carrier-tube axle designs use C-clips to retain the axles into the housing. The C-clip fits over a groove cut in the end of each axle and fits inside a recess cut in the side gear. You can see the C-clip just above the cross-shaft in the center of this photo.*

# C-Clip Eliminator Kit Installation

Several aftermarket manufacturers offer C-clip eliminator kits for most of the carrier-tube axles that use C-clip axle retention. Specific steps and instructions vary with the manufacturer and the specific axle design. The original kits seemed to have flaws, but newer designs have been greatly improved. Discard your old axles and original C-clips.

Mark 1/4 inch from the end of the axle tube/brake bracket with a magic marker.

Use a hacksaw or a cutoff wheel to cut off the axle housing ends.

Remove both axle bearings from each side (axle end).

Deburr any rough edges.

Apply a moderate amount of supplied silicone to both the brake plate and the C-clip eliminator.

Install C-clip eliminator.

Slide in the new axles designed for use with the C-clip eliminator.

Tighten the four (typically) retaining nuts.

Some designs are recommended for drag race–only applications. Strange and Moser offer street kits that feature better seals (up to two seals per side) and bearings. Note that the Moser C-clip eliminator kit replaces the factory C-clip axle retention and provides a safety hub with sealed, press-on bearings. The latest version has an extra internal seal to help prevent leakage. While the technology applies, on-the-shelf kit availability is currently limited as of this writing.

These C-clip eliminator kits typically require new axles. Check with the manufacturer to see if they are required and if they are included in the kit.

# REBUILDING *AMC* DIFFERENTIALS

Dana axles were installed in AMC, Jeep, and Chrysler vehicles. In addition, Chrysler and AMC axles were also used on these vehicles. This chapter covers the AMC 20 axle only.

The two most apparent ways of identifying one axle from another are the number of bolts that are used to attach the cover or center section and the shape that these bolts are in. This shape also matches the gasket surface of the cover. The AMC 20 uses twelve attaching bolts and the shape is almost round, making it one of the easiest axles to identify. The Chrysler 9¼-inch axle also uses twelve attaching bolts, but is in the shape of an octagon.

AMC production vehicles used the AMC 20 axle or one of several Dana axles. Various Jeep production models used the AMC axle, many Dana axles, and some Chrysler axles, such as the 8¼-inch. These axles fall into two basic groups: banjo and carrier-tube. Banjo axles feature a one-piece main housing, shaped like a banjo, with a center section that is removed toward the front of the car. The only banjo axle in this group is the Chrysler 8¾-inch axle. The AMC 20 is a carrier-tube axle. With carrier-tube axles, the axle tubes press into the housing and the cover

is bolted to the rear. As such, the ring-and-pinion are removed toward the rear.

Most AMCs equipped with the AMC 20 are RWD vehicles. Introduced in 1968 and used in production until 1986, the AMC 20 was installed in passenger cars, such as the Hornet, V-8 Javelin, and Gremlin, along with Jeep vehicles such as the Wagoneer. It was also used in the Hummer H1. The AMC 20 has an 8.875-inch ring gear diameter, which makes it a heavy-duty design, and readily available

in aftermarket hardware such as optional ratios. The AMC 20 was offered in open and limited-slip configurations.

The AMC 20 axle has a rich history in drag racing with AMX and Javelin V-8s, but these axles are also used for other applications. A lot of off-road Jeeps with big tires and high numerical gears, such as 4.56:1, have used this axle. Off-road Jeeps produce lots of torque and certainly put the product to the test on an almost daily basis.

*The AMC 20 has a 12-bolt attaching pattern on its circular cover, which makes it easy to identify. On the AMC 20 axle, AMC letter codes are generally stamped on the small pad at the passenger's side of the center housing or carrier. The code can be one letter or two letters. (The Chrysler 9¼-inch is the only other axle that uses 12 attaching screws; its cover has an obvious octagon shape.)*

## Identification of AMC Rear Ends

Be sure you can accurately identify the AMC axle and not confuse it with the Dana and Chrysler carrier-tube units. The Dana 44 and 60 and the 8¼-inch Chrysler axle use a 10-bolt pattern, but the Dana axle has an uneven shape while the Chrysler cover is oval or round. The 9¼-inch Chrysler uses twelve bolts, and has an octagonal pattern. Only the AMC unit also uses twelve bolts, but has a round pattern, and it also has a ring gear diameter of 8.875 inches.

The purpose of discussing the other axles is to illustrate that counting the bolts helps narrow the field but doesn't eliminate all possibilities. The round shape and the twelve bolts identifies it as an AMC 20.

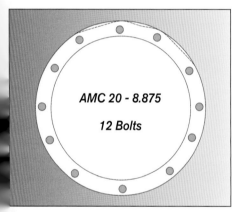

The AMC 20 is the only 12-bolt attaching pattern in the form of a circle, so it's one of the easiest axles to identify. This is looking at the rear of the axle.

### AMC Rear Axle Cover/ Gasket Dimensions

| Axle | Design | Dimensions (inches) |
|---|---|---|
| AMC 20 | All | 10¹⁄₃₂ x 10²⁵⁄₆₄ |

The AMC 20 rear axle cover, gasket shape, and dimensions are almost round and measure about the same in height and width.

Once the basic axle has been identified, specific details, such as model or model number and build date, can be useful. On the Chrysler and Dana axles, some of this information (manufacturing date and part number) may be stamped on the rear of the right axle

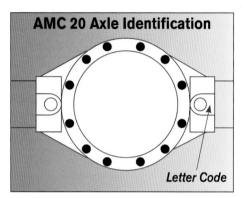

### AMC 20 Axle Identification

Letter Code

This is the rear view of the AMC 20 axle and 12-bolt cover. The AMC letter codes are generally stamped on the small pad at the right side of the center housing or carrier. The code can be a one-letter code or a two-letter code. (See the chart below.)

tube or on the rear of the center carrier housing, which is near the axle tube entry and spreader pilot hole. If the axle has been worked on, the tag may be gone or may no longer represent that actual ratio installed. It is helpful but double-check. On the AMC 20 axle in particular, the number of teeth on the pinion and ring gear is typically stamped in a one- or two-letter code near the right axle tube entry and spreader pilot hole as you are looking at rear of housing.

Another piece of valuable axle information is the axle's bolt circle. Most AMC cars used the standard 4½-inch bolt circle. Jeeps also use the 5-on-4½-inch bolt circle but other bolt circles are also used.

### Ratio

Once you know it is an AMC 20, the next step is to determine the axle ratio. Most AMC axles have the ratio stamped on an axle pad. The chart "AMC 20 Identification" on page 35 lists the letter codes

### AMC 20 Identification

| 1981 Axle Ratio Codes | LLD Models | WLD Models | | |
|---|---|---|---|---|
| 2.73 (15:41) | AA | DD | | |
| 3.31 (13:43) | BB | CC | | |
| 3.73 (11:41) | GG | HH | | |

| 1982 & Newer | Prior to 8-17-81 | | After 8-17-81 | |
|---|---|---|---|---|
| Axle Ratio Codes | LLD Models | WLD Models | LLD Models | WLD Models |
| 2.73 (15:41) | AA | DD | D | DD |
| 3.31 (13:43) | BB | CC | B | BB |
| 3.54 (11:39) | A | N | A | AA |
| 4.10 (10:41) | L | M | C | CC |
| 3.73 (11:41) | H | HH | | |
| 4.65 (9:41) | G | GG | | |

LLD = Less Locking Differential
WLD = With Locking Differential

The above chart helps identify the various production axle ratios and the usage of the locking differential, sometimes called a limited-slip differential or a Sure-Grip. These are specifically listed for the 1981–1982 models, which are typical.

*Count the actual number of teeth on your pinion; this pinion gear has 10. This is one piece of necessary gear information for determining the gear ratio.*

*The second step in calculating the actual ratio is to count the number of teeth in the ring gear. This pinion has 41 teeth.*

used. The limited-slip is also identified with a letter code. While helpful information, it does not definitively identify the ratio, so don't rely on it exclusively. The axle ratio could easily have been changed several times after the vehicle was originally produced.

The best way to determine the actual axle ratio is to count the teeth on the ring gear and on the pinion. Then you divide the pinion number into the ring number. For example, if there are 41 teeth on the ring gear and 10 teeth on the pinion, the ratio is 4.10:1 (41 ÷ 10 = 4.10).

### Open or Limited-Slip Differential

To determine which type of differential you have, jack up the car/axle with wheels off the ground. Turn the driveshaft and count the turns for one complete revolution of the tires.

Use chalk to mark both the tire and driveshaft tube. This method is suitable for a limited-slip differential because both wheels turn together in the same direction. If the vehicle has an open differential, the opposite-side tire turns backward. This means that the size between the side gears and the pinion gears is a factor. The AMC 20 has 39 to 43 ring gear teeth while the

pinion has 8 to 13 teeth. Currently available ratios for this axle are 3.31 to 4.88:1.

For example, the 4.88 ratio has 8 pinion teeth and 39 ring gear teeth.

Remember that the differential case changes at ratios above 3.07:1 (numerically lower numbers) on the AMC 20 axles. (See Chapter 7 for more details.)

### Width

Refer to "Basic Rear Axle Widths" in Chapter 1. With the wheels off, it is much easier to measure the axle's total width, wheel mounting face to wheel mounting face. On AMC 20 axles with the typical tapered axle end, it is not as easy to define the wheel-mount location as it is on the flanged axles used on other axle designs because the flanged axle shafts end in a flat, vertical surface while the tapered axle shaft ends in a ramp of taper with no clear step.

On leaf-spring suspension vehicles, the spring seats are welded to the outer ends of the axle tubes. The distance from the center of one spring seat to the other spring seat is an important width for mounting the axle in the car. All AMC 20 axles discussed here use 3-inch tubes.

The ends of each axle tube have a flange and a mounting face and bolt pattern that holds the brake hardware. (See Chapter 10 for more details.)

### Yoke/Flange

The driveshaft's rear yoke attaches to the axle's yoke through a single or double U-joint. The width of the yoke or U-joint should be measured. There are two styles of U-joints: straps and two bolts per side or a small U-bolt with two nuts per side. (See Chapter 10 for more details.) The typical passenger car rear U-joint uses a strap and two bolts per side. However, the early Dana 60 in the mid-1960s Chrysler B-Body cars use U-bolts and nuts. The U-bolt attaching method is a popular upgrade in off-road Jeeps and trucks.

The U-joint varies between straps and U-bolt style. The straps or U-bolts are only used in the rear U-joint. The 1310 and 1330 model numbers are from Spicer, while the 7260 and 7290 numbers are Chrysler numbers. The aftermarket uses two styles of U-joints in the same part to connect various driveshafts to various rear axles. Two vertical caps are one style, and two horizontal caps are the other.

The yoke is designed to slide over the pinion's splines, so the number of splines is an important factor. The yoke must match the splines on the pinion shaft. The AMC 20 uses 28 splines, so there

| Current Aftermarket AMC 20 Rear Axle Ratios | | |
|---|---|---|
| **Axle Ratio (:1)** | **Ring Gear Teeth** | **Pinion Teeth** |
| 3.31 | 43 | 13 |
| 3.54 | 39 | 11 |
| 3.73 | 41 | 11 |
| 4.10 | 41 | 10 |
| 4.56 | 41 | 9 |
| 4.88 | 39 | 8 |

*All AMC 20 axles use the same number of attaching bolts, which is 12.*

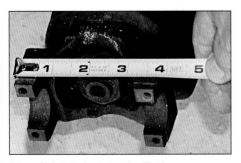

*Most U-joints look basically the same. To distinguish U-joint sizes, such as the 7260 from the 7290, use a ruler or tape to measure the width.*

won't be any problems matching splines to the pinion shaft; such an AMC 20 yoke matches an AMC pinion. Note that several Chrysler axles have two different splines, which can cause some confusion.

If the axle housing or complete assembly is being swapped, the length of the axle housing in the side view must be checked. Each design of axle has a different length. (See chart "Axle Length in Side View" on page 13.) If a swap is being performed and there is a difference in side-view lengths, the driveshaft's length must be revised to compensate, or a new driveshaft fabricated taking this length adjustment into account.

### Wheels

The bolt circle drilled into the axle shafts dictates the bolt circle of the wheels. The 4½-inch bolt circle is the most common. The position of the axle under the car (widths and wheel well location and size) determines the best wheel offset and tire clearances. (See Chapter 1 for more details.)

### Axle Bolt Circles

| Jeep/AMC | 5 bolts on 5.0 inch |
|          | 5 bolts on 4.5 inch |

*The axle shaft dictates the bolt pattern which must be reflected in the wheels. Aftermarket manufacturers make axles with virtually any bolt pattern. The key is making sure that the wheel bolt circle and the axle shaft bolt circle match.*

### Axle Tube Size

Most AMC 20 rear axles use 3-inch axle tubes.

### Spring Seat

Many RWD and 4WD AMC/Jeep vehicles use a leaf-spring rear suspension. Leaf springs are also used in 2WD Jeeps and AMC models. The leaf spring's center-bolt head pilots into the center hole in the spring seat to locate the rear suspension and, therefore, the axle.

The spring seat is welded to the outer ends of the axle tubes, and the spring is held onto the spring seat by two large U-bolts per side. The orientation of the two spring seats on the axle tubes determines the driveshaft angle. The spring seat doesn't generally control height, but in some off-road applications, it is mounted to the top of the axle, which moves the spring above the axle and greatly increases the rear height. The driveshaft angle is basically determined by the relationship between the pinion centerline and the bottom surface of the spring seat. The seat is welded to the axle tube, so you need to add thin angled shims (1, 2, or 3 degrees) to adjust the driveshaft axle between the spring and the seat.

If the driveshaft angle needs to be corrected for any reason, angled shims are placed under the spring seat after the seats are welded on. These shims maintain the proper/desired driveshaft angle. If you plan on installing new spring seats, take the shim angle into account so the shims are not required while the vehicle's driveshaft angle is maintained. If you work on your vehicle, you must get the shims installed correctly *every* time. Leave one out, put one or both in backward, and you'll probably break something, such as the driveshaft or rear axle. Weld the new seats at the desired angle and you don't have to worry about it.

### Other Things to Check

The complete axle assembly does not need to be removed for the typical rebuild. With carrier-tube axles, remove the assembly and set it up on an axle fixture to help with the build-up process.

### Tapered Axle Shafts

All AMC 20 axles use tapered axle shaft ends. They were also used in a few early-model (1964 and earlier) Chrysler 8¾-inch axles. Don't be fooled by the similarity of the descriptions. The AMC 20 uses a splined outer end on the axle shaft, while the early Chrysler uses a keyway. Both use a large nut on the end of the axle.

## AMC Rear Axle Set-Up Specifications

| Axle Model | Pinion Bearing Preload, New | Pinion Bearing Preload, Used | Ring Gear Backlash | Ring Gear Bolts to Case | Side Bearing Caps |
|---|---|---|---|---|---|
| AMC 20 | 15–25 in-lbs | 6–8 in-lbs | .005–.009 inch | 65 ft-lbs | 65 ft-lbs |

*The rear axle set-up specifications are common to all AMC 20 axle rebuilds. These numbers are very helpful as you begin to re-assembly your axle after the new parts have been installed.*

### 4WD

The typical 4WD vehicle does not always use the same axle design in the front and rear locations. It is very common that the front axle in the 4WD application is a Dana. (See Chapter 6.) The AMC 20 axle is mainly used in the rear location.

### Brake Lines

The brake lines can stay attached if the axle assembly is not being removed. However, it might be helpful if the parking brake cable is disconnected.

### Electrics and Speed Sensor

On mid-1980s-and-newer vehicles, a speed sensor was sometimes attached to the rear axle housing, which is used with anti-lock brakes. These speed sensors came into rear axle use in the mid 1980s, and that was about the same time the production of the AMC 20 ended. That means that there are probably no remaining examples in as-produced AMC 20 axles.

### C-clips

AMC 20 axles are retained by a castle nut and cotter pin on the top of the hub, and therefore do not use C-clips to retain the axle shafts. AMC 20 axles have a thrust block in the center of the differential. Once the castle nut has been removed, a special axle puller is fastened to the hub and then the axle shaft is drawn out of the axle tube. The axle shaft endplay is set using shims on the left side only.

Other carrier-tube axles do use C-clips to retain the axle shafts. If you have one these axle assemblies, first remove the rear cover, remove the C-clips from each axle, and then remove the axle shafts.

### Differential Case

AMC 20s with a limited-slip or Sure-Grip assembly come with a one-piece differential case, similar to the one-piece open differential. When switching ratios from a high ratio (2.73:1 or lower numerically) to a lower ratio (3.08:1 or higher numerically), the differential case has to be changed. (See Chapter 7 for details.)

### Gaskets

Be sure that you have new cover gaskets (or RTV), bearings, and a rebuild kit (which includes hardware) *before* starting your rebuild project. Also remember to get fresh rear axle oil (Sure-Grip fluid, if required).

## AMC 20 OTB Carrier-Tube Axle

All AMC 20 axles are carrier-tube designs. Several features identify the typical carrier-tube axle. First, they have a center housing (carrier) with two tubes (one from each side) pressed into it. There is also an inspection plate or cover bolted to the rear of the center housing. Carrier-tube axles require the ring and pinion to be removed toward the rear, one at a time. In other words, ring-and-differential assembly is removed out the back.

Many racing and off-road uses and conditions require stronger axle shafts

*There are lots of different styles of differentials and their cases. This is a Dana/AMC 20 version designed for the AMC 20 axle. It is a one-piece differential case. All of the internal parts for this style of differential go in through this window in the case. (See Chapter 7 for information on Sure-Grip differentials.)*

*You can buy components individually but if you're rebuilding an axle, you should buy a complete rebuild kit before you start working on an axle. Generally, these kits include the two pinion bearings (front and rear) and two bearings for the differential (left and right are the same), plus other hardware, such as the crushed sleeve and gaskets.*

*All of the hardware, such as the ring gear, differential, and pinion, is removed out the back on the AMC 20 axle and other carrier-tube axles. Typically, it is not required to take the complete axle assembly out of the vehicle but it can be helpful with a carrier-tube axle to sit it on a special axle rebuilding fixture such as the one shown here.*

than the basic production units. As axle housings were narrowed to gain tire clearance, aftermarket manufacturers, such as Strange, Mark Williams, and Moser, created new and shorter axle shafts and took over the leadership role in producing high-strength axles for off-road use. In addition, the use of spools has created an additional demand for stronger and stronger axle shafts. A "spool" is a solid or locked differential. They are a solid, one-piece unit designed for light weight and equal torque distribution. The spool itself is generally very strong but it puts a large amount of load into the axle shafts so sanctioning bodies for various competitions require XHD axles with their use.

## AMC 20 Carrier-Tube Axle Disassembly

This step-by-step process can be applied to the standard passenger car, Jeep, and light-duty-truck semi-floating rear axle. Many styles of carrier-tube axles are available, including the AMC 20, Dana 44, Dana 60, Chrysler 8¼-inch, and Chrysler 9¼-inch. In the following procedure, I detail the process for the AMC 20.

1 Confirm that you have everything you need: tools, parts, gaskets, cleaners, and sealers.

2 Use a flathead screwdriver to pry off the dust caps on the axle shaft.

3 Remove the cotter pins and axle shaft nuts from both sides. Straighten the ends of the cotter pin with a flat-blade screwdriver and pinch the ends together with pliers. Once straight, pull out the cotter pin with pliers or channel locks. Then use a 1/2-inch-drive ratchet and large socket to remove the nut.

4 Use a floor jack to lift the vehicle. Install jack stands under the frame rails on both sides of the vehicle, so both rear wheels are off the ground. You do not need to remove the complete axle assembly in order to rebuild/recondition the differential or change the axle ratio.

*The dust cap goes on the end of tapered axle shafts and hides the castle nut and cotter pin. The cap can be pried off with a small screwdriver.*

5 Use a socket and ratchet or impact gun to remove the lug nuts and then the wheels.

6 If present, remove the retaining clips on the axle studs and the brake drum assemblies. This allows access to the flanged/hub axle shaft ends. The brake drum removes from the hub, which stays attached to the axle shaft and must be removed with a hub puller.

### Disc Brakes

While disc brakes were available on the front, few production cars are equipped with rear disc brakes. Although disc brake rotors are removed similarly to drum brakes, the disc brake caliper must be removed first. ∎

*The basic hub puller is used for axles that have tapered axle shafts. On the AMC 20 with the wheel off and the brake drum removed, the hub puller is attached to the hub using wheel stubs. Two of the legs attach next to each other and the third goes opposite those two. The center-threaded adjuster is lowered to push on the end of the axle shaft. Torque is applied through the nut by a socket and breaker bar.*

**TECH TIP**

## Full-Floating Axles

Full-floating axles are commonly used for heavy-duty, off-road applications and disc brake conversions. Aftermarket companies make kits to convert C-clip axles to non-C-clip axles. Conversions are also offered for flanged axles. Whether a limited-production option or an aftermarket conversion, the rebuilding procedure in this book focuses on the standard production hardware. Since these axles are more than 25 years old, many changes may have been made to them over the years. Someone may have added an ARB air locker or a Detroit Locker, or changed the axle shafts to a full-floating design, etc. You just need to recognize when the axles have been altered. ■

7 Release the parking brake.

8 Clean all dirt from the area around the housing cover.

9 Install the axle hub puller onto the wheel studs.

10 Remove the axle nut. Turn the threaded adjuster on the hub puller to remove the axle hub.

11 Remove the axle shaft and bearing using a threaded axle shaft puller that's compatible with the AMC 20. Note that the axle bearing is pressed onto the shaft and must be removed in an arbor press.

12 Remove and discard the axle-shaft inner oil seal using a seal puller. The fingers of the seal puller fit inside the seal itself and then the slide hammer pulls the seal out. Smaller seal pullers

## Axle Shaft Serration Depth

For the AMC 20 axle, it is very important to correctly set the engagement depth of the axle shaft splines.

You need to follow these steps:

- Install the brake drum and retaining screws.
- Adjust the brakes shoes properly.
- Install the wheel.
- Lubricate two thrust washers with chassis grease and install the washers on the end of the axle shaft.
- Lower the vehicle to ground.
- Apply parking brake. You need to take caution because the hub must be pressed onto the axle shaft to the specified dimension in order to form the hub serrations properly.
- Tighten the axle shaft nut until the distance from the hub outer face to the axle shaft outer end is 1⁵⁄₁₆ inches.
- Remove the axle shaft nut and one thrust washer. Reinstall the axle nut. Tighten the nut to 250 ft-lbs of torque. Install a

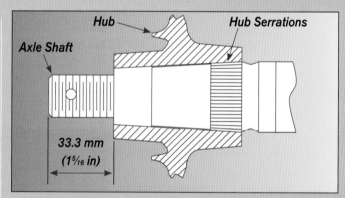

replacement cotter pin. If the cotter pin hole is not aligned, tighten the nut to the next castellation. Do not loosen the nut to align the cotter pin hole.

- Scribe or mark the driveshaft tube and the yoke so you can reassemble in the same relationship to maintain dynamic balance.

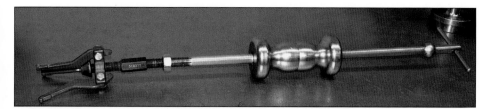

*This seal remover has three fingers. The fingers of the seal puller fit inside the seal itself and then the slide hammer pulls the seal out. Smaller seal pullers may use a separate hammer and have only one finger and a fixed two-finger.*

may use a separate hammer and have only one finger and a fixed two-finger.

**13** Rotate the axle shaft hub to allow access to the brake backing plate nuts. Remove the nuts and discard. Remove backing plates. Typically you find four nuts per plate on the AMC 20 axle and a plate on each side. This is not required if the axle housing stays in the vehicle during rebuild.

**14** Mark the driveshaft at the U-joint and pinion flange with a scribe or Sharpie marker.

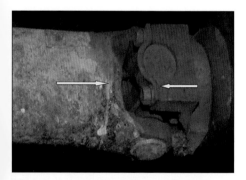

*Mark both the driveshaft and the yoke before you take them apart to enable you to re-assemble them to maintain the dynamic balance of your drivetrain. Use one or two marks, just below the U-joint cap on the yoke and a matching set on the driveshaft tube.*

**15** Disconnect prop-shaft from the axle yoke. Push the driveshaft forward and support it in a near-horizontal position, out of your way. The transmission leaks when removing the driveshaft.

To prevent any leaking, install a plastic cup on the seal.

**16** Use duct tape to tape the U-joint and hold cups together.

**17** Rotate pinion several full revolutions and use an inch-pound torque wrench to measure the torque required to rotate the pinion gear (turnover torque). Record the measurement in your assembly notebook. Torque range should be about 15 to 25 in-lbs.

**18** Place an oil drain pan below the axle cover.

**19** Remove the drain plug. (If there is no actual drain plug, follow the next three steps. If there is a drain plug, remove it to drain the oil and proceed to Step 22.) The oil fill plug is only used to fill, and is too high to function as a drain. However, it will be required to be open at assembly to allow oil to be added.

**20** Remove the housing cover bolts. Leave one bolt threaded into the top of the housing but loose. Carefully pry the cover loose at the bottom.

**21** Allow the oil to drain from rear axle at the bottom of cover.

**22** Remove the rear cover and the last screw and clean the inside, scrap old gasket material off with a gas-

ket scraper and wipe with clean rag. Last step (optional) is to wipe with cleaner that leaves no oil or grease residue like Brakleen.

**23** You now have access to the differential. You should verify the type of differential: open versus limited-slip or locker style. (See page 131 for the limited-slip in-car test procedure.)

**24** Inspect the axle shafts, especially in the bearing and seal area, and look for wear and grooving. If the axle shafts show any significant wear or damage, replace them. Also closely inspect the splines on the inner end of the shaft, the seal, and the wheel bearing areas on the outer end of each shaft. Look for signs of high heat—discoloration to actual burned/blackened appearance along with signs of scuffing. The shaft and splines should be straight.

**25** Use a seal puller to remove the axle shaft seal from the housing bore. Be sure you have a replacement seal. A seal puller has two or three fingers to reach inside the axle tube along with a small slide hammer. Insert your fingers around the inner lip of the seal and pull the tool's slide hammer until the seal pops out.

**26** Measure the differential side play by placing a flat-blade screwdriver or small pry bar between the left side of the axle housing and the differential case flange. Use a prying motion to determine if side play is present. If side play is found, add the necessary number of shims if there's excessive side play and remove shims if not enough side play is present at reassembly. Keep in mind that you are going to re-set side play when you re-assemble the axle, so it is mainly for reference. However, these procedures

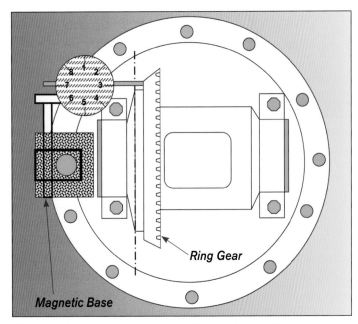

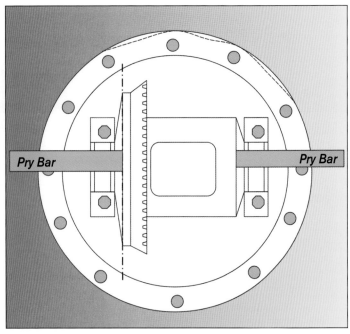

*Measure ring gear runout on the differential case. Mount a dial indicator onto the flat surface of the carrier housing, which is the left side of this drawing. Slightly depress the stem of the indicator when the plunger is at right angles to the back of the ring gear.*

*Pry the differential loose by using one pry bar on each side or alternate sides with one. You can also use a large screwdriver in a similar way.*

are uncommon so a little extra practice helps at rebuild time.

27 Measure side play and runout. These checks taken during disassembly are very useful at reassembly. To measure, use a dial indicator. This step is more important if the current axle assembly had problems, such as an exploded rear end or being locked up during use.

28 At reassembly, measure the ring gear runout by turning the ring gear several full revolutions and reading the dial indicator. Mark the ring gear and differential case at the point of maximum runout. Marking the differential case is an important step when checking the differential case runout later on. This step is important if problems existed with the current axle setup. The indicator reading should be no more than .006 inch. If runout exceeds .006 inch the differential case may be damaged, and a damaged case may be responsible for excessive runout. If the

differential case is damaged, replace it. However, there may be another reason for high runout and a new ring gear and bearings should fix it.

29 To check the clearance between the differential bearing cap and the bearing cup, try to insert a piece of .003-inch feeler gauge between them. It should not fit. If the clearance is more than .003 inch, it could be caused by the bearing cup turning in the carrier, which causes excessive wear. If this has occurred, the carrier may have to be replaced or major repair is required. If major repair is required, you need to take the carrier to a professional shop.

30 Mark each half of the differential case if it is a two-piece case. Most AMC 20 production-based axles use a one-piece differential; therefore, there is no reason to mark it. However, most aftermarket differentials are two-piece types and they should be marked for reinstallation.

31 Loosen the four main cap bolts, but do not remove the bearing caps.

32 Loosen the bearing-cap attaching bolts until only a few threads are still engaged, and pull the bearing caps away from the bearings. This prevents the differential assembly from falling out

*Use a punch to mark the carrier housing and the main caps for reinstallation. Place one mark on the left and two marks on the right. Note the two dots above the main cap in the center of this photo and the two dots on the differential case just to the right of the main cap.*

*Remove ring gear and differential assembly. Re-install the differential case after the ring gear has been removed to check for runout. Leaving the caps in the housing helps you find them at reassembly.*

or becoming damaged when it is pried out of the axle housing.

**33** Remove the bearing caps.

**34** Tie the differential bearing shims to the caps.

**35** Keep the bearing cups with their respective bearing cones.

**36** Use the bearing removal tool to retrieve the differential bearings from the case.

**37** Use a yoke holder to remove the drive pinion nut and washer. If you use an air impact gun on the pinion

nut, a large pair of channel locks can serve as the yoke holder. If you are using a socket and manual ratchet/breaker bar, you need to hold it more securely, which requires a yoke holder similar to the one shown on page 25.

**38** Remove the drive pinion yoke using a flange puller tool.

*The yoke remover is a smaller puller with two fingers and a center adjusting screw. The fingers generally go over the outside of the yoke saddles and the center adjuster pushes on the pinion stem. Once set up, a small socket and ratchet is all that is required to removed the yoke.*

**39** Install the rear cover with two bolts to prevent the pinion from falling out of the housing during removal.

**40** Remove the drive pinion oil seal.

**41** To remove the pinion, push/tap/drive the pinion stem rearward and out of the bearing using a non-metallic, plastic, rubber, or rawhide hammer. Catch it in your hand or on the reinstalled cover.

*Tap the nose of the pinion with a non-metallic hammer (or use a brass drift). Be prepared for the pinion to fall into the case. To catch it, use towels, your hand, a helper, or use the rear cover and some towels.*

**42** Remove the front bearing and spacer. This collapsible spacer is used to control preload. Discard this spacer; it is not re-usable.

**43** Remove the rear cover, pinion gear, and rear bearing if the cover was reinstalled.

*Once the pinion is loose, reach into the housing (remove cover if reinstalled) and carefully pick up the gear and remove it rearward. The rear bearing comes with the pinion.*

**44** Remove the front and rear bearing cups from the housing using bearing pullers, which come in all sizes because of the many sizes of bearings.

*This is a yoke holder. If you use an air impact gun to remove the pinion nut, the yoke holder can be a large pair of channel locks. If you are using a socket and manual ratchet/breaker bar, you need to hold it more securely, which requires a yoke holder similar to the one shown on page 25.*

*The bolt-on yoke holder attaches by two bolts diagonally opposite each other on the yoke saddles. The trick with various yoke holders is that the torque wrench, breaker bar, or air impact gun has to pass through the center of the tool to apply torque to the pinion nut.*

*A bearing remover/installer can be used to push bearings into place or to hammer out bearings/races after being pressed into place. Bearing pullers come in all sizes because of the many sizes of bearings in an axle. The puller is selected based on the size of the bearing and its location (length of handle). However, a brass drift or punch and a hammer may be used in a pinch. The bearing race (on the left) selects the installer/remover (on the right).*

The puller is selected based on the size of the bearing and its location (length of handle). However, a brass drift or punch and a hammer may be used if you can't find a puller.

*The pinion bearing remover has two pieces that separate so they can fit behind the pinion bearing, once the pinion has been removed from the axle. After the two shells have been fitted behind the pinion bearing, the threaded bars on each side can be tightened. This assembly is installed in an arbor press and then the bearing is pressed off. The tool has threaded attachments that allow the bearing to be removed using a ratchet (not shown).*

**45** Check and record the number of shims on either side of the bearings. Replace the pinion bearings (from the rebuild kit).

**46** Mark all shim thicknesses and locations. You can hang the shims in order on a wire or spare coat hanger or place a tie-rap around each pack and place in a zip-lock bag.

**47** Remove the ring gear from the differential housing only if the ring gear is being replaced.

**48** Remove and discard the ring gear screws, which have right-hand threads (all AMC 20 axles use right-hand threads).

*Remove ring gear, if being replaced. Use a non-metallic hammer and brass drift punch to tap the ring gear loose. Cushion the ring gear's fall to the workbench with shop towels.*

*Attach a dial indicator to the carrier housing so that the pointer is perpendicular to the ring gear surface of the differential case flange. This is between the outer edge and the ring gear attaching bolts holes.*

**49** Optional: If the ring gear runout was more than .006 inch in step 30, re-measure the differential case flange runout. Install the differential case and respective bearing cups and adjusters in the housing.

**50** Install the bearing caps and bolts and lightly tighten the bearing cap bolts.

**51** Attach the dial indicator to carrier housing so that the pointer is perpendicular to the ring gear surface of the differential case flange (between the outer edge and the ring gear attaching bolts holes).

**52** Rotate the differential case several complete revolutions while noting the total indicator reading. This indicator reading must not exceed .003-inch runout. If the runout is more than .003 inch, the differential case must be replaced.

**53** Use a socket and ratchet to remove the two bearing cap bolts and remove the differential case assembly from the housing.

**54** Remove the drive pinion and bearing. Drive out the front and rear pinion bearing cups from the carrier housing. Select a bearing driver or use a long punch and hammer to remove the cups. Remove the shim with the rear bearing and record its thickness. Press off the rear bearing in arbor press.

**55** Use a bearing puller to remove the rear bearing cone from the drive pinion.

**56** Use a punch to remove the pinion shaft lockpin in the differential. Some differentials use a threaded pin with a hex head that thread into the case.

**57** Measure and record the differential side-gear-to-case clearance for assembly reference. Insert equal-thickness feeler gauges between each side gear and the differential case (or behind it) to measure the clearance. Do not remove one feeler gauge before the both gears have been measured. In other words, use one feeler gauge on each side to measure the clearance.

**58** Use a punch to remove the pinion shaft from the differential housing. Remove the thrust block from inside

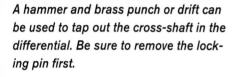

*A hammer and brass punch or drift can be used to tap out the cross-shaft in the differential. Be sure to remove the locking pin first.*

the differential. Once the cross-shaft is out, slide the thrust block out through the side gear/axle hole.

**59** Clamp the case and rotate by hand the differential housing side gears until the differential pinions appear at the case window opening. Lift the two pinions and thrust washers from the housing. If the side gears are hard to rotate, try inserting an axle shaft end into the side gear and use the shaft to rotate the gear. Once removed, tag and bag the parts.

**60** By hand, lift the differential side gears and thrust washers from the case one at a time.

**61** Use a bearing puller to remove the differential bearing cones from the differential case.

**62** Remove the shims and record their thickness.

**63** Use mineral spirits or another suitable cleaner to thoroughly clean all parts. Dirt is the enemy of any moving part. Cleaning allows you to see cracks, especially small ones in your hardware. It also allows you to observe the surface for scuffing and any discoloration.

## AMC 20 Carrier-Tube Cleaning and Inspection

With the differential completely disassembled, it is time to check all the parts and see what you have. Obviously wearable parts such as bearings that are replaced do not need to be checked

**1** Clean all parts with a parts brush and mineral spirits or a dry cleaning solvent. Dry the bearings cones with compressed air or lint-free towels.

**2** To clean the axle housing tubes, insert a long, stiff wire (length greater

*To remove all the gasket material, scrape the gasket surfaces on both the housing and the cover. Use an even and careful scraping motion. Position the scraper at about a 45-degree angle to the scraping surface and make sure you don't deeply scratch or mar the flange area.*

than the one axle tube) into the axle tube from the outer end. Attach a clean cloth to the wire in the center housing and pull the cloth from the center outward. Scrape the carrier cover gasket surface.

**3** Check the axle housing and differential bearing caps for sharp edges. Both should be smooth with no raised edges.

*Inspect your differential housing for cracks. The open differential is a one-piece design; some limited-slip units are also one-piece designs, but most feature a two-piece housing. Lockers are also two-piece designs.*

**4** Inspect the differential pinion shaft or cross-shaft for excessive wear in the contact area of the pinions. The shaft should be smooth and round with no scoring.

*This cross-shaft is worn and scuffed. (You can tell because the wear surface is not smooth) and therefore it should be replaced. Note that the turning slot is at the top and the lock pin hole is at the bottom. It is very difficult to show scuffed surfaces in photographs. Scuffing looks like deep scratches in a smooth surface. This end of the cross-shaft is scuffed and should be replaced.*

**5** Inspect the thrust block for excessive wear or cracks. Replace the thrust block if it is damaged.

6 Inspect the differential case for an elongated or enlarged pinion shaft hole. The pinion shaft can be used to check the basic hole size, but also check for scuffing, which is best done visually. Inspect the differential carrier housing for cracks or other damage. Check the machined thrust washer surfaces inside the differential case.

*This is the back of a side gear with its thrust washer. Inspect your differential side gears and pinions. Check the gears for cracked or chipped teeth. They should have smooth teeth with a uniform contact pattern. Side clearance must not exceed .007 inch. Replace thrust washers with those from the rebuild kit. (See Chapter 7 for limited-slip details.)*

7 Confirm that the new ring and pinion gears are a matched set (same numbers).

8 Inspect the ring gear and pinion for worn or chipped teeth or damaged attaching bolt threads. Always replace as a set. Be sure the mounting face of the ring gear is flat. Slide the large, flat file over the rear mounting face to remove nicks and sharp edges.

*The mounting surface of the ring gear should be flat. Pass a large, flat, file over the back face of the ring gear to remove high spots and dents.*

9 Inspect the differential bearing cones, cups, and rollers for pitting or other visible damage, such as overheating. If replacement is necessary, remove the bearing cones from the case using a bearing puller. Replace the cup and cone as a set only.

*This is done using a special differential bearing remover. There are several pieces to the tool. The differential has been installed on this tool and now I'm ready to remove the bearing. There are two pieces that fit around the differential bearing and the end of the case. The tall, threaded adjuster fits on top of the end of the case. Once the two halves have been fitted around the bearing, the outer sleeve is dropped over it and the bearing removal can begin. An air impact gun or large socket/ratchet is applied to the top of the threaded adjuster to actually remove the bearing.*

10 The axle shaft splines should be smooth and straight and not show signs of excessive wear. To remove flaws and rough spots, polish the area with 600-grade crocus cloth.

11 Clean the axle shaft bearings with mineral spirits and dry with a lintless towel or compressed air. Inspect all surfaces for damage or excessive wear. Rollers should not be flattened, chipped, or grooved. Replace as required.

12 Use mineral spirits or a spray degreaser to clean the axle shaft oil seal bores at both ends of the housing. Dry with compressed air. Inspect these areas for damage or wear; they should be free of rust or corrosion. This applies to the brake support plate and housing flange face surfaces.

13 Inspect the drive pinion bearing cones, cups, and rollers for excessive damage or overheating. Note that the pinion bearing was pressed off in an earlier step, or you can do it here. Look carefully for discoloration and a burned/blackened appearance. Also examine these parts for physical damage, such as flat-sided rollers and scuffed cups/cones/rollers. Replace as sets if required.

*Here is the arbor press with the pinion installed in the process of removing pinion bearing. The pinion bearing remover tool is installed behind the bearing and the press will remove it smoothly. Be sure to catch the pinion below the support.*

14 Inspect the yoke for cracks or worn splines. Replace if required.

15 Inspect the drive pinion bearing shim pack for broken, damaged, or distorted shims. Place the shims on a flat bench or table surface to verify shim straightness. Replace if necessary during pinion bearing preload adjustment.

# AMC 20 Carrier-Tube Assembly

## AMC 20 Axle Torque Specifications

| Component | Ft-lbs |
|---|---|
| Differential Bearing Cap Bolts | 87 |
| Ring Gear to Differential Case Bolts | 55 |
| Drive Pinion Flange Nut | collapse spacer |
| Carrier Cover Bolts | 15 |
| Brake Support Plate Retaining Bolts | 32 |
| Driveshaft Bolts (Rear) | 16 |
| Spring Clip (U-bolt) Nuts | 100 (9/16 x 18) |
|  | 55 (1/2 x 20) |
| Wheel Stud Nuts | 80 |
| Shock Absorber Stud Nuts (Lower) | 45 |
| Axle Hub Nut | 250 (minimum) |

*There are a lot of bolts in an axle assembly and each one should be torqued to a specific torque specification. It can be handy to have all of these torques listed in one chart so they can easily be found when required during assembly.*

*Use an inch-pound torque wrench to measure the pinion bearing preload. With the torque wrench on, slowly rotate the pinion flange and record the maximum torque reading. Note that the pinion gear mainly sits in the center housing or carrier while the inch-pound torque wrench has to fit on the yoke end of the pinion gear.*

*This test is often best performed with the housing nose-up to keep the handle of the torque wrench in a flat circle, not going up and down or upside down, which makes it difficult to read.*

AMC 20 carrier-tube axles are similar to Dana 60s and 8¼-inch Chryslers. Here I focus on the AMC 20.

1 Always count the actual teeth on the ring gear and pinion to verify that you have received the correct parts. Dividing the number of ring gear teeth by the number of pinion teeth determines the actual ratio. For example, if the ring gear teeth count is 41 and the pinion gear teeth count is 10, the ratio is 4.10:1 (41 ÷ 10 = 4.10).

For street use, use ratios in the range of 2.5 to 3.5:1. For dual-purpose applications, use ratios in the range of 3.5 to 4.1:1. For drag racing, use ratios at 4.10:1 and higher (numerically lower). Overdrive transmissions and/or add-on units change these basic numbers. The blueprinting clearances and specifications are listed in an earlier section.

2 Clean all parts thoroughly, blow-dry, and inspect. Metal pieces from previous miles of wear and general dirt circulate in used oil, but you also need to check for cracks, scuffing, and discoloration that would indicate too much heat. In addition, check all new parts for damage.

3 Lubricate all components with rear-axle lubricant.

4 Reinstall the main caps in their original locations. Typically torque the main caps to 87 ft-lbs. (See the chart above for torque values.)

5 Remember that you are going to make adjustments to the pinion depth, pinion bearing preload, backlash, and carrier bearing preload as discussed in the following pages.

6 With two-piece differentials, which include some limited-slip units, the two halves were marked at disassembly. Align the marks to properly reassemble them in the same relationship. Torque the differential case bolts to 45 ft-lbs.

The AMC 20 axle uses a one-piece limited-slip differential similar to many Dana axles. These units use clutches and can be rebuilt. (See Chapter 7 for more information.)

# Ring-and-Pinion Gear Setup

The pinion gear depth must be measured and adjusted before the final assembly installation of the gear. There are several ways to set the pinion depth. The initial pinion depth is set according to the plus/minus numbers found on the old pinion and the new pinion. This approach is fine if you are using a good, original axle. However, if you have a brand-new axle housing or one that was broken or severely damaged, you must go through a more detailed measuring process. You need to go through this more detailed process if you didn't have the plus/minus numbers from one or both of the pinions. (See sidebar "How to Set Pinion Gear Depth" on page 49.)

Ring-and-pinion gear sets are machined and manufactured in matched sets. Each set has a number, typically two digits, etched or stamped on the end face of the pinion and around the outside diameter of the ring. The number on the pinion and on the ring must match for the parts to be a matched set.

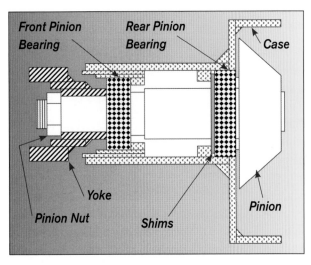

Front Pinion Bearing
Rear Pinion Bearing
Case
Yoke
Pinion Nut
Shims
Pinion

*The pinion depth is the distance in inches between the pinion gear end face and the axle shaft centerline. Installed shims set the distance between the pinion rear bearing cup and the axle housing. There are several ways of measuring the pinion depth; adding shims or various thicknesses adjusts the depth.*

*Numbers on the pinion head face can be painted (shown), etched, or stamped on. The end face of the pinion also has a number with a plus (+) or minus (-) sign in front of it. It indicates the pinion position in relation to the axle shaft centerline, where the tooth contact is best and offers the quietest operation. The number represents the variance in the pinion depth and is the amount in thousandths of an inch that the set varied from the standard setting.*

## Pinion Gear Depth Measurement and Adjustment

This section is not required for most axle rebuilds. In most cases you have shim thickness numbers, both on the the new gear set and the old gear set. If this is the case, you can skip to the marking pattern step.

However, if you have no numbers (old gear or can't read), any number is not available, you have a brand-new housing, or you have a broken housing (welded on to repair, etc.), you need to refer to sidebar "How to Set Pinion Gear Depth" on page 49.

1 Once the starter shim thickness has been calculated, install the rear bearing on the pinion gear with the larger

diameter of the bearing facing the pinion head. Then press the bearing against the rear face of the pinion head.

2 Clean the pinion bearing bores in the axle housing (carrier) thoroughly. This is important to the correct depth measurement and adjustment.

3 Once the bearing bore is thoroughly clean, add the proper shim and drive the bearing cup into the housing using a hammer and a handle sized for the bearing. Be sure that the shim is centered in the bore—chamfered side toward the bottom of the bore.

4 Install the rear pinion bearing cup into the housing using a bearing installation tool. (See top photo on page 44.)

5 Lubricate the front and rear pinion bearings with rear axle lubricant. Also rotate the pinion several complete revolutions to help set the rollers.

*Pressing the pinion bearing onto the pinion stem in a basic arbor press can be done with no special fixtures.*

6 Use a hammer and drift to drive the pinion gear into the rear bearing cup and housing. Make sure it is squarely positioned in the bearing cup and you strike it evenly as it's driven into the bearing cup. A bearing driver works best but a hammer and punch also work.

7 Install the front pinion bearing and the yoke onto the splines of the pinion gear. Tap the yoke with a non-metallic hammer and it should slide into place. Do not install the oil seal or the collapsible spacer at this time.

8 Install the original or used pinion nut onto the pinion and tighten the nut only enough to remove any bearing endplay. Snug with a wrench. At this time, *do not* use the new pinion nut and *do not*

*Install the large washer on the stem of the pinion before the large nut. Lube the bottom side of the washer with axle lube prior to installation.*

# How to Set Pinion Gear Depth

The pinion shim chart below helps determine the approximate shim thickness for the initial pinion depth measurement. However, the chart does not provide the exact shim thickness required for the final depth adjustment and must not be used as a substitute for an actual pinion adjustment.

The head of the drive pinion is marked with a plus (+) or a minus (–) sign, followed by a number ranging from zero to 4.

To use the chart, measure the thickness of the original shim using a vernier caliper or micrometer. Note the pinion variance numbers marked on the old and new pinion gears. Refer to the New Pinion Marking and Old Pinion Marking columns. The place where the two numbers intersect provides the approximate amount of shim change needed for your starter thickness.

## Pinion Shim Chart

| | | New Pinion Marking | | | | | | | |
| | **-4** | **-3** | **-2** | **-1** | **0** | **+1** | **+2** | **+3** | **+4** |
|---|---|---|---|---|---|---|---|---|---|
| **+4** | +.008 | +.007 | +.006 | +.005 | +.004 | +.003 | +.002 | +.001 | 0 |
| **+3** | +.007 | +.006 | +.005 | +.004 | +.003 | +.002 | +.001 | 0 | –.001 |
| **+2** | +.006 | +.005 | +.004 | +.003 | +.002 | +.001 | 0 | –.001 | –.002 |
| **+1** | +.005 | +.004 | +.003 | +.002 | +.001 | 0 | –.001 | –.002 | –.003 |
| **0** | +.004 | +.003 | +.002 | +.001 | 0 | –.001 | –.002 | –.003 | –.004 |
| **-1** | +.003 | +.002 | +.001 | 0 | –.001 | –.002 | –.003 | –.004 | –.005 |
| **-2** | +.002 | +.001 | 0 | –.001 | –.002 | –.003 | –.004 | –.005 | –.006 |
| **-3** | +.001 | 0 | –.001 | –.002 | –.003 | –.004 | –.005 | –.006 | –.007 |
| **-4** | 0 | –.001 | –.002 | –.003 | –.004 | –.005 | –.006 | –.007 | –.008 |

(Old Pinion Marking runs down the left side)

For example, if the old pinion is marked –2 and the new pinion is marked +3 (or just 3), find the –2 line in the column on the left. Then, move to the right (in the same row) until you are in the +3 column. The intersecting number is the amount of shim thickness change that is required.

In this case the change is –.005 inch. This is the amount that is to be subtracted from the old shim thickness. (If you have a plus number, it is the amount to add to the old shim thickness.)

An axle shop has lots of shims waiting for pinion adjustments. Shims come in all sizes and many, many thicknesses, so you can properly set the pinion depth for any differential. There are shims for the differential and for both the front and rear pinion bearing. Typically the rear pinion bearing shims are the largest in diameter.

*To select the proper thickness shim, proceed as follows: The head of the drive pinion is marked with a plus (+) or a minus (–) sign, followed by a number ranging from 1 to 4 or 0 (zero). This is Step 2 in the calcualtion and results in the shim thickness to be installed. If the old and new pinions have the same marking and if the original bearing is being reused, use the same mounting shim thickness. If the old pinion is marked zero, and the new pinion is marked +2, try a .002-inch-thinner shim. If the new pinion is marked –2, try a .002-inch-thicker shim. Axle shops have lots of shims waiting for pinion adjustments.*

install the collapsible spacer because the pinion must be removed after the depth measurement.

**9** Determine the thickness of the rear pinion bearing mounting shim suitable for the carrier by using a gauge block and cross-arbor. The master gauge block fits directly on top of the pinion head. The two master bearing discs come in several sizes based on the axle design and fit into the main caps. The cross-pin/arbor fits between the two discs. The dial indicator/gauge fits on top of the block and its indicator rest on the arbor.

**10** Position the crossbore arbor into the differential bearing bores and

*A gauge arbor (the cross-bar in the photo) has three basic pieces, not counting the dial indicator/measuring hardware. The two metal discs are inserted into the differential case's main bearing bores. (They are sized to fit exactly.) Then the main caps are installed. The disc in the right-side main can be seen here. Then the cross-arbor is slid across between the two discs in the sized holes in their centers. From this basic setup, the gauge block and indicators are used to measure from the across-arbor (the rod) down to the pinion head.*

secure with the bolts. Tighten the bolts. Place the differential bearing caps over the discs and securely tighten the main cap bolts. Be sure the gauge discs are completely seated before installing the bearing caps.

**11** The selection of a rear pinion bearing mounting shim is based on the thickness of shim (gauge block) that fits between the crossbore arbor and the gauge block. Position the gauge block (part of a gauge-arbor tool kit) on the rear face of the pinion gear. Do not allow the gauge block to contact the pinion gear teeth.

**12** Mount the gauge tool clamp strap and holding screw tool onto the housing. Extend the holding screw until it is firmly against the gauge block to hold the block in position.

**13** Loosen the thumbscrew in the end of the gauge block and allow the spring-loaded plunger to contact the gauge arbor at the center of the shaft.

**14** Tighten the thumbscrew to lock the plunger in the gauge. Be careful not to disturb the plunger position.

**15** Remove the differential bearing caps and remove the gauge arbor and discs.

**16** Remove the gauge block and measure the distance from the end of the anvil to the top of the plunger head using a 2- to 3-inch micrometer. (This dimension represents the measured pinion depth.) Record the measurement in your assembly notebook.

**17** Remove the pinion nut and the axle yoke from the pinion gear. Remove the pinion gear and the front bearing. Then remove the rear pinion bearing cup from the housing. Use a yoke puller to remove the yoke, which is a medium-size, two-finger design with center-threaded adjuster. Remove the rear pinion bearing cup using a cup remover, driver handle, and hammer. Remove the front bearing cup in a similar fashion (opposite direction).

**18** Remove the starter pinion depth shim from the housing and measure the shim thickness. Add the starter shim thickness to the measured pinion depth, then subtract the desired pinion depth. The result represents the actual shim thickness needed for the correct pinion depth adjustment.

Remember, this is an optional step for most rebuilds.

## Pinion Gear Installation and Bearing Preload Adjustment

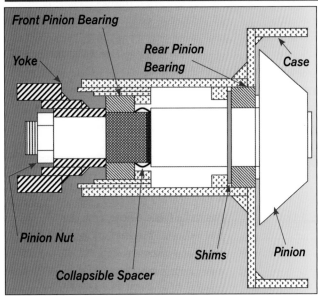

Front Pinion Bearing

Yoke

Rear Pinion Bearing

Case

Pinion Nut

Shims

Pinion

Collapsible Spacer

*The pinion gear bearing must be preloaded to compensate for expansion caused by heat and load during operation. A collapsible spacer, installed between the front bearing and a shoulder on the pinion gear, maintains the preload. With the use of a collapsible spacer, the front bearing shims are not used. Remember that this collapsible spacer cannot be re-used.*

the necessary number of shims were added. (See "How to Set Pinion Gear Depth" on page 49.) Using two hands, carefully pass the yoke end of the pinion through the rear bearing cup from the rear of the carrier until your other hand can grip the pinion splines.

**1** Install the correct-thickness pinion depth shim (calculated above) in the rear bearing cup bore in the housing. Be sure the shim is centered in the bore—the chamfered side faces the bottom of the bore.

**2** Install the pinion rear bearing cup in the housing bearing cup bore.

**3** Install the pinion gear and rear bearing into the rear bearing cup. The rear bearing has been pressed on and

**4** Install the new collapsible spacer onto the pinion. The spacer slides down the pinion shaft over the splines and into position.

**5** Install the front bearing onto the pinion. The bearing slips over the splines and into the front bearing cup. If the bearing is reversed, it does not seat properly in the cup. Note that the cup or bearing race was installed.

**6** Install the new pinion oil seal using a seal installer tool. In most cases any flat metal object, sized to the bearing seal, will serve to tap the seal into place.

*The Pinion seal is on the end of the housing. Therefore it can be tapped in easily but an installer (shown) can be helpful. In most cases, any flat metal object, sized to the bearing seal, serves to tap the seal into place.*

**7** Install the yoke. Line up the splines and tap the yoke onto the spline.

**8** Thread the new pinion nut and place the washer onto the pinion and tighten only enough to remove any bearing endplay. Rotate the pinion when tightening the nut to seat the bearing evenly. Caution: Do not exceed the specified preload torque and do not loosen the pinion nut to reduce preload if the desired torque is exceeded.

*Try to keep torque wrench as flat as possible as you rotate it. A steady hand gives the best reading. Check the pinion-rotating torque using an inch-pound torque wrench. The rotating torque must be 15 to 25 in-lbs.*

**9** Continue tightening the pinion nut in small increments to collapse the spacer and preload the bearings. When a very slight increase in pinion turning effort is felt, the spacer has collapsed—and you don't want to crush the spacer, so stop tightening the nut and remove the tools.

**10** If the specified preload torque is exceeded, remove the pinion nut,

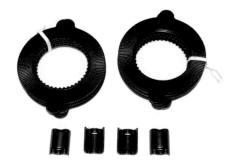

yoke, oil seal, and collapsible spacer and install a new, replacement collapsible spacer and seal.

**11** Install the yoke and new pinion nut and adjust the preload torque again.

*Differential cases may be one-piece as shown on left or two-piece, bolt-together units. The one-piece unit may be an open or limited-slip unit while the two-piece units may be limited-slip or lockers. Re-assemble a two-piece unit keeping the same component orientation. Typically differential case bolts are torqued to 45 ft-lbs. Aftermarket limited-slips or lockers may be one or two piece designs and tend to come fully-assembled, ready to install. If you have a limited-slip differential, there may be clutch disc and plates inside that can be replaced. Rebuild kits are generally available for clutch-disc units.*

*If you have a limited-slip differential, always replace the clutch discs during any rebuild. This disc package for the AMC 20 Sure-Grip includes the round disc and plates with two ears, plus a Belleville washer (in each pile). The four clips at the bottom are used to hold the clutch packs together. One pile installs to the right side and the other to the left.*

*In a limited-slip clutch pack, you find a Belleville washer (at the top), discs and plates (in the middle), and four clips to hold the clutch packs together (at the bottom).*

## AMC 20 Carrier-Tube Differential Assembly Prep

*Position each new differential bearing cone on the hub of the differential case (with the cone taper away from the ring gear) and carefully press on the bearing cones or use a bearing installation tool with a hammer or an arbor press.*

The AMC 20 uses a one-piece limited-slip differential similar to the Dana axles. See Chapter 7 for specific details on differentials. The standard or open differential is also a one-piece design and the basic steps for assembly are listed below and on page 134. Set out all the parts next to the case: pinions, side gears, cross-shaft, washers, and differential bearings.

1 Install the thrust washers onto the side gears. Install the assembled side gears and washers into the differential case.

2 Place new, replacement thrust washers onto the differential pinions. To

*To begin putting the differential back together, place the thrust washer onto the back side of the side gear (the ones with teeth on the inside diameter). Lubricate both side before the install.*

help with installation, mate the washer lips with the shaft bores in the pinions (to help maintain washer position) during installation.

3 Install the assembled differential pinions and thrust washers into the case. The pinion and washer are meshed with the two side gears already in the case. The side gear must be rotated to take the pinion out of the window and over to the opposite side. Then the second pinion can be meshed with the side gears. The side gear is rotated to move both pinions over to line up with the cross-shaft holes. If the side gears do not rotate easily, try inserting the end of an axle shaft into the side gear and rotate the gear using the shaft. Mesh the pinions with the side gears, so the shaft bores in the pinions are aligned (180 degrees opposite each other).

4 To mesh the pinion gears, rotate the side gears inside the differential until the shaft bores in the pinions are aligned with shaft holes in the case.

*Then install the pinion thrust washers onto the back side of the pinion gears. Lubricate both sides before installation.*

5 Install the thrust block. Once pinion gears are in place, insert the block through the axle hole and side gear into position. Align the bore in the thrust block with the pinion shaft bores in the case.

6 Install the differential pinion shaft. Tap the cross-shaft with a brass drift and hammer. Be sure to align the lockpin bore in the shaft with the lockpin bore in the case. Use the slot in the bottom of the cross-shaft and a large, flat-blade screwdriver to fine-tune. As the cross-shaft gets close to position, use a pin to help align them. Install the lockpin.

*One end of the cross-shaft has a slot in it. This slot and a large screwdriver can be used to help align the lockpin hole with the hole in the case during assembly. The height alignment can be done using a brass drift and hammer.*

## Differential Bearing Endplay Adjustment

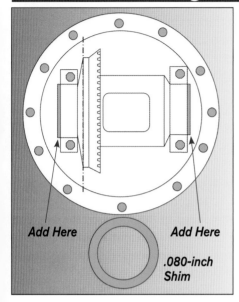

Add Here    Add Here

.080-inch Shim

*Place a bearing cup over each differential bearing and install the differential assembly into the axle housing. Install .080-inch shims on each side of the differential bearing cup and the central carrier housing. Install the bearing caps and finger tighten the bolts.*

1 Mount a dial indicator so that the end contacts the ring gear mounting face of the differential case. (See sidebar "Dial Indicator Use" on page 23.)

2 Use a large, flathead screwdriver or small pry bar to pry between the shims and the housing. Pry the assembly to one side and zero the indicator, and then pry the assembly to the opposite side and read the dial indicator. Do not attempt to zero or read the indicator while prying.

3 The reading on the indicator is the shim thickness that must be added to arrive at zero preload and zero endplay. Repeat the procedure before finalizing your calculation.

4 Install the shims as necessary to adjust the bearing endplay to zero. Install the same thickness shim at each bearing. Endplay shims are available in thickness ranges of .080 to .110 inch in .002-inch increments.

5 When the bearing endplay is eliminated, a slight bearing drag should be noticed.

6 Install the bearing caps and tighten the bolts to the specified torque, which is 87 ft-lbs for an AMC 20.

7 Optional: Attach a dial indicator to the axle housing and check the ring gear mounting face of the differential case for runout. Replace the case if runout exceeds .002 inch. The differential case may be damaged. If you checked runout at disassembly and it passed, it should still be okay but it is always a good idea to check. If it wasn't done at disassembly, do it now.

8 Remove the bearing caps and remove the differential assembly. Retain the shims used to eliminate differential bearing side play.

## AMC 20 Ring Gear Installation

*Examine the ring gear mounting surface for nicks or burrs and de-burr as required. Remove the sharp edge on the chamfer on the inside diameter of the ring gear by using a large, round or half-round file (shown) or an Arkansas stone.*

Set the ring gear, differential, and new ring gear bolts on your workbench. Remember that these bolts are right-hand thread. You should have discarded the old bolts so they don't get mixed with the new ones.

*Place the ring gear onto the differential case and align the bolt holes. Using new ring gear screws (right-hand threads) insert the screws through the case flange, into the ring gear, and finger tighten. Install all screws before tightening any of them.*

*When fitting a new ring gear to a differential case, torque down the bolts in a crisscross pattern, in steps of 25 and 55 ft-lbs or 20, 40, and 55 ft-lbs. This allows the ring gear to sit correctly on the case and prevents cocking the ring gear. Tighten each screw to 55 ft-lbs using an alternating tightening pattern for final setting.*

## Ring Gear Backlash Adjustment

1 Slide the differential assembly into position in the housing. The ring gear should drop into place and the bearing should drop between the cap pedestal. Install the previously selected bearing endplay shims on the housing as well. Each shim pack (left and right) should have the same total thickness.

2 Move the ring gear backward and forward and note the backlash reading on the dial indicator. The backlash should be .005 to .009 inch (.008 inch is desired).

Adjust the backlash. To increase it, install a thinner shim at the ring gear side of the case and a thicker shim at the opposite side. To decrease the backlash, install a thicker shim at the ring gear side of the case and a thinner shim at the opposite side. In either case, do not change the total thickness of the two shims.

For example:

The bearing side play was removed with a .090-inch shim on each side (.180 inch total).

The backlash was found to be .011 inch (more than the desired .009 inch).

To correct the backlash, .004 inch was added to the shims on the ring gear side of the differential and the same amount was subtracted from the shims at the opposite side.

The result was a .094-inch shim on the ring gear side (.090 + .004 inch) and a .086-inch shim on the opposite side (.090 − .004 inch).

The new backlash was approximately .007 inch (.011 − .004 inch). Note that the total shim thickness remained unchanged at .180 inch (.094 + .086 inch).

3 Remove the differential assembly after adjusting the backlash.

*Install the differential bearing cap bolts and tighten to the specified torque. Mount the dial indicator on the housing. Position the indicator end so that it contacts the drive side of the ring gear tooth at a right angle to the tooth face.*

## Differential Bearing Preload Adjustment

1 The differential bearings must be preloaded to compensate for heat and loads during operation. To preload the bearings, increase the existing shim thickness at each differential bearing by .004 inch for a total of .008 inch in extra thickness for preload. Caution: Do not hammer the shims into the bearing bores because this bends and distorts the shims. As a result, the preload is incorrect.

2 Install the differential bearing preload and side-play shims in the axle housing bearing bores.

3 Install the bearing cups onto the differential bearings. The cups must cover the bearing rollers completely. Cups are placed on differential bearing by hand, one at a time. Note that the differential bearings were pressed onto the case.

4 Position the differential so that the bearings just enter the axle housing bearing bores. Note that tipping the bearing cups slightly eases the entry of the cups into the bores. Keep the differential assembly square in the housing and push it in as far as possible.

5 Tap the outer edge of the bearing cups with a plastic or wood mallet until the differential assembly is seated in the housing. Squarely drive the bearing cups down into the bores.

6 Install and align the differential bearing caps using the reference punch marks made at disassembly. Place some axle lube on the cap bolts and tighten the bearing cap bolts to 87 ft-lbs. (See Step 32 on page 42.)

7 Preloading the differential bearings may change the backlash setting. Therefore you need to recheck the backlash and correct if necessary.

## Carrier-Tube Gear Tooth Contact Pattern

At this stage, you need to perform this crucial procedure. You've taken backlash and other detailed measurements, but that does not guarantee the correct ring gear and pinion contact pattern. Consequently, you need to verify and set the correct contact pattern of the differential so it performs at its best. If the contact pattern is too close to the heal or toe, the differential will be loud, prematurely wear, and could possibly fail. Setting the correct pattern is the key to obtaining low gear noise and long wear, which directly correlates to durability and your satisfaction.

The gear tooth contact pattern discloses whether the correct rear pinion bearing mounting shim has been installed and the drive gear backlash set

properly—the final setup test.

Running the contact pattern determines the axle has been properly set up. Basically you adjust the depth of the pinion and the left-to-right location of the differential case. The shape and general location of the contact pattern tells you which way to adjust these items.

To obtain the tooth contact pattern, apply a thin film of hydrated ferric oxide, commonly known as yellow oxide of iron, on both the drive and coast side of the ring gear teeth. Using a round bar or large screwdriver (between the carrier housing and the differential case flange), apply a load against the backside of the ring gear and rotate the pinion several 360-degree revolutions in both directions. This procedure

leaves a distinct contact pattern on both the drive and the coast side of the ring gear teeth.

Maintain backlash between the ring gear and the pinion within the specified limits until the correct pattern is obtained.

Compare your observed contact pattern to the pattern examples shown on pages 21–23 in Chapter 2, to determine if all adjustments have been made properly. The correct contact pattern is very well centered on both the drive and coast sides of the teeth. When the tooth contact patterns are obtained by hand, the actual contact area tends to be small. Under actual operating loads, the contact area increases while centered on the smaller area.

## AMC 20 Carrier-Tube Axle Shaft Assembly and Installation

Once the differential installation is complete, you now need to start assembling the rest of the axle. Gather the axles, bearings, and seals that are going to be used. Remember that axle grease is very messy, so you might want to consider using rubber gloves for these steps.

1 Inspect the axle shaft seal journal for scratches and other damage. If light scratches are present, polish with 600-grade crocus cloth.

2 Use brake cleaner to clean the axle housing flange face thoroughly and install a new gasket followed by the brake support plate assembly on the driver's side of the axle housing.

3 Install new axle shaft oil seals in the axle housing. Use the proper size seal and tap into place with a hammer. You can use a similarly sized piece of metal and a hammer or select a sized seal

installer. You may also use a proper-sized socket if available or a block of wood, sized for the seal. Coat the inner lip of the oil seal with axle lube. This is messy, so use rubber gloves.

4 Lubricate the wheel bearings with multi-purpose grease (if required). Put a small dollop of grease in your hands and tap the bearing onto the grease and then the grease slides into the races.

5 Slip a new gasket (silicone sealer) over the studs of the axle housing ends.

6 Apply a silicone-type sealer to the flange and the brake support plates, carefully slide the axle shafts into the housing, and engage the splines in the differential side gear. Use a brush or your finger to apply a small amount of axle lube to the shaft's splines. Carefully insert the shaft into the axle tube. Once the shaft reaches the side gear, the shaft

should be centered in the tube. Rotate the shaft slightly to align the splines on the shaft with those in the side gear by turning the shaft by the flange using one hand and supporting the shaft's weight with the other hand.

7 Install and tighten the retainer plate nuts to 35 ft-lbs. Once the retainer plate is lined up with the support plate and the axle tube flange, install the nuts or bolts (typically four or five). Some axle tubes have studs pressed into the holes in the flange and use nuts; some use bolts. Tighten in an alternating pattern.

8 Check axle endplay on the left side only. To check axle shaft endplay, mount a dial indicator. The correct endplay should be .004 to .008 inch, with .006 inch preferred. Correct the endplay as necessary by adding shims to increase endplay or removing shims to decrease endplay.

## AMC 20 Carrier-Tube: Carrier Cover

**1** Thoroughly clean the gasket surfaces of the cover and the rear axle housing. You may want to try a degreaser. (See Step 2 on page 45.)

**2** Use a new gasket (or RTV) to assist in holding the gasket in place. Apply a thin coat of gasket sealer to both sides of the gasket. Install the cover assembly into the axle housing. Thread on the nuts and tighten the cover to the axle housing to 25 ft-lbs. Note that aftermarket services gaskets for the axle covers while the factory often recommends a bead of RTV.

Tip: With a new ratio, add a ratio tag to one of the attaching bolts. You can make the tag from metal (aluminum) and stamp in the correct numbers along with any Sure-Grip/open information.

## AMC 20 Carrier-Tube: Driveshaft

**1** Install the driveshaft into the transmission. The keyway spline on the driveshaft must match up with the end of the output shaft on the transmission. If it is not aligned correctly, the driveshaft won't install on the output shaft.

### AMC Axle Chart

| Axle | Ring Gear Diameter | Axle Type | Style | Lube Capacity |
|------|--------------------|-----------|-------|---------------|
| AMC 20 | 8.8 inches hypoid | Semi-floating | OTB | 76 ounces (4.75 pints) |

*OTB = Out-the-back*

*In many cases, if you use higher numerical axle ratios (4.56 or 4.88:1 versus 2.91 or 3.23:1, etc.) you may have to use less fill volume than the amount listed.*

**2** Install the rear universal joint of the driveshaft into the saddle of the yoke, aligning the marks made at disassembly and tighten the clamp screws to 15 ft-lbs.

**3** Install the brake drums. To do that, torque down the two bolts (to 25 ft-lbs) that hold the wheel cylinder to the flange. Use locking washers.

Install the bleeder screw on the wheel cylinder. Slide the wheel cylinder links into the dust boot. Install the clip for the parking brake lever that mounts to the larger shoe, and mount the shoe to the backing plate. Bolt the shoe onto the backing plate. Use pliers to install hold-down springs for both shoes, which fasten the shorter shoe onto the backing plate.

Install the parking cable by sliding the end into parking brake lever. Slide the parking brake strut into position and face the spring toward the front. Install the adjusting screw correctly. Install the adjusting screw on the backing plate. Hook the adjuster cable on the support plate. Hook the brake return springs on the shoes and mounting posts. Install the adjuster lever spring on the brake shoe and the lever arm. Slide the parking brake into the cable guide and place the drum brake cover over the wheel lugs.

**4** Install the rear wheels and tighten the lug nuts to 55 ft-lbs.

**5** It is very important to fill the unit with oil! Replace the drain plug if removed and tighten. Use the recommended lube based on the ring and pinion manufacturer or the Sure-Grip manufacturer specifications or recommendations. Use a syringe to fill the axle because typically there is limited room for other oil-fill approaches. A general lube recommendation is as follows: 75W-90 for street, 140W for race. There are also synthetic oils, such as 75-140 synthetic, that may offer wider coverage. Replace the oil fill plug.

**6** Connect all brake lines (if disconnected) and bleed the brakes if the lines were opened up.

**7** Re-connect any electrical wires for sensors that were removed or air lines/electrical wires required for special locker differentials.

**8** Remove the jack-stands and lower the vehicle. The unit should now be ready.

### Break-In Procedure for New Rear Axle Gear Set

On any new ring-and-pinion set with new bearings, especially the higher numerical ratios, excessive heat can build up in the rear end. This over-heating situation can cause durability problems, such as softening, with the gear teeth and bearings. Avoid over-heating by performing the proper break-in procedure. All new axle gear sets require a break-in period.

Be sure that the axle has been filled to the correct fluid level with the proper axle lubricant before driving the vehicle. The oil rating must be GL5 or higher—follow the ring-and-pinion manufacturer's suggestions.

### Street Vehicles

On basic street vehicles, bring the axle to normal operating temperature by driving it (unloaded) for approximately 10 to 20 miles. Do not run full-throttle (heavy) accelerations or create any shock loads (hard launch). Stop and let the vehicle cool completely (about 30 minutes). Repeat this procedure two or three times. As an option, you can also drive gently for 100 to 200 miles with no heavy loads.

### Off-Road and Trail Vehicles

Drive the vehicle (unloaded) off-road or on-trail for approximately 15 minutes. Do not use full-throttle accelerations. Stop and let it cool for about 30 minutes. Repeat this procedure two or three times.

### Circle Track Race Vehicles

Run approximately six to eight laps at slow speed and then let the vehicle cool for 30 minutes. Repeat for six to eight laps, then two or three laps at full speed, and then cool again for 30 minutes.

### Drag Race Vehicles

Perform an initial run-in, such as a one part-throttle run down the drag strip and then let the vehicle cool, typically for 15 to 20 minutes. Drag race cars are only driven short distances and heat is not commonly a problem with the proper lube and backlash installation.

### Trailer Towing

If trailer towing is intended, an additional break-in of 200 to 300 miles is required without the trailer. This is very important! To properly break in a new gear set, a minimum of 500 miles (general street break-in of 200 miles plus the additional 300 miles for trailer towing use) of driving is essential before towing. On the first actual trailer tow, drive 15 miles and stop. Repeat two more times (45 miles total) to fully break-in the gears.

Since the AMC 20 axle went out of production in 1986, upgrades have been left mainly to the aftermarket. Fully fabricated axle housings and brand-new, stamped axle housings are available for many styles of axles, but they haven't been offered in the AMC 20 style yet.

The most popular use of the AMC 20 in performance applications is in off-road usage. In these vehicles, low-speed, high-torque conditions tend to twist the axle tubes in the carrier or center housing. The production axle has the axle tubes spot-welded into the carrier in one position. If the tube is welded to the carrier for the full 360 degrees, it can turn a standard axle into a heavy-duty piece for minimal expense.

### Optional Additional Step

It is optional to change oil after first 500 miles—consult your ring gear manufacturer. Remember, there are acceptable noise levels that may vary from manufacturer to manufacturer. Break-in of gears is paramount to gear life. The initial run-in should be at low speeds. This enables gears to run in without overheating.

## AMC 20 Upgrades

The AMC 20 carrier-tube rear axle has been around for many years. It was installed in the vast majority of AMC/Jeep performance cars and trucks. In the 1980s and early 1990s, there wasn't much new hardware available for rear axles upgrades beyond the basic ratio options and Sure-Grips and service items. Today there are many more gear ratios than ever before.

### Ratios

Rear axle ratios have been available from the mid-3s to the 5s. Overdrive ratios or add-ons in the transmission area are used on the other end of the scale for the low overall numbers, such as 2.5 and 3.0:1.

### Bearings

Rear axles wear out pinion, differential, and axle shaft bearings. Since they are commonly replaced, they maintain their availability along with other service items. While they may not always be available individually, they are readily available in service or repair kits. For rear axles, always replace parts as sets.

### Limited-Slips

In the AMC 20 rear axle family, the clutch-type Sure-Grip has maintained service parts and general availability. The newer cone-type Sure-Grip was only serviced as an assembly because there was no clutches or discs to be replaced. These basic cone-style Sure-Grips are still available. There is also a group of new limited-slips, or lockers, and some function as air lockers, some as electric. There are many different styles and technologies.

### 4-wheel Disc Brakes

Brakes may not be considered a rear axle part but they bolt directly to the axle housing and in many cases must be removed to allow the rear axle to be rebuilt. Also, all original AMC 20 axles used drum brakes. Starting in the mid 1990s, aftermarket manufacturers began offering disc-brake conversion kits for these axles. This allows owners of many of these older cars/trucks to upgrade their braking systems to 4-wheel disc brake systems. Manufacturers now offer better drum brakes, such as upgrading production 9-inch to 10-inch drums.

# REBUILDING CHRYSLER AXLE ASSEMBLIES

In this chapter, I cover the 7¼-, 8¼-, 8¾-, 9¼-, and 9¾-inch Chrysler differentials. Most of these assemblies have been offered since 1960 in RWD passenger cars. All of these axles are carrier tube design, except for the 8¾-inch axle, which is a banjo design.

The 7¼ and 8¼ were commonly installed in production cars, and the 8¼ was used in certain Jeep applications.

The 8¾ and 9¼ differentials were typically installed in high-performance muscle cars. The 8¾ differential was smaller than the Dana 60 yet bigger than the 8¼. Among the 8¾-inch differentials, the 741, 742, and 489 castings are the ones to seek out because these cases offer the largest bearings for high-performance use. In addition, they are offered with the limited-slip clutch packs. But as time has gone by, the 741, 742, and 489 are typically difficult to find, so if you're in the market to buy a Chrysler axle and can't find an 8¾, the 9¼ differential is certainly a viable alternative.

The 9¼ was widely used in the many models of Chrysler vehicles, and widely installed in B-, C-, R-, J-, and M-Body models. The stout pinion shaft diameter and the 31-spline 9¼ axles could take drag strip launches and high-performance street use. This axle is available in open and limited-slip internals, so if you're going to drive your car hard, you need to opt for the limited-slip version.

Banjo axles feature a one-piece main housing, shaped like a banjo, with a center section that is removed toward the front of the car (OTF). Carrier-tube axles have a definite center housing with the

*The Chrysler 8¾-inch axle is the only banjo axle in this book. (All the other axles are carrier-tubes.) The housing is a one-piece unit. Thus the ring and pinion in the center section remove from the axle housing as an assembly through the front of the housing. There is no bolt-on cover on the rear (shown).*

*The bolts on the front of an 8¾ hold the center section in the housing, which allows the whole center section to be removed and taken to the workbench to be rebuilt. The bracket sitting over the yoke is the pinion snubber.*

axle tubes pressed into this housing and a cover bolted onto the rear of the housing. The ring and pinion are removed toward the rear (OTB).

Another way to tell the difference between them is to find out which side has the bolts. If the front side is holding the center section in place it is a banjo. If the rear side is holding the rear cover in place it is a carrier-tube.

Before you start the disassembly process on a rear axle rebuild, make sure that you have made your basic rear-end removal choice and that you have addressed any rear-end swapping concerns. Also, keep in mind that most Chrysler rear-wheel-drive vehicles built

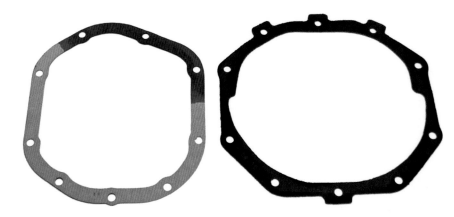

*Two styles of Chrysler 7¼-inch axles are the 9-bolt (left) and 10-bolt (right). The 9-bolt was used from 1960 thru 1986. The 10-bolt version was used from around 1986-1997.*

before the mid 1990s used leaf-spring rear suspensions. This was true of both passenger cars and trucks. A leaf-spring rear suspension uses a solid rear axle and two leaf springs. This style of rear suspen-

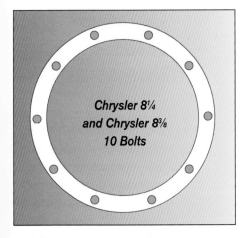

**Chrysler 8¼ and Chrysler 8⅜ 10 Bolts**

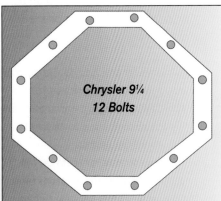

**Chrysler 9¼ 12 Bolts**

*The Chrysler 9¼-inch axle uses a unique octagonal, 12-bolt attaching pattern, which makes it easy to identify. These axles were used in the larger cars in the 1970s and early 1980s and are also common in trucks.*

*This is the 10-bolt, round gasket as used on the Chrysler 8¼-inch axle and the 8⅜-inch axle. These axles were common in passenger cars in the 1970s and early 1980s and also used in trucks and some Jeep models.*

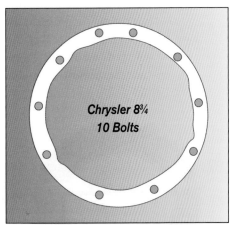

**Chrysler 8¾ 10 Bolts**

*The Chrysler 8¾-inch axle is the only banjo axle in the Chrysler group. Being a banjo axle means that the axle dissembles toward the front, or that the pinion removes OTF. This means that the bolts are on the front side of the housing, and the gasket mounts on the front side as well. It is also a 10-bolt pattern.*

sion is relatively easy to change from one axle assembly to another, but there are several things to check out before starting any swap.

## Identification of Chrysler Rear Ends

The banjo axle is a one-piece unit when viewed from the rear. The center section with the ring and pinion is unbolted and removed toward the front of the vehicle for disassembly. The 8¾-inch axle is the only Chrysler banjo axle.

There are five carrier-tube axles that are semi-floating, hypoid gear designs. (The number of bolts that hold the rear cover on and the shape of the rear cover gasket can identify the axle.) The two Dana axles—the 60 and the 44 (or 9¾ and 8½-inch)—both use a 10-bolt pattern in the shape of an offset hexagon. The Chrysler-built 7¼-inch axle has a 9-bolt cover, the 8¼-inch axle has a symmetrical (almost round) 10-bolt cover and the 9¼-inch axle has a 12-bolt octagon-shaped cover.

Once the basic axle has been identified, specific details like the model, model number, and build date can be useful. Some of this information is stamped on the rear of the axle.

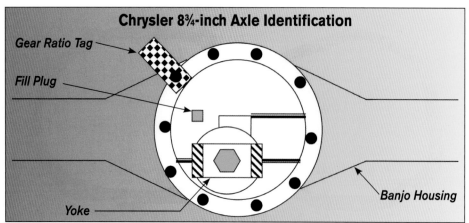

**Chrysler 8¾-inch Axle Identification**

Gear Ratio Tag

Fill Plug

Yoke

Banjo Housing

*First you need to know whether your axle is a Chrysler 8¾-inch banjo axle. You also need to know the axle ratio. Most Chrysler axles and Sure-Grips have the ratio stamped on a metal tag attached to one of the bolts that hold the cover onto the center section (typically at the 10 o'clock position). Sure-Grip information is shown in the same way if that option was included in the original production. While it is helpful information, never trust it. The axle ratio could easily have been changed several times after the vehicle was originally produced.*

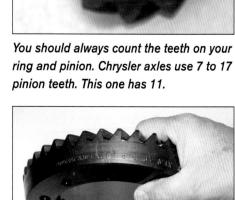

*You should always count the teeth on your ring and pinion. Chrysler axles use 7 to 17 pinion teeth. This one has 11.*

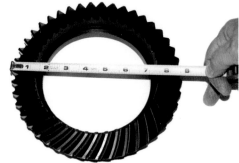

*There can be a lot of information located on the ring and pinion. On the outside of the ring gear, the manufacturer stamps/ etches all kinds of data, such as the part numbers, gear ratios, dates, etc. It should all be written down in your assembly sheet or book. Chrysler tends to use 7-digit part numbers on the left of the ring gear edge to identify it.*

The most useful piece of information is the ratio. It is typically found on a small metal tag under one of the attaching bolts, in the form of an actual teeth count. If the axle has been worked on, this tag may be gone or it may no longer represent the ratio that is currently installed. An "SG" on the metal tag or a separate tag identifies the production Sure-Grip. Always double-check.

Another piece of valuable axle information is the axle's bolt circle. Some of the early A-Body cars used 4.0-inch bolt circle

wheels/axle shafts while most cars used the standard 4½-inch bolt circle. Some trucks use a bigger bolt circle. (See Chapter 1 to learn how to measure the bolt circle.)

*Ratio*

The best was to determine the actual axle ratio is to count the teeth on the ring gear and on the pinion. Then divide the pinion number into the ring number. For example, the 43 teeth on the ring gear and 11 teeth on the pinion, then the ratio is 3.91:1 (43 ÷ 11 = 3.91).

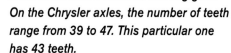

*So you can determine the actual ratio, you need to count the teeth on the ring gear. On the Chrysler axles, the number of teeth range from 39 to 47. This particular one has 43 teeth.*

*This particular one has 43. Be sure to check and double-check your basic specifications. Ring gear diameter is one such specification to check; this one is about 8¾ inches.*

*As the number of teeth on the ring gear changes for different ratios, the diameter varies slightly, but you won't confuse it for an 8¼-inch ring. The manufacturer often places a lot of information on the ring and pinion, including part number stamps/etches, gear ratios, dates, etc. on the outside of the ring gear. It should all be written down in your notebook. The factory (Chrysler) often places a seven-digit part number on the left lip of the ring gear edge.*

### Gasket/Cover Shape

All 8¾-inch axles use 10 bolts and the same gasket shape. The three Chrysler carrier-tube axles each used different numbers of bolts and different shapes for the cover attaching pattern and bolts.

### Width

Refer to the track drawing on page 36 in Chapter 1. With the wheels off, it is much easier to measure the axle's total width, wheel-mounting face to wheel-mounting face. The spring seats are welded to the outer ends of the axle tubes. All banjo and carrier-tube Chrysler axles use 3-inch tubes except the 7¼-inch. There is a small hole in the flat of the spring seat, which locates the leaf spring rear suspension. The distance from the center of one spring seat to the other is an important measurement for mounting the axle in the car.

The ends of each axle tube have a flange and a mounting face and bolt pattern that holds the brake hardware. (See Chapter 10 for more details.)

### Yoke/Flange

The rear yoke (or flange) of the driveshaft attaches to the axle's yoke through a single or double U-joint. If the axle housing or complete assembly is being swapped

or changed, the length of the axle housing (in the side view) has to be checked. Each axle's design's length is different. (See Chapter 1.) If a swap is being performed and there is a difference in lengths, the driveshaft's length must be revised to compensate or a new driveshaft must be fabricated to take this length into account.

The style of U-joint cap varies between attaching methods (straps and U-bolts). The straps or U-bolts are only used in the rear U-joint. The U-joint numbers 1310 and 1330 are from Spicer while the 7260 and 7290 numbers are from Chrysler. The aftermarket uses two styles of U-joints to connect various driveshafts to various rear axles: two vertical caps and two horizontal caps. (See Chapter 10 for more information.)

### Wheels

The bolt circle drilled into the axle shafts dictates the bolt circle of the wheels. The way the axle sits under the car—widths and wheel well location and size—determines the wheel offset and tire clearances.

### Axle Tube Size

Most Chrysler rear axles use 3-inch tubes. The exception is the 7¼-inch axle, which uses 2½-inch tubes. (See Chapter

3.) The 1986-and-newer 7¼-inch axles have swedged tubes that are 3 inches in diameter at the outer ends. The 3-inch tubes can all use the standard spring seats. The aftermarket makes 2½-inch spring seats. Since the spring seat is welded to the axle tube, you need to use a new one if you are moving the spring seat. Do not try to cut off and re-use the old ones.

### Basic Features

The vast majority of RWD Chrysler products built prior to 1994 (the introduction of the Ram pickup truck) used a leaf-spring rear suspension. The head of the center bolt of the leaf spring pilots into the center hole in the spring seat to locate the rear suspension and, therefore, the axle. The spring seat is welded to the axle and the spring is held onto the spring seat by two large U-bolts on each side. The location of the two spring seats on the axle tubes determines the driveshaft angle. If the driveshaft angle needs to be corrected for any reason, angled shims are placed under the spring seat. Any shim found there should be maintained to keep the driveshaft angle at its current number. If you plan on installing new spring seats, take the shim angle into account so the shims are not required and make sure the driveshaft angle is maintained.

The width of the yoke should be measured. Note whether there are straps and two bolts per side or a U-bolt style of U-joint with two nuts per side. The typical passenger car rear U-joint uses a strap and two bolts per side, except for the early Dana 60 in the mid-1960s Chrysler B-Body 4-speed cars, which use U-bolts and nuts. To determine the difference between U-joints, such as the 7260 and 7290, the easiest method is to measure the width.

A pinion snubber is located on top of the axle housing just above the U-joint on most RWD passenger cars. The pinion snubber is bolted to the top of the housing with two or three bolts. Some models use two while others use three. On this particular case/carrier, there are three bosses. There is generally a boss for a third or fourth bolt, but it is not machined. Pinion snubbers are generally not used on trucks or might be optional. The pinion snubbers function as part of the rear suspension, but they do bolt directly to the axle. They do not have to be removed to rebuild the axle.

The yoke is designed to slide over the pinion splines, so the number of splines is important. The two popular ones are 10 (coarse) and 29 (fine), which were used on the pre-1969 Dana 60 and the 1970-and-later Dana 60 respectively. On the 29-spline pinion, the splines or grooves are much closer together.

On the 29-spline pinion, the splines or grooves are much closer together than on a 10-spline (above).

The driveshaft angle is basically determined by the relationship between the pinion centerline and the bottom surface of the spring seat. Because the seat is welded to the axle tube, any adjustment to the driveshaft axle is done by adding thin-angled shims (1, 2, or 3 degrees) between the spring and the seat, which adds complications.

## Other Things to Check

For the typical rebuild, you do not have to remove the complete axle assembly. On banjo axles, the center section is removed leaving the housing still in the car. On carrier-tube axles, the ring and pinion are removed toward the rear individually leaving the housing in the car.

The main difference is that the center section of the banjo is rebuilt on your workbench while similar rebuilding procedures are done to the carrier-tube housing in the vehicle.

There are three pinion sizes for the Chrysler 8¾-inch axle: small, large (shown), and tapered. The small stem is 1⅜ inches in diameter while the large stem is 1¾ inches in diameter. These stems are not tapered and maintain one thickness from the splines to the backside of the gear head. The 741 and 742 axles (refers to last three digits of the casting number) look identical.

### Tapered Axle Shaft

All Chrysler axle designs feature flanged axle shafts except one—the early model 8¾-inch, found on 1964-and-earlier B-Body cars, such as the Coronet/Belvedere. (See Chapter 2.)

This version of the 8¾-inch axle has tapered axle shafts and the brake drum/hub is pressed onto the end of the tapered axle shaft. This axle design is very difficult to work on. It is popular to swap in a flanged axle design. The easiest and best one is the 1965–1966 B-Body 8¾-inch, which is flanged and has the same width as the original.

*The 8¾-inch axle does not use C-clips to retain the axle shafts. The axle shafts must be removed using a standard axle shaft puller. The carrier-tube axles do use C-clips to retain the axle shafts, so the rear cover must be removed first, then the C-clips, and then the axle shafts are removed from the axle tubes.*

The tapered pinion is considered to have a 1⅞-inch diameter, but it is larger under the gear head and tapers to a smaller diameter at the splines.

### Brake Lines

The brake lines can stay attached if the axle assembly is not being removed. However, it might be helpful to disconnect the parking brake cable.

### Speed Sensor and Electrics

On cars from the mid 1980s and newer, you may find a speed sensor attached to the rear axle housing, which is used with anti-lock brakes. The axle can remain attached if it is not being removed. Note that since the last 8¾-inch axle was produced in 1974, the speed sensor is likely to only be found in one of the newer carrier-tube axles, such as the 8¼- or 9¼-inch. (See Chapter 6, page 103, for a photo of a speed sensor.)

There may also be an electric line or an air line for an electric or air-controlled Sure-Grip/locker assembly. It can remain attached if the axle is not being removed.

*An open differential has two side gears (at the top and bottom inside the differential window), two pinion gears (left and right inside the window), and a cross-shaft (runs left to right). The case is a one-piece design and everything inside has to come out through this window.*

### Differential Case

To identify whether the differential is a limited-slip unit, a Sure-Grip or locker assembly comes with its own differential case. However, switching ratios from a high one (low number such as 2.45) to a lower one (high number such as a 4.10), the differential case has to be changed. This special differential case situation also exists in carrier-tube axles. (See Chapter 7.)

This situation does not exist on the 8¾-inch axle; it uses the same case all the way, high to low ratios.

### Chrysler 8¾-Inch Banjo Axle

The Chrysler 8¾-inch banjo axle was first used in the 1957 model year, and through the 1974 model year. The 1974 Barracuda and Challenger (E-Body cars) were the last models to use it.

The 8¾-inch axle was last used in the A-Body cars (Duster, Dart, Valiant) in the 1972 model year. The A-Body version is the narrowest of these popular performance axles. Also, they all have 4.0-inch bolt-circle axle shafts/wheels.

*While the 8¾-inch axle does not have the unique differential, the carrier-tube axles do, such as the 8¼-inch. On the 8¾-inch,* the solution to the pinion getting smaller as the ratio number gets larger (going from 3.08 to 4.10:1 for example) is to make the ring gear thicker. Note the distance from the backside of the ring gear itself to the bottom of the teeth.

All the larger body styles use 5-on-4½-inch bolt circles. Custom wheels using a 4.0-inch bolt circle are hard to find so it is a common conversion to swap these axles to a more readily available 4½-inch pattern. This requires new (aftermarket) axle shafts and modified rear brakes or a disc brake conversion kit. Another approach is to swap-in a 1973–1976 A-Body axle assembly, which has the 4½-inch bolt circle and is an 8¼-inch design.

There are three basic types of 8¾-inch banjo axles: small stem pinion, large stem pinion, and tapered pinion. These axles are referred to by their nicknames: 741 for the small stem, 742 for the large stem, and 489 for the tapered pinion. These numbers come from the last three digits of their part numbers, which are cast into the left side of the housing, parallel to the pinion.

Two basic 8¾-inch rear axle designs were offered in 17 years of production. The early version has tapered axle shafts, which means that the brake assemblies are attached to the axle shaft with a keyway and large nut. This design was used until the 1964 model year. In 1965 the 8¾-axle was introduced with flanged axle shafts and redesigned brake hubs. The newer

*With a 4.10:1 or higher ratio, the distance from the backside of the ring gear to the bottom of the teeth is much greater. The teeth themselves are the same height.*

(1965–1974) flanged axle assemblies are considered much easier to work on. Note that the 1965–1966 B-Body 8¾-inch axle assemblies are a good selection to swap into the earlier 1962–1964 B-Bodies that used the tapered axle shaft design. The three different center sections, 741, 742, and 489 as complete assemblies, called pigs, are interchangeable between the two 8¾-inch axle designs.

The 1966 through 1970 B-Body Dana 60 axles used 23-tooth splines on the axle shaft and side gears while the newer and wider E-Body design (1970–1972) and the 1971–1979 B-Bodies use 35-spline axle shafts and side gears.

The three different styles of 8¾-inch ring-and-pinion assemblies are identified by a Chrysler part number that is cast into the center section housing on the driver's side of the case. The small-stem case has two casting part numbers, 1820657 (used in production until 1964) and 2070741 (1965–1968). The large-stem housing uses a casting part number of 2070742. The tapered pinion version was introduced in 1969 to replace the large-stem unit and uses a casting part number of 2881489. These numbers are actual casting numbers and should only be used for identification purposes. The aftermarket uses the last three digits of these casting numbers to identify their ring and pinions.

Another method of identifying the ring and pinion is the size or diameter of the pinion shaft or stem.

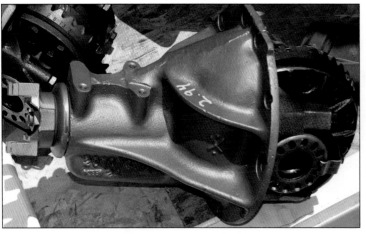

*This is the left side of an 8¾-inch center section, or pig. The Chrysler seven-digit casting number (such as 2070741) is located on the bottom, toward the front (to the right of the yoke at the bottom). This particular center section is a small-stem unit. The three different casting numbers are each seven digits long, so it is very popular to refer to them by their last three digits. In this case, 741.*

## Chrysler 8¾ Axle Torque Specifications

| Axle | Small and Large Stem | Tapered Pinion |
|---|---|---|
| Case ID Number | 741 or 742 | 489 |
| Differential Bearing Cap Bolts | 90 ft-lbs | 90 ft-lbs |
| Ring Gear to Differential Case Bolts-LH | 55 ft-lbs | 55 ft-lbs |
| Drive Pinion Flange Nut | 240 ft-lbs min. | 170 ft-lbs min. |
| Carrier to Axle Housing Bolt Nuts | 45 ft-lbs | 45 ft-lbs |
| Axle Shaft Retaining Nuts | 35 ft-lbs | 35 ft-lbs |
| Driveshaft Bolts (Rear) | 15 ft-lbs | 15 ft-lbs |
| Spring Clip (U-bolt) Nuts | 45 ft-lbs | 45 ft-lbs |
| Wheel Stud Nuts | 65 ft-lbs | 65 ft-lbs |
| Shock Absorber Stud Nuts (Lower) | 50 ft-lbs | 50 ft-lbs |

One point to remember is that a 20- or 40-year-old muscle car may not have the same axle ratio as when it was built. This is true whether or not the small tag on one of the attaching bolts is still attached. For example, a 1968 Charger R/T with an HP 440 engine that was produced with a 3.23:1 ratio in a 742 case may now have a 4.10:1 ratio, Sure-Grip in a 489 case. To be sure, use the casting number on the side of the housing that is now installed in your car.

All three versions of the 8¾-inch banjo remove toward the front (OTF). This style of axle is sometimes referred to as a Hotchkiss design. The 8¾-inch axle does not use C-clips to retain the axle shafts. They are pulled out at the brake area using a standard axle puller. The center section of the banjo removes OTF, and it's sometimes called a third member or a pig. Having an axle that uses a third member or removable center section makes it easier and quicker to swap gear ratios.

Two styles of Sure-Grip differentials were used in the 8¾-inch axle assemblies. As assemblies the Sure-Grip can be swapped from one version to another. A full range of axle ratios (from 3.55 to 5.13) is used in the 8¾-inch axles. All ratios use the same dimensions for the differential case.

Many axles use different ring-to-pinion centerline dimensions for the differential case that is used with larger gear ratios, such as 4.10 to 4.56 on the Dana 60. (See Chapter 7 for more details.) In the 8¾-inch axle, this problem is solved by using thicker ring gears as the ratio numbers get bigger.

The three different styles of 8¾-inch axles all tend to look very similar, especially installed under a car. Therefore it is best to use the 7-digit casting number (last three digits actually) cast into the center section housing on the driver's side, parallel to the pinion. Typically only the last three digits of this part number are required: 741, 742, 489.

In the set-up procedure for an 8¾-inch axle, you have to adjust the depth of the pinion shaft relative to the fixed centerline of the ring gear and axle shafts. The depth is adjusted to obtain the proper contact pattern between the ring and pinion. This depth adjustment is accomplished by adding shims of different thicknesses shims pinion. Because the factory no longer carries many of the desired sizes, depth-adjusting shims must be found in the aftermarket. Many aftermarket suppliers have rebuild kits that include them.

## Chrysler Banjo Axle Disassembly

The three most common styles of Chrysler banjo axles are: small stem, large stem, and tapered pinion. Here, I focus on the large stem (742 case) and the tapered pinion (489 case) because they are the strongest and most popular versions. They also have the most ratios available. The following procedure applies to open differentials only.

## Chrysler 8¾ Center Section Removal

1 Confirm that you have all the required tools, parts, gaskets, cleaners, and sealers.

2 With a floor jack or a car lift, raise the vehicle high enough off the ground to install jack stands under the frame rails on each side of the vehicle. Both rear wheels should be off the ground.

3 Remove the lug nuts from rear wheel assemblies and then remove the wheels

4 Remove the clips holding the brake drums onto the axles and then remove the brake drum assemblies.

### TECH TIP — Disc Brakes

Disc brakes were commonly installed in the front and rarely used in production on the rear. This axle rebuild process covers rear axles with drum brakes because they were used almost exclusively on the rear. While the disc brake rotors remove somewhat similarly, you must remove the disc brake caliper first. Today, there are many manufacturers that build disc brake conversion kits for these vehicles originally equipped with drum brake. ∎

5 Spray on brake cleaner and wipe away all dust and dirt. Keep in mind that asbestos is often used in brake pads, so make sure not to get the dust on clothing or to inhale it.

6 Locate the access hole in the axle shaft flange. Rotate the flange as required to remove the retainer nuts (typically five). The right axle shaft has the threaded adjuster in the retainer plate. Locate the

adjuster lock under one of the attaching studs and use a socket and ratchet to simply remove it.

7 Remove the parking brake strut. With parking brake cables, it is generally best to release the forward cable adjustment first before working on the parking brake at the rear.

8 Bolt your flanged axle shaft removal tool to the axle shaft flange and remove the axle shaft. Slip the puller base over the lug nuts and then tighten down the lug nuts over the puller. The puller shaft is snugged down on top of the axle shaft. Use a wrench or ratchet and socket to drive the puller down on the axle and the hub will then lift off of the axle tube.

*A slide hammer is used to remove flanged axle shafts. The bracket (on left end) slips over three wheel studs and three wheel nuts secure it to the axle shaft's flange. The long bar fits into the center. The right end of the shaft has a bulge so that the slide cannot pass. Once attached, the slide is moved from the left side to the right side and stops at the bump, which applies force to the axle shaft, pulling it out. Several strikes are often required.*

(A tapered axle shaft requires a heavy-duty axle puller.)

9 Remove the brake assembly and foam gaskets. If you have rear disc brakes, remove the caliper bolts and hang the rear caliper from the frame with a piece of wire. If you have drum brakes, loosen the brake shoe adjustment first. Then, with the wheel off, remove the small retaining clip on several of the wheel studs (if they are used or still installed). Then slip the brake drum off over the wheel studs and set aside.

10 Slip the seal removal tool under the lip of the seal in the axle end. Simply pry out the oil seals from both axle housing ends, or use a seal removal tool. The fingers of the seal puller fit inside the seal itself and then the slide hammer pulls the seal out. Smaller seal pullers may use a separate hammer and have only one finger and a fixed two-finger.

11 Use a Sharpie marker or a crayon to mark the driveshaft at the U-joint and pinion flange.

*A basic hub puller is used for axles that have tapered axle shafts. On the early 8¾-inch axles (1963/1964 and earlier) with the wheel removed, the hub puller with three legs is attached to the hub/drum assembly using the wheel stubs. Two of the legs attach next to each other while the third leg fastens opposite of them. The center threaded adjuster is brought down to push on the end of the axle shaft. Use a breaker bar and nut to apply torque to the nut.*

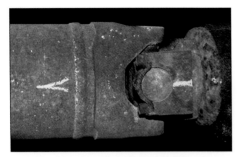

*Scribe or mark the driveshaft tube and the yoke so you can reassemble them in the same relationship to maintain dynamic balance.*

**12** Disconnect the prop-shaft. Push it forward and support it in near-horizontal position out of your way. Pry the U-joint out of the yoke and then push the driveshaft forward by hand. Or remove the driveshaft and install a plastic cap to keep the transmission from leaking.

**13** Tape the U-joint caps on the driveshaft.

**14** Position the oil drain pan below the axle housing to prepare for draining the rear axle fluid.

**15** Remove all nuts, except the top and bottom ones. These two nuts should be at the end of the stud. Loosen the center housing assembly (carefully push up on the nose of the center section) and pry as required.

**16** Drain the banjo housing. Oil comes out the bottom when the nose is pushed up and tends to be very messy. Once the oil drain is complete, set the drain pan aside, out of your way.

**17** Remove the last two nuts and lift the carrier assembly out of the banjo housing. It is very heavy so use caution.

## Chrysler Banjo Center Section Disassembly

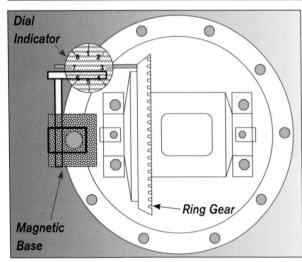

*Attach the dial indicator to the housing and set up the indicator/pointer contacts the back face of the ring gear in a perpendicular position. Rotate the ring gear through several complete revolutions. Use the pinion flange to rotate. Note the total indicator reading. Mark the ring gear and the differential case at the point where the runout is at the maximum. The total dial indicator reading, called TIR-total indicator reading, should be .005 inch or less. If the runout exceeds .005 inch, the differential case may be damaged. A second reading is recommended after the ring gear has been removed. Note that when measuring runout, the reading can go from plus .003 to a minus .003; the indicator points to the two numbers. Total indicator reading means .006 or the range that the dial shows. You can go back and re-zero the dial so it reads 0 at the minus .003 position and then it will go from 0 to .006 or a TIR of .006; it is sometimes more work to take the extra readings.*

**1** Mount the center section assembly in an axle rebuilding stand or mount securely to your work station.

**2** Place a flat-blade screwdriver between the main bearing cap and the differential case. Pry the case in one direction and then in the other direction. Watch the indicator dial to see if any side play is present. If side play is measured, remove the adjuster lock and loosen the adjuster slightly then retighten the adjuster to eliminate the side play.

**3** Install the yoke holding tool. Hold the yoke (and flange) and remove the

*If you use an air impact gun to remove the pinion nut, the yoke holder can be a large pair of channel locks. If you are using a socket and manual ratchet/breaker bar, you need to hold it more securely, which requires a yoke holder similar to the one shown in Chapter 2. The bolt-on yoke holder attaches by two bolts diagonally opposite each other on the yoke saddles. The trick with various yoke holders is that the torque wrench, breaker bar, or air impact gun has to pass through the center of the tool to apply torque to the pinion nut*

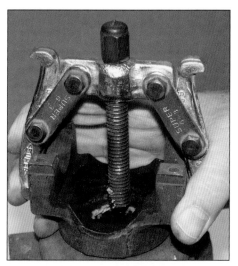

*Once the yoke is engaged with the pinion splines, install the large washer and large nut on the pinion (left). Lube the bottom side of the washer with axle lube. Install the yoke puller, tighten it down on shaft, and remove the yoke.*

*Use a wrench or socket and ratchet to remove both differential bearing adjuster lock screws and locks (one per cap) and center between the two main cap bolts (top and bottom).*

drive pinion nut and Belleville washer. If you use an air impact gun on the pinion nut, the yoke holder can be a large pair of channel locks. However, if you are using a socket and manual ratchet/breaker bar, you need to have a firmer grasp on the yoke, so you need to securely hold it. Use a yoke holder similar to the one on page 25 in Chapter 2.

4 Using a seal removal tool, extract the drive pinion oil seal from the housing. The fingers of the seal puller fit inside the seal itself and then the slide hammer pulls the seal out. Smaller seal pullers may use a separate hammer and have only one finger and a fixed two-finger.

5 By hand, remove the front pinion bearing cone, shim pack, and bearing spacer (if used). No tools are required. Put a catch tray under the housing and simply tip the housing upside down. The parts fall right out.

6 Remove the differential and ring gear assembly with the bearing cups. The ring gear and differential assembly lifts right out of the housing once the main caps and bolts are removed. Be sure that you have a place to set it down.

The differential bearing cups must be kept with their respective bearing cones. Each cap is machined in place on the differential case and therefore must not be switched or reversed. Mark caps before removal.

*Use a 3/4-inch socket to loosen the four main bearing cap bolts. There are two on each side.*

*Using a spanner wrench, slightly back off the adjusters. Remove the four bearing cap bolts, two caps, and two bearing adjusters.*

*The seal remover has three fingers. These fingers fit inside the seal itself and then the slide hammer pulls the seal out. Smaller seal pullers may use a separate hammer and have only one finger and a fixed two-finger.*

7 Mark the differential case for reinstallation if it's a two-piece Sure-Grip. A Sharpie mark indicates proper alignment upon reinstallation. The open differential is a one-piece unit and doesn't require marking. They are already marked so that they are properly aligned at re-installation.

*Use a punch or magic marker to mark the main caps for re-installation. Also mark the bearing adjusters for proper location at re-assembly. Be sure to verify that they were not marked at an earlier rebuild. Here, the main cap screw is at the middle left. The parting-line (middle) is below the head of the bolt. There are two dots (close together) just to the left of the parting-line and two more just to the right.*

8 Remove drive pinion rear bearing from the pinion using a bearing puller. Remove the shims once the

*Push/tap the pinion rearward by directly tapping the nose of the pinion stem with a non-metallic hammer, or use a brass drift. Remove the press-off pinion bearings. Inspect shims on either side of bearings. Then write down how many shims you find on either side. Replace the pinion bearings; do not re-use them.*

bearing is off. You can hang the shims in order on a wire or spare coat hanger or place a tie-rap around each pack and place in a zip-lock bag.

*The pinion bearing removal tool has two pieces that separate so they can fit behind the pinion bearing. The pinion must be removed from the axle first. Once the removal tool's two shells have been fitted behind the pinion bearing, tighten the threaded bars on each side. Install this assembly in an arbor press and press off the bearing. The tool has threaded attachments that allow the bearing to be removed using a ratchet (not shown).*

*Reach into the housing and carefully lift out the pinion and the rear bearing. Cushion the pinion's fall into the housing with towels or your hand.*

## Chrysler Banjo Axle Case Disassembly

1 Mount the differential case and ring gear assembly in a vise securely mounted to a bench and equipped with soft jaws (brass).

*Remove and discard the ring gear screws. They have left-hand threads on the 8¾-inch axle.*

2 Remove only the ring gear from the differential housing if the ring gear is being replaced.

*If the ring gear is worn or damaged, use a non-metallic hammer and brass drift punch to tap the ring gear loose and remove it.*

3 Install the main bearing caps, cap bolts, and bearing adjusters. Lightly tighten the bearing cap bolts and then screw in both adjusters with a spanner wrench.

4 Tighten the cap bolts and adjusters to prevent any side play in the bearings.

5 Install the dial indicator on the housing and set it up on the differential case flange between the outer edge of the flange and the edge of the ring gear bolt holes.

**6** Rotate the differential case several complete revolutions while noting the total indicator reading. This indicator reading should not exceed .003 inch. If the measured runout exceeds .003 inch, the differential case must be replaced.

*If the ring gear mounting flange runout exceeded .005 inch in Step 12, re-install the differential case (without ring gear) and the respective bearing cups in the carrier.*

**7** Use two feeler gauges of equal thickness to measure the side gear. Insert them between the differential case and the side gear, so one is inserted at the top and one toward the bottom or one to the left and one to the right. Install new thrust washers if the clearance exceeds .012 inch.

**8** Remove the differential pinion shaft lock pin from the backside of the ring gear flange using a punch or flat-nose drift and hammer. The hole is only reamed part way through, making it necessary to remove the lock pin from one direction.

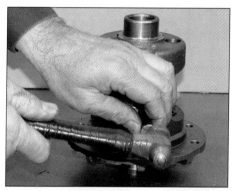

*Once the lock-pin is tapped out, remove the pinion shaft from the differential housing using a brass drift and hammer along with the cross-shaft centerline.*

**9** Remove the two differential side gears and thrust washers from inside the differential case. Then lift the pinion and side gears out of the case one at a time with their thrust washer.

**10** Thoroughly clean and inspect all parts. Dirt is the enemy of any moving part. Cleaning allows you to see cracks, especially small cracks in your hardware. It also allows you to observe surface for scuffing and any discoloration.

**11** Using your hand, rotate the differential housing side gears until the differential pinions appear at the differential case window opening. Remove the two pinions.

**12** Remove the two differential side gears and thrust washers from inside the differential case. Note that the side gears are the large ones on the left and right. The cross-shaft sits vertically in the middle. The pinion gears are at the top center and bottom center. The thrust washers are next to each gear. The thrust block is to the right of the cross-shaft and the lock pin is to the right of the top of the cross-shaft. These are the basic parts of the open differential.

## Cleaning and Inspection

With the differential completely disassembled, it is time to check all the parts and see what you have. Obviously wearable parts such as bearings that are replaced do not need to be checked

**1** Clean all parts with mineral spirits or a dry cleaning solvent, except for the bearings, and dry with compressed air.

**2** Inspect the differential bearing cones, cups, and rollers for excessive wear, pitting, flat areas, or other visible damage, which may be discoloration to actual burned/blackened appearance. Identify any physical damage, such as flat-sided rollers or scuffed cups/cones/

*Remove the differential assembly and ring gear. This is done using a special differential bearing remover. There are several pieces to the tool. This view is fully assembled into the differential bearing and ready to remove it. There are two pieces that fit around the differential bearing and the end of the case. The tall, threaded adjuster fits on top of the end of the case. Once the two halves have been fitted around the bearing, the outer sleeve is dropped over it and the bearing removal can begin. An air impact gun or large socket/ratchet is applied to the top of the threaded adjuster to actually remove the bearing (see page 26 for partial assembly of this tool).*

rollers. If replacement is necessary, remove bearing cones from the case using a bearing puller.

3 Inspect the differential case for an elongated or enlarged pinion shaft hole. The machined thrust washer surface areas and counterbores must be smooth.

*Check the differential case for damage, excessive wear, or discoloration due to excessive heat. Cracks mostly commonly form in the towers. Scuffing and discoloration are mostly likely on the bottom surface inside the towers and the bearing (not visible at bottom). Note that this is only half the differential.*

4 Inspect the case for cracks or other damage. Most common areas to check are machined surfaces and thin sections.

5 Inspect the differential pinion shaft lock pin for damage or looseness in the case. Replace pin if required. The pin could be worn and beaten-up, but you hope the hole in the case is in good condition, so replacing the pin solves the problem.

6 Inspect the ring gear and pinion for worn or chipped teeth or damaged attaching bolt threads. Also inspect the teeth for any centered wear pattern or scuffing. You should be able to look at

*Thoroughly inspect the cross shaft and lock pin. These components need to be free of cracks, chips, marring, and excessive wear. This cross-shaft (left) is worn and scuffed (its wear surface is not smooth) and should be replaced. The lock pin is at the right.*

*The two side gears are the larger gears in the differential. The center hole in the side gear is also splined to match the axle shaft. Check for broken teeth, scuffing, damaged surfaces, and excessive heat. If the side gears have been exposed to excessive heat, the side gears are blackened.*

the ring gear and determine the wear pattern from the previous setup. If the ring and pinion are being replaced, the main inspection is done on the new parts. However, the old parts can provide a lot of telltale information about the condition of the rear axle assembly, so examine them also. Look for physical damage on new parts, mainly machining errors or problems, such as chips, burrs, or sharp edges. Always replace the ring and pinion as a set. Be sure the mounting face of the ring gear

*The thrust block is in the center, unless a Sure-Grip is used. Check for damage in the top and bottom surfaces.*

is flat. Slide the large, flat file over the rear mounting face to remove nicks and sharp edges.

7 Inspect the drive pinion bearing cones, cups, and rollers for excessive wear, flat-sided bearings, chips, or damage. Only inspect the parts that are going to be re-used. Look for flattened or scuffed rollers or any discoloration in the bearings. Also examine the cups for scuffing or discoloration. If required, replace as sets.

8 Inspect the drive pinion for damaged bearing journals or excessively worn splines. Whether new or used, splines should be straight and not worn, scuffed, or discolored. The gear itself should have a smooth wear pattern on the teeth (used). There should be no chips or cracks, and no discoloration on the teeth or bearing surfaces.

9 Inspect the yoke for cracks or worn splines.

10 Inspect the drive pinion bearing shim pack for broken, damaged, or distorted shims. Replace any if required during pinion bearing preload step.

## Chrysler Banjo Axle Assembly

The three common styles of Chrysler banjo axles are: small stem, large stem, and tapered pinion. In the following procedure, I assemble the large stem (742 case) and the tapered pinion (489 case). They are the strongest and most popular versions and also have the most ratios available.

Several special steps are required for the crushed-sleeve version, which is a tapered pinion of 489-case design. The tapered pinion uses a crush sleeve, which is also called a collapsible spacer.

1 You need to select the correct gear ratio for your vehicle and application. To do so, count the actual teeth on the ring gear and pinion to verify that you have received the correct parts. Divide the number of ring gear teeth by the number of pinion teeth to determine the ratio. For example, if the ring gear teeth count is 43 and the pinion gear teeth count is 11, the ratio is 3.91:1 (43 ÷ 11 = 3.91).

For street use, use ratios in the 2.5 to 3.5 range. For street/strip applications, use ratios in the 3.5:1 to 4.1:1 range. For drag racing, use ratios of 4.10:1 and higher (numerically lower). Overdrive transmissions and/or add-on units change these basic numbers.

2 Clean all parts thoroughly, dry-wipe (or air dry), and inspect. Check all new parts for damage. Closely inspect the pinion gear for cracks and chips and examine the shaft for wear. In addition, look closely at the ring gear teeth for chips, cracks, and any excessive wear. An excessively worn pinion gear has a blunted or rounded gear edge; as a result the ring gear teeth may also be damaged.

3 Lubricate all parts before assembly with rear axle lube.

4 Re-tap or chase the threads then blow out the holes. You need to re-tap the threads so the bolt threads are firmly engaged and the torque specifications are accurate. Dirty threads don't provide an accurate torque reading and bolts can work loose. The main caps were marked at disassembly, so reinstall them in their original locations and torque to 90 ft-lbs. (See chart on page 64.)

5 The adjustments to be made are pinion depth, pinion bearing preload, backlash, and carrier bearing preload. These adjustments are explained in the following sections.

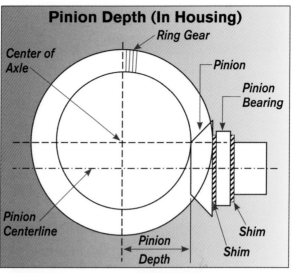

**Pinion Depth (In Housing)**

Ring Gear
Center of Axle
Pinion
Pinion Bearing
Pinion Centerline
Shim
Shim
Pinion Depth

*The basic rebuild kit should include four bearings, the pinion nut, the collapsible spacer (if used), and gasket.*

*Some differentials, which include some limited-slip differentials, have two halves, which were marked at disassembly. Reassemble the pieces in the same relationship. Torque the differential case bolts to 45 ft-lbs. (See Chapter 7 for details.) Aftermarket Sure-Grips or lockers may be one- or two-piece units and tend to come fully assembled, ready to install. This could be a one-piece open unit or an older (pre-1969), two-piece Sure-Grip unit.*

*There is more than one way to set the pinion depth, which is based on the plus/minus numbers that are found on old and new pinions. This approach is fine if you are using a good, original axle. However, if you have a new axle housing or one that was broken or severely damaged, you must go through a more detailed measuring process. That process must also be used if one or both of the pinions don't have the plus/minus numbers.*

*The 1970-and-newer production Sure-Grip assemblies are two-piece units, and they are serviced as an assembly. No clutches or discs are inside the newer units, so they are not similar to the clutches in the older units. (See Chapter 7 for more information on Sure-Grip differentials.) Note the two separate bolt circles, a smaller one inside the basic ring gear bolts. The newer, two-piece Sure-Grip units thread in the differential bolts from the ring gear side.*

# Chrysler 8¾-Inch Limited-Slip Differential

The Chrysler 8¾-inch axle uses a two-piece limited-slip differential. (See Chapter 7 for details.) The standard or open differential is a basic one-piece design, and the basic assembly steps. The design of the Chrysler Sure-Grip version changed in mid 1969.

While the early units use a disc-style clutch unit, the newer unit, built from 1969 and on, uses a cone-style clutch. These are both two-piece units, but the early disc-style clutch unit has the differential bolts on the left side, opposite the ring gear. The newer, cone-style clutch unit has the bolts on the same end as the ring gear—a second bolt circle inside the ring gear bolts.

The cone-style unit was not designed to be serviced in the field because the differential required machining. However, this unit could be remanufactured and oversized cones installed and fully remachined. That would be more expensive than a new, complete unit. Oversized cones are installed at a remanufacturing facility, but you cannot realistically install these at home in your garage. Chrysler recommends replacing the assembly rather than attempting to service it.

Several two-piece differentials include some limited-slip units and most lockers. The two halves were marked at disassembly. Reassembly follows the same procedure. The differential case bolts are torqued to 45 ft-lbs. Aftermarket limited-slips or lockers may be one- or two-piece units and tend to come fully assembled, ready to install. (See Chapter 7 for more information on limited-slip differentials.)

*Note the vertical marks just above the ring gear. Two-piece differentials include some limited-slip units and most lockers. The two halves should be marked at disassembly (on the parting line in the center here). Reassembly should follow the same procedure. Typically, the differential case bolts are torqued to 45 ft-lbs. Aftermarket limited-slips or lockers may be one- or two-piece units and tend to come fully assembled, ready to install. (See Chapter 7 for more information on limited-slip differentials.)*

*The early-style 8¾-inch Sure-Grip is a two-piece design and is based on clutch discs and plates for operation. It has screws that hold it together and they enter opposite the ring gear.*

6 With the differential case mounted in a vise, install the thrust washers on the side gears and position them inside the case. One is installed on each side of the case. The ring gear flange runout was checked at disassembly with a dial indicator maximum reading of .003 inch. (See illustration on page 66.) If this was skipped, it should be done before reassembly.

7 Place the thrust washers on both differential pinions and side gears. Install the side gears first. Push the pinions through the large window in the differential case and mesh the pinion gears with the side gears. Orient the pinions to be exactly 180 degrees opposite each other.

*Once the dual cross-shaft is assembled, add the four pinions. Then place the two side gears to the case; one to each half before the pinion assembly is added.*

*At the initial stages of assembling the differential, place the thrust washer onto the back side of the side gear.*

*Install the pinion thrust washer onto the back side of the pinion gear.*

8 Rotate the side gears 90 degrees to align the pinions and thrust washers with the differential pinion shaft holes in the case. Rotate the side gear to move the pinions into position. If required, insert an axle shaft into the side gear and use it

to turn the gear itself. You only need to turn one side gear to get the pinion gears to move into position.

9 Start from the side of the differential case with the pinion shaft lock pin hole. By hand, slide the slotted end of the pinion shaft into the case and the conical thrust washer. The cross-shaft needs to be approximately flush with the case. Then you align the pin hole in the case with the pin hole in the cross-shaft and then insert the pin. Only insert the shaft through one of the pinion gears.

*With an early-style Sure-Grip, two cross-shafts must be mated together and then the small thrust pin inserted to hold them together. (Refer to Chapter 7, page 137 for complete instructions.)*

*These are the clutch discs and plates used in the older-style Sure-Grip differential. The plate/disc is round and the clutch disc has four tabs. Each style can be flat or dished (Belleville shaped). (See Chapter 7 for more details.)*

*With an open differential, use your hand to insert the thrust block through the side gear hub, so that the slot is centered between the side gears. Be sure not to leave this small part out!*

10 While maintaining alignment, push the pinion shaft into the case until hole in the shaft lines up with the hole in the case.

*If you have an early-style Sure-Grip differential, the two case halves must line up as they were marked at disassembly. Look for the faint vertical lines to match up the two case halves. Also the Vs in the cross-shaft ends that are positioned above the pinions must match the notches in the case. Here, they are both up and down.*

Line up everything and easily thread the screws on the older-style Sure-Grip differential. Then torque the screws in an alternating pattern.

This early-style Sure-Grip unit is assembled and ready for the ring gear.

Study the backlash and pinion depth drawing on page 49. Find the new, matched ring-and-pinion set for number(s). Record them on your build sheet. The key number for reassembly is the one marked on the pinion gear face. It could be a zero (0), a minus 1 (-1), or a plus 2 (+2). These numbers are combined with the existing shim numbers for the proper shim thickness. Note that a +1 is shown here.

**11** Install the pinion shaft lock pin into the case hole from the pinion shaft side of the drive gear flange. It should slide in part way. You then use a brass drift/punch and hammer to move into position.

**12** Place the ring gear onto the differential case pilot (inner diameter of ring gear with chamfer). Align the threaded holes in the ring gear with those in the case.

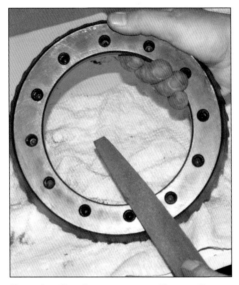

Examine the ring gear mounting surface for nicks or burrs and de-burr as required. Use a large, round file (shown) or an Arkansas stone to lightly chamfer the inner edge of the ring gear.

**13** Mount the case in a vise between brass jaws and torque each screw to 55 ft-lbs. Torque them in an alternating sequence and use a two-step torqueing process. First torque to 25 or 30 ft-lbs, then torque to 55 ft-lbs.

With new differential case bearings, position each cone on the hub of the case with the taper away from the ring gear and then press on the cones. An arbor press or shop press may be used.

Insert the new ring gear attaching screws with left-hand threads through the flange on the case and into the ring gear. After all screws have been properly started, tap the ring gear against the differential case flange with a non-metallic mallet. When fitting a new ring gear to a differential case, torque down the bolts in a cross-over pattern, using new bolts. Torque them down in increments of 25 to 30 ft-lbs at a time until the final specification is reached. This allows the ring gear to sit correctly on the case and prevents cocking the ring gear.

## Chrysler Banjo Axle Carrier Housing Prep

*Bearing pullers come in all sizes because of the many bearing sizes in an axle. The puller is selected based on the size of the bearing and its location (length of handle). However, a brass drift or punch and a hammer may be used in a pinch. The bearing race (on the left) selects the installer/remover (on the right).*

1 Place the pinion bearing cups squarely in the bores of the carrier housing, one toward the front and one at the rear. The most common method of bearing cup installation is to tap them into position with a bearing race installer and hammer.

2 Tap the bearing cups into position, fully seated. Check from the opposite direction to verify position.

3 Set the pinion bearing preload and depth of mesh. The 8¾-inch axle features three types of pinions. The method of determining pinion depth of mesh and the bearing preload are the same for the small- and large-stem pinions. However, the sequence of making the two adjustments is different.

The small-stem pinions require the bearing preload adjustment be made first, while the large-stem pinions require the depth of mesh adjustment be made first. The large-stem pinion uses a collapsible spacer for bearing preload, and therefore the depth of mesh must be set first.

The position of the drive pinion in relation to the drive gear (depth of mesh or drive pinion depth) is determined by the location of the bearing cup shoulders in the carrier and by the portion of the

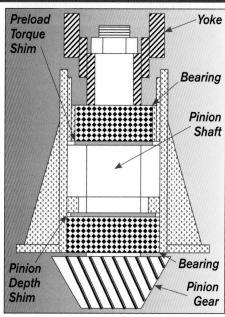

*The pinion shims for pinion depth and preload torque are placed between the bearing and the case. The proper thickness must be calculated/measured.*

pinion in back of the bearing. The plus/minus numbers on the ends of the old and new pinions and the current shim package are used to determine the suitable thickness of the rear pinion bearing mounting shim for the carrier.

## Chrysler Banjo Pinion Bearing Preload and Pinion Setting (Large Stem)

These steps focus on the most popular and stronger large-stem axle (742 case) and the tapered-pinion axle (489 case). The 489 case details are in the next section on the collapsible spacer.

1 If the differential assembly was acceptably quiet before disassembly, you can use the drive pinion and the original components for reassembly. If replacement parts are being installed, a complete re-adjustment is required. Therefore, a shim with the proper thickness must be selected and installed. Remove the old pinion bearings, if they were not removed

in the disassembly process. Install new bearing races using a bearing driver.

2 The ring gear and pinion are manufactured, lapped, and sold in matching sets only. The adjustment position, in which the best tooth contact is obtained, is marked on the end of the pinion head. To obtain the proper pinion setting in relation to the ring gear, the correct-thickness mounting shim must be selected before the drive pinion is installed in the carrier.

Pinion bearing mounting shims are available in increments of .002 from .084

to .100 inch for small-stem or large-stem step-type pinions. Shims are also available in .020- to .038-inch in increments of .001 inch for large-stem pinions with a collapsible spacer, which are also called tapered pinions. Note: The original shim thickness should have been checked and recorded at disassembly.

3 To select the shim with the proper thickness, note that the head of the drive pinion is marked with a plus (+) or a minus (−) sign, followed by a number ranging from 0 to 4. Shims are available in .002-inch increments.

## Chrysler Banjo Depth of Mesh Large Stem and Large Stem with Collapsible Spacer: First Step (Covers 742 and 489 cases)

*A gauge arbor (the cross-bar in the photo) has three basic pieces, not counting the dial indicator/measuring hardware. The two metal discs are inserted into the differential case's main bearing bores. (They are sized to fit exactly.) Then the main caps are installed. The disc in the right-side main can be seen here. Then the cross-arbor is slid across between the two discs in the sized holes in their centers. From this basic setup, the gauge block and indicators are used to measure from the across-arbor (the rod) down to the pinion head.*

This section is not required for most axle rebuilds. In most cases you have shim thickness numbers, both on the the new gear set and the old gear set. If this is the case, you can skip to the marking pattern step.

However, if you have no numbers (old gear or can't read), any number is not available, you have a brand-new housing, or you have a broken housing (welded on to repair, etc.), you need to refer to sidebar "How to Set Pinion Gear Depth" on page 49.

## Chrysler Banjo Pinion Bearing Preload Large Stem: Second Step

1 Pinion shims are chamfered on one side and must be installed on the pinion stem with the chamfered side toward the pinion head.

2 Always make sure that the bearing cones are lubricated with hypoid gear lubricant.

3 Install the front pinion bearing, universal joint flange, Belleville washer (convex side facing up), and nut. The bearing slips down over the splines and into the front bearing cup. If the bearing is reversed, it does not seat properly in the cup. Note that the cup or bearing race has been installed. Do not install the oil seal!

4 After the correct pinion depth of mesh has been established and the correct bearing preload obtained, remove the drive pinion flange. Apply a light coat of sealer to the drive pinion oil seal and carrier housing bore. Install the drive pinion oil seal with a sealer installation tool.

5 Install the pinion flange, washer, and nut. Hold the flange securely using special yoke holding tool and tighten nut to 240 ft-lbs.

*If the bearings are being replaced, place the new bearing cup in position in the carrier and drive the cups in place with a suitable drift. (Note: This was done in earlier step.) After properly positioning the bearing cups in the carrier, assemble the drive pinion mounting shim (chamfered side toward the gear) on the drive pinion stem. Install the tubular spacer (if so equipped) and the preload shims on the pinion stems. Insert the pinion assembly into the carrier.*

*Carefully point the nose of the pinion into the rear bearing cone and housing.*

*To properly seat the bearing rollers in the bearing cups, rotate the drive pinion after tightening the flange nut to 240 ft-lbs. The preload torque required to rotate the pinion with the bearings oiled should be 20 to 30 in-lbs for new bearings and 0 to 15 in-lbs for used bearings. Use a thinner shim pack to increase preload and a thicker shim pack to decrease preload. Try to maintain steady pressure and speed as you rotate the torque wrench.*

## Pinion Bearing Preload Large Stem with Collapsible Spacer: Second Step (489 Case only)

1 After installing the correct pinion bearing mounting shim behind the rear pinion bearing cone, continue with the installation of the pinion assembly into the carrier housing.

2 Install the new collapsible spacer followed by the new front pinion bearing cone on the pinion stem. Press the front pinion bearing cone onto the pinion stem, being careful not to collapse the spacer. Use caution and go slow. Watch

*Pressing the pinion bearing onto the pinion stem in a basic arbor press can be done with no special fixtures.*

the gap between the bearing race and the shoulder of the differential case. As the clearance or gap closes down, slow down until race just touches the shoulder.

3 Apply a light coat of sealer to the drive pinion oil seal and the carrier housing bore. Install the drive pinion oil seal with a seal installer.

*The pinion seal is on the end of the housing. Therefore it can be tapped in easily but a correctly sized installer (shown) can be helpful. In most cases, any flat metal object, sized to the bearing seal, serves to tap the seal into place.*

4 Install an anti-clang washer and universal joint flange (the yoke), Belleville washer (convex side facing up),

and the large nut. Tap the yoke onto the pinion with a non-metal hammer to move it into position.

5 Tighten the pinion nut to 170 ft-lbs. Using an inch-pounds torque wrench, rotate the pinion to determine preload. To set an accurate preload, make two full turns for warmup and then practice to get a steady, consistent reading. The correct preload specifications are 20 to 30 inch-pounds for new bearings or 10 inch-pounds over the original if the old rear pinion bearing is being reused.

If the preload is not correct, continue to tighten the pinion nut in small increments until preload on the bearings is correct. A minimum of 170 ft-lbs of torque is required. Under no circumstances should the pinion nut be backed off to lessen the preload. If this is done, a new pinion-bearing collapsible spacer must be installed and the nut retightened until the proper preload is obtained.

## Chrysler Banjo Axle Differential and Ring Gear Installation into Carrier

Assemble the differential unit taking care that the bearings, especially the side bearings, are sitting correctly in the bearing housing, not cocked or sitting at a slight angle.

1 Hold the differential and ring gear assembly with the bearing cups assembled onto their respective bearing cones, and carefully install the assembly into the carrier. Gently guide the carrier into the housing assembly. Correctly orient the ring gear in the case and align the bearings with the pedestals and set the carrier inside the housing. Set the carrier assembly into the housing with the original side shims (if used) and new bearings.

2 Install the differential main bearing caps on their respective sides. Line up the identification marks, which were added on the cap and the carrier housing pedestals at disassembly.

*Using spanner wrenches, turn the adjuster in until the cups are properly square with the bearing cones. The end play should be eliminated with some backlash existing between the drive gear and the pinion. Backlash is usually .006 to .010 inch.*

3 Install the main cap bolts and tighten them by hand so the carrier is held in the housing while you install the other components. You will tighten the main caps to final torque spec later.

4 Install the differential bearing adjusters, on their respective sides, making sure that the identifications mark lines up. Screw in the adjuster by hand. Do not attempt to apply any excessive pressure at this time. The side adjusters should mate against the outside edge of the bearing.

5 Tighten one differential bearing cap bolt on each side to 85 to 90 ft-lbs.

## Chrysler Banjo Axle Ring Gear and Pinion Backlash

Install the dial indicator and fixture on the housing to properly measure backlash. (Refer to Chapter 2 for mounting the dial indicator.) When properly set, the correct ring gear and pinion backlash is .006 to .008 inch at the point of minimum backlash.

1 Measure backlash between the ring gear and pinion at four positions,

*Attach a dial indicator to the carrier flange so the pointer of the indicator is squarely contacting one ring gear tooth face on the drive side. A gear tooth has a top and bottom, which are along for the ride. The drive side is the front face of the tooth and the coast side is the back side of the tooth. Most wear occurs on the drive side. Use a dial indicator with a magnetic base before checking the ring gear wear pattern.*

approximately 90 degrees apart. (Every 90 degrees means four marks on the ring gear. If you have a 40-tooth ring gear, that's a mark every 10 teeth.) After the point of least backlash has been determined, mark the ring gear. Do not rotate the ring gear from the point of least backlash until all adjustments have been made.

2 Using a spanner wrench, turn both bearing adjusters equally and in the same direction until the backlash between the ring gear and the pinion is .0005 to .0015 inch. (This backlash variation allows alignment and installation of the bearing adjuster lock, lockwasher, and attaching screw.) The adjuster should only be turned in the clockwise direction and not backed off.

*The adjuster lock is held on the center bolt. The main cap bolts are on either side of it. The adjuster lock has two feet that fit into the holes in the ring. The feet must be inserted before you try to install the bolt. Install the adjuster lock on the bearing cap, back-face side of the ring gear. Tighten the lock screw to 15 to 20 ft-lbs.*

## Chrysler Banjo Axle Differential Bearing Preload

1 Turn in the bearing adjuster (tooth side of the ring gear) one notch at a time (notch refers to an adjuster lock hole) until the backlash between the ring gear and the pinion reaches a minimum of .006 to .008 inch. This preloads the differential bearings and establishes the correct backlash.

2 Tighten the remaining two differential bearing cap bolts to 85 to 90 ft-lbs.

3 Install the remaining adjuster lock, lockwasher, and attaching screw. Tighten to 15 to 20 ft-lbs.

## Chrysler Banjo Axle Gear Tooth Contact Pattern

At this stage, you may think that that the contact pattern is adequately set. But even after taking all the detailed measurements, you need to set the contact pattern.

The gear tooth contact pattern shows whether the correct rear pinion bearing mounting shim has been installed and the drive gear backlash has been set properly. This is the final setup test.

The correct pattern provides low noise and long wear, which directly cor-

relates to durability, performance and reliability of the axle assembly, but it also enhances the driving experience. Few things are more annoying that a whining ring and pinion that reduces torque.

Running the contact pattern determines the axle has been properly set up. Basically you adjust the depth of the pinion and the left to right location of the differential case. The shape and general location of the contact pattern tells you which way to adjust these items.

To obtain the tooth contact pattern, apply a thin film of hydrated ferric oxide, commonly known as yellow oxide of iron, on both the drive and coast side of the ring gear teeth. Using a round bar or large screwdriver (between the carrier housing and the differential case flange), apply a load against the backside of the ring gear and rotate the pinion several 360-degree revolutions in both directions. This procedure leaves a distinct contact pattern on both the drive and the coast side of the ring gear teeth.

Maintain backlash between the ring gear and the pinion within the specified limits until the correct pattern is obtained.

Compare your observed contact pattern to the pattern examples shown on pages 21–23 in Chapter 2, to determine if all adjustments have been made properly. The correct contact pattern is very well centered on both the drive and coast sides of the teeth. When the tooth contact patterns are obtained by hand, the actual contact area tends to be small. Under actual operating loads, the contact area increases while centered on the smaller area.

Prepare to lift the carrier assembly into position. It is heavy so this should be given some planning.

## Chrysler Banjo Axle Differential and Carrier

*Thoroughly clean the gasket surfaces of the carrier housing and the rear axle (banjo) housing. You may want to try a degreaser. Install the new gasket. To assist in holding the gasket in place, apply a thin coat of gasket sealer to both sides.*

## Chrysler Banjo Axle Shaft Assembly

1 Using a new gasket, install the carrier assembly into the axle housing. Tighten the nuts holding the carrier to the axle housing to 45 ft-lbs. Use an alternating pattern.

2 Install the retainer plate and seal the assembly onto the axle shaft.

3 Lubricate the wheel bearings with multi-purpose grease.

4 Install a new axle shaft bearing cup, cone, and collar on the shaft using a bearing installer.

5 Inspect the axle shaft seal journal for scratches and polish it with 600-grade crocus cloth if necessary.

## Chrysler Banjo Axle Shaft Installation

1 Clean the axle housing flange face thoroughly and install a new gasket followed by the brake support plate assembly on the driver's side of the axle housing.

2 Apply a thin coating of multi-purpose grease to the outside diameter of the bearing cup prior to installing it in the bearing bore.

3 Install a foam gasket on the studs of the axle housing and carefully slide the axle shaft assembly through the oil seal and engage the splines in the differential side gear.

4 Lightly tap the end of the axle shaft with a plastic or wood mallet to position the axle shaft bearing in the housing bearing bore. Position the retainer plate over the axle housing studs.

5 Install the retainer nuts and tighten to 30 to 35 ft-lbs. Start tightening on the bottom nut, then follow an alternating pattern (left/right) to complete the procedure.

6 Repeat steps 4 and 5 for the passenger's side of the axle housing. Install a foam gasket on the studs of the axle housing.

7 Turn counterclockwise the threaded adjuster of the right axle shaft assembly until the inner face of the adjuster is flush with the inner face of the retainer plate. Carefully slide the axle shaft assembly through the oil seal and engage the splines in the differential side gear. Look inside the axle housing to verify that the axle spline has fully engaged the side gears.

8 Repeat steps 6 and 7 for the passenger's side of the axle housing.

## Chrysler Banjo Axle Shaft Endplay

1 Be careful when setting the axle shaft endplay; both rear wheels must be off the ground, otherwise you get a false endplay setting.

2 Using a dial indicator mounted on the left brake support, turn the axle adjuster clockwise until both wheel bearings are seated and there is 0 endplay in the axle shafts. Back off the adjuster counterclockwise approximately four notches (notches refer to adjuster lock holes) to establish an axle shaft endplay of .013 to .023 inch.

3 Lightly tap the end of the left axle shaft with a non-metallic mallet to seat the right wheel bearing cup against the adjuster, and rotate the axle shaft several rotations so that a true endplay reading is indicated.

4 Remove one retainer plate nut and install an adjuster lock. If the tab on the lock does not mate with notch in the adjuster, turn the adjuster slightly until it does. Reinstall the nut and tighten to 30 to 35 ft-lbs.

5 Recheck axle shaft endplay. If it is not within the tolerance of .013 to .023 inch, repeat the adjustment procedure.

6 Remove the dial indicator.

## Chrysler Banjo Axle Driveshaft

1 Install the driveshaft into the transmission if removed.

2 Install the rear universal joint of the driveshaft into the saddle of the yoke aligning marks made at disassembly and tighten the clamp screws to 15 ft-lbs.

3 Install the brake drums and drum retaining clips, if used.

4 Install the rear wheels and tighten to 55 ft-lbs.

5 It is very important to fill the unit with oil! Replace the drain plug if removed and tighten. Use the recommended lube based on the ring-and-pinion manufacturer or the Sure-Grip manufacturer specifications or recommendations. Use a syringe to fill the axle because typically there is limited room for other oil-fill approaches. A general lube recommendation is as follows: 75W-90 for street, 140W for race. There are also synthetic oils such as 75-140 synthetic that may offer wider coverage. Replace the oil fill plug.

### 8¾ Axle Chart

| Axle Diameter | Ring Gear | Axle Type | Style | Lube Capacity | Gen. Ratios |
|---|---|---|---|---|---|
| 742 | 8.75 inches | Semi-floating hypoid | OTF | 64 ounces (4.0 pints) | 3.55 to 5.13:1 |
| 489 | 8.75 inches | Semi-floating hypoid | OTF | 70 ounces (4.4 pints) | 3.23 to 5.13:1 |

OTF = out-the-front

*Fill a syringe with axle lube. It may take more than one application to get 4.0 to 4.4 pints into the axle.*

### Fill 8¾ Axle

Corporate service manuals show the 741 and 742 case versions of the 8¾-inch axle (up to 1968) to have a 4.0-pint fill capacity while the 489 case version (1969 and newer) is shown to have a 4.4-pint fill capacity. This is related more to the lower numerical axle ratios (2.9:1 and 3.2:1 versus 3.5:1 and 3.9:1) used in the newer axles compared to the old axles. The lower numerical ratios require thinner ring gears, which allows for more fill volume. In any case, if you use higher numerical axle ratios (4.56:1 versus 3.55:1) you may have to use less fill volume from the amount listed. ∎

# Chrysler Carrier-Tube Axle

Sure-Grips are now only available from the aftermarket. The special differential cases are dictated when the ratio changes from 2.45:1 and 2.71/2.76:1 axle ratios, if produced.

### Chrysler OTB 7¼, 8¼, 9¼ Carrier-Tube Axles

Chrysler has installed six different axles in its vehicles since 1960, not counting FWD vehicles: 7¼-, 8¼-, 8¾-, 9¼-, Dana 60 (9¾-inch), and Dana 44 (8½-inch). The only banjo axle is the 8¾-inch design. The others are carrier-tube axles, which remove the ring and pinion individually OTB. Dana builds the Dana 60 (9¾-inch) and the Dana 44 (8½-inch). See Chapter 6 for more details.

Several features identify a typical carrier-tube axle. First, these axles have a center housing with two tubes (one from each side) pressed into it. There is also an inspection plate or cover bolted to the rear of the center housing. A carrier-tube axle requires the ring and pinion to be removed OTR, one at a time, ring and differential assembly first.

When viewed from the rear, you see that a banjo axle is a one-piece unit. On banjo axles, the center section with the ring and pinion can be unbolted and removed OTF.

The 7¼-inch-diameter ring gear axle has a 1⅜-inch-diameter pinion stem. The axle housing is stamped with casting number 2070051, 3507881, or 3723675 depending on the year it was pro duced.

The 8¼-inch-diameter ring gear axle has a 1⅝–inch-diameter pinion stem. The axle housing is stamped with casting number 2852905, 3723598, or 3723599 depending on the year it was produced.

The 9¼-inch-diameter ring gear axle has a 1⅞-inch diameter pinion stem. The axle housing is stamped with the casting numbers 3507890, 3507891, or 3723199

depending on the year it was produced.

There are two types of 7¼-inch Chrysler carrier-tube axles: a nine-bolt version used up to 1985 and a ten-bolt version used from 1986 and newer. The 8¼-inch axle was used in the 1974–1976 A-Body cars (Duster/Dart/Valiant) plus the 1976-and-newer F-Body cars. The 1974–1976 A-Body cars received disc brakes on the front and drums on the rear and both packages came with a 4½-inch bolt circle. The 1960–1972/3 A-Body cars used 4.0-inch bolt circle wheels. To gain the 4½-inch bolt circle, it is common to swap a 1974-and-newer A-body axle into an older pre-1973 A-Body.

### 7¼-inch Carrier-Tube Axle

The Chrysler 7¼-inch axle was Chrysler's first carrier-tube axle design that was used in production cars. It was introduced in the 1960 model year and was used in lightweight cars, such as the A-Body with six-cylinder and small V-8 engines.

A casting number located in the center housing can identify the 7¼-inch axle housing (nine-bolt version). The number is located on the bottom right side of the housing toward the front. There are three casting numbers for the 7¼-inch axle: 2070051, 3507881, and 3723675. The early 7¼-inch axle used 2½-inch axle tubes, which means that the commonly available 3-inch spring seats that get welded to the outer ends of the tubes to hold the suspension springs in place do not fit. Some aftermarket suppliers offer 2½-inch spring seats for this application.

The newer 7¼-inch axles have 3-inch tubes and can use the 3-inch spring seats. To make this conversion, the tubes are swedged down to the smaller size as they enter the center housing.

On the 7¼-inch axle, the differential case changes between the 2.47:1 and numerically smaller ratios and the 2.76:1

and numerically higher ratios. Both the 2.47:1 and 2.76:1 ratios were only used in production applications. Note that not many 2.47 ratios were produced.

Sure-Grips (production and aftermarket) are available for the 7¼-inch axles, but very few were installed in these axle housings. If you want a Sure-Grip, you have to get one from an aftermarket supplier.

### 8¼-inch Carrier-Tube Axle

The 8¼-inch carrier-tube axle design was introduced in 1969. The performance community did not notice it until it was installed in the 340 Dusters and Darts (A-Bodies) in 1973. It was also installed on the 1973-and-newer 318/340/360 Road Runners and Chargers (B-Bodies).

There is a wide selection of ratios available for the 8¼-inch axle, including the Sure-Grip from 1973-on.

The axle tubes are the standard 3-inch diameter so that the commonly available 3-inch spring seats can be used.

A casting number cast into the bottom of the housing identifies this axle housing. This casting number is located on the passenger's side toward the front of the housing. The 8¼-inch casting numbers are 2852905, 3723598, and 3723599.

The 1960–1973 A-Body cars were built with 4.0-inch bolt circle axles and 4.0-inch bolt circle wheels. In 1973, these A-Body cars were introduced with disc brakes and the standard 4½-inch bolt circle axles/wheels. This 4½-inch package only came on the 8¼-inch axles. It was not used on the 8¾-inch axle. The 4½-inch axle shafts from the 8¼-inch axle do not fit in the 8¾-inch banjo axle.

Special differential cases are dictated when the ratio changes from 2.45:1 and 2.71:1 axle ratios. Note: The

2.45:1 and lower numerical ratios were only used in production applications, typically passenger cars.

### 9¼-inch Carrier-Tube Axle

The 9¼-inch axle is the newest and largest Chrysler carrier-tube axle design. It was introduced with the 1973 model cars in the B-Body station wagon models. In the next few years, it replaced other 9-inch axles in heavy-duty applications. The 9¼-inch axle is more commonly found in large cars and heavy trucks.

Like the other Chrysler axles, the 9¼-inch axle can be identified by the casting number, which is cast into the center housing toward the bottom at the rear. The casting numbers are: 3507890, 3507891, and 3723199.

There was a Sure-Grip available for the 9¼-inch axle in production; however, Note that it is not known whether the 2.45:1 and lower numerical ratios were actually used in production applications.

Here I focus on the 8¼-inch axle but tips for the 7¼- and 9¼-inch axles are also included. The 8¼-inch axle was used in popular performance cars in the muscle car era.

## Chrysler Carrier-Tube Axle Disassembly

**1** Before you start the rebuilding procedure, you need to get all the necessary tools, materials, gaskets, parts or rebuild kit together, so you have everything you need.

**2** Use a floor jack or a car lift to raise the vehicle off the garage floor. Place jack stands under the frame rails on both sides. If you need to replace the axle tubes or housing itself, remove the entire axle assembly from the vehicle. If you are going to rebuild the differential, it is not necessary to remove the complete axle assembly to rebuild/recondition the differential or change the axle ratio.

**3** Use a lug wrench, impact gun, or breaker bar and socket to remove the rear wheel lug nuts. Then remove wheels and place them away from the work area.

**4** Remove the retaining clips (on axle studs) and then the brake drum assemblies, which allows access to the flanged axle shaft ends. If used, a small screwdriver or pliers allows you to remove the clips. They are not always used and may not have been re-installed to the last shop trip. All 8¼- and 9¼-inch axles use C-clips. (The 7¼-inch axle may or may not.)

**5** Use water and a soap agent to clean all dirt from the area around the housing's rear cover. If the rear housing has leaked, use mineral spirits or a degreaser to strip the oil and grease from the housing and the cover.

**6** Use a scribe or Sharpie to mark the U-joint and pinion flange. You look for a flat spot, such as under the cup on the yoke and then on the driveshaft tube opposite. (See top photo on page 66.) This maintains the dynamic balance of the drivetrain.

**7** Disconnect the prop-shaft and push it forward while supporting it in near-horizontal position. Then move it out of your way. If you remove the driveshaft from the transmission, the transmission may leak. Insert a plastic plug to prevent the transmission from leaking. (See page 30.)

**8** Tape the U-joint to hold the cups together to keep everything in position for re-assembly.

**9** In preparation to drain the axle housing, place an oil drain pan below the axle cover.

**10** You can remove the fill plug. But after all, it is used to fill the differential and positioned too high to function as a typical drain. So you are effectively able to drain the axle housing by removing the plug.

**11** To completely drain the rear axle housing, you need to remove the housing cover bolts. Leave on the cover bolt attached at the top of the housing but make sure it's loose, so the housing cover separates from the housing at the bottom but remains attached at the top. This way the cover won't fall into the drop pan.

**12** Use a small pry bar or a large flathead screwdriver to pry the cover loose at the bottom. This breaks the seal between the housing and the cover, but be careful because you don't want to mar or damage the mounting surface. If you do damage it enough, the axle housing could leak. Once the cover is loose, let the oil drain from the differential housing into the catch pan.

**13** Remove the last bolt and remove the rear cover. Look at the cover for any obvious signs of damage or decay. If it's in good condition, properly store it in preparation for reassembly.

**14** You now have access to the differential; check for open versus limited-slip differential type. If you see clutch pack coil springs inside the differential it is a limited-slip differential. If there are no springs and you simply see the pinion and side gears, it's an open differential. However, there is a conclusive test for determining differential type and you should follow the procedure in Chapter 4, page 36, to make sure.

**15** Reach into the axle housing and by hand rotate the differential case to access the pinion shaft lock screw. Once the side of the case faces you, use a wrench or socket and ratchet to remove the pinion shaft lock screw. Once the screw has been removed, you can remove the pinion shaft.

**16** Remove the pinion shaft. If the cross-pin needs to be driven out, use a brass drift and a mallet. Take your

*Turn the differential and check the C-clips on the axle shaft ends. The C-clip sits nestled in a recess machined into the side gear.*

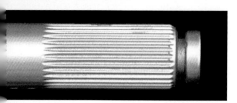

*The C-clip fits over a machined notch in the end of each axle shaft. Once the C-clip is installed, the axle shaft is pulled outward and the C-clip fits into its recess in the side gear. Then the cross-shaft can be installed.*

ime and be patient when driving it out. Use the correct-size pin and squarely trike it to drive it out. Before the notched cross-shaft is removed, the ring gear must be removed from the differential case. Therefore, remove the retaining bolts that secure the ring gear to the differenial housing.

With a notched cross-shaft, rotate the notch toward the correct axle and push the axle in. The C-clip is easily seen in the differential housing so snag it with your finger or a flathead screwdriver. Lift it out of the differential case. Then repeat for the other axle, rotating the notch toward the opposite axle. Leave the special cross-shaft in place until the ring gear has been removed. Note that notched cross-shafts are required with lower (numerically higher such as 4.5 versus 3.00) ratios.

*Many axles have pressed lock pins on the cross-shaft but the 8¼ uses a threaded lock pin. Remove it with a small wrench.*

*This is an actual C-clip that drops into the notch cut in the end of the axle shafts.*

**17** By hand, push the axle shaft inward, toward the center of the vehicle.

**18** Remove the C-clip/lock inside the differential housing that's located in the recessed groove at the end of each axle shaft. Do one side at a time.

**19** Carefully slide the axle shafts out of the axle tubes. Do not let the axle shafts bang around inside the tubes as you're sliding them out because you must not damage the axle shaft seal and bearing. Try to keep the axle shaft centered in the axle tube as you slide it out of the axle tubes. Support the axle shaft using one hand on the flange and the

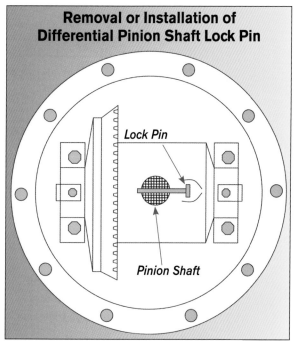

**Removal or Installation of Differential Pinion Shaft Lock Pin**

Lock Pin

Pinion Shaft

*Remove the pinion shaft. The cross-pin may need to be driven out. Use a brass drift if needed. Note that a notched cross-shaft can't be removed until the ring gear is removed from the differential case. With a notched cross-shaft, rotate the notch toward the proper axle, push the axle in, and remove the C-clip. Then repeat for the other axle, rotating the notch toward the opposite axle. Leave the special cross-shaft in place until the ring gear is removed. Note that notched cross-shafts are required with higher (bigger numbers) ratios.*

other hand on the shaft itself once it is far enough out to allow access.

**20** Slide or drive the pinion shaft with a drift and hammer into the differential case and through the pinion gears. Insert the lock screw back into the differential case to secure pinion shaft. Only hand tighten it because you will remove the pinion shaft later.

**21** Inspect the axle shafts, especially in the bearing and seal area. If there is excessive wear or the splines are chipped, stripped, or in any other way damaged, you need to replace the axle shafts.

**22** Remove the axle shaft seal from the housing bore. Place a slide-hammer-style bearing removal tool into the axle tube and move it past the bearing seal.

**23** Measure the differential side play using a dial indicator.

**24** Side play and runout checks taken during disassembly need to be performed at reassembly.

**25** Turn the ring gear several full revolutions and read the dial indicator. Mark the ring gear and differential case at the point of maximum runout. This differential case marking will be very important later in checking the differential case runout. Total indicator reading should be no more than .005 inch. If runout exceeds .005 inch, the differential case may be damaged.

**26** Mark each half of the differential case, if it is a two-piece (a Sure-Grip), for reinstallation (optional). Mark it on two opposite flat sections near the parting line. You're marking it so the case halves line up. Note that the cone-style Sure-Grip used in newer axles is not serviced, and must be replaced as a complete unit. (See Chapter 7 for details.)

**27** Use a wrench or a socket and ratchet to remove the adjuster lock from the center of each main cap.

*Mark the carrier housing and the main caps for reinstallation. Use a punch to make one mark on the left and two marks on the right. The main cap bolt head is toward the bottom, the two dots are slightly above the bolt. The two dots on the housing/casting are just above the parting line.*

**28** Loosen the hex adjuster using a special tool. Although it does not have a specific name, this tool has a 3-foot-long single shaft; one end fits into the adjuster on each side of the differential (remove the adjuster lock from each main cap) and the other end takes a socket wrench or torque wrench. The tool has a long extension and is inserted through the axle tube on each side.

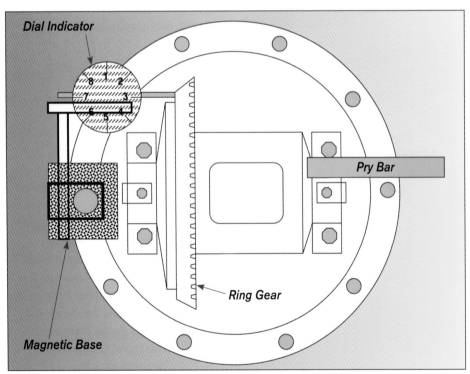

*To measure the differential side play, place a small pry bar or flat-blade screwdriver between the left side of the axle housing and the differential case flange. Next using a prying motion, determine if side play is present. There should be none. If side play is present, use a threaded adjuster and a long, special tool to reach in through the axle tube to remove the side play.*

*Loosen the four main cap bolts but do not remove the bearing caps.*

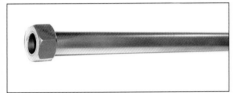

*One of the unique features of the 8¼ and 9¼ axles is that they require a long (around 3 feet) tool with a large hex on the end to reach in through the axle tubes to the center section to adjust the side clearance. This tool is made by Yukon.*

**29** If you decide to replace the wheel bearings, you will be a special wheel bearing puller for these wheel bearings. Basically it is a unique add-on to the standard slide hammer.

**30** Use a wrench or ratchet and socket to remove the four cap screws while holding the differential assembly in place. Carefully remove the two main bearing caps, adjusters, and then the differential assembly with ring gear. Be prepared to lift the differential housing from the axle housing and place it in a safe place for further servicing. Make sure to tag and bag the parts (left/right), so they are assembled in the correct position.

**31** You need to keep all the related parts together, so the differential is correctly assembled with the right parts. When removing the differential from the case, keep the bearing cups with their respective bearing cones. Also keep the threaded adjusters with their respective bearings.

**32** Using an inch-pound torque wrench, measure the pinion bearing preload by rotating the pinion flange slowly with the torque wrench; record the maximum torque reading.

**33** Remove the drive pinion nut while holding with special yoke holder tool. The trick with various yoke holders is that the torque wrench, breaker bar, or air impact gun has to pass through the

center of the tool to apply torque to the pinion nut.

**34** Use a flange puller tool to remove the drive pinion yoke as described earlier on page 85.

*The yoke remover is a small puller that has two fingers and a center adjusting screw. The fingers are placed over the outside of the yoke saddles and the center adjuster pushes on the pinion stem. Once set up, a small socket and ratchet is all that is required to removed the yoke.*

*Using a spanner wrench, turn both bearing adjusters equally and in the same direction until backlash between the ring gear and the pinion is .0005 to .0015 inch. (This backlash variation is given to permit alignment and installation of the bearing adjuster lock, lockwasher, and attaching screw.) The adjuster should only be turned in the clockwise direction and not backed off.*

*This is a basic slide hammer with a tool attached to the end, which is used for pulling the axle bearings from 8¼ and 8¾ axles. The foot on the end rotates to horizontal (it's vertical in photo) and this allows it to slip inside the bearing. Then it rotates to vertical and you can pull out the bearing.*

*There are two different techniques for removing the pinion nut and its washer. If you use an air impact gun on the pinion nut, the yoke holder can be a large pair of channel locks. If you are using a socket and manual ratchet/breaker bar, you need to hold it more securely, which requires a yoke holder similar to the one shown on page 25 in Chapter 2. Two bolts are used to attach the yoke holder on the yoke saddles, which are diagonally opposite each other. The trick with various yoke holders is that the torque wrench, breaker bar, or air impact gun has to pass through the center of the tool to apply torque to the pinion nut.*

**35** Remove the drive pinion oil seal. Follow the seal removal process described earlier on page 84.

**36** To remove the pinion, use a hammer and punch to take or drive the pinion stem rearward and out of the bearing in the housing. This procedure can damage the bearings, so both the bearing cones and cups must be replaced. Also discard the collapsible spacer.

**37** Use a bearing puller (driver) to remove the front and rear bearing cups from the housing. You can also use a punch or drift and hammer. You may need to use the extension handle and a hammer to drive them out. Remove the press-off pinion bearings. Press off.

**38** Measure the shim thickness on both sides of the bearing and record it on a piece of paper in your notebook, so you can correctly set gear depth on reassembly. Also you need to note the shim order and their location. Inspect the shims for cracks, straightness, and any damage. If the shims are in good condition, retain them or replace with shims of the same thickness. Replace pinion bearings.

**39** Use a socket and ratchet to remove all the bolts that hold the ring gear to differential housing. Remember, these have left-hand threads, so you need to turn them to the right (clockwise) to loosen them.

**40** Once the ring gear screws have been removed, discard them. You need new bolts or screws for proper re-installation of the ring gear.

**41** Use a ratchet and socket to remove the bearing cap bolts and bearing caps. Carefully lift the differential case

*Once all of the ring-gear bolts have been removed (left-hand thread on Chrysler axles) then the ring gear can be tapped off with a brass punch and hammer. Rags are piled at the bottom to catch the ring gear to keep it from being damaged.*

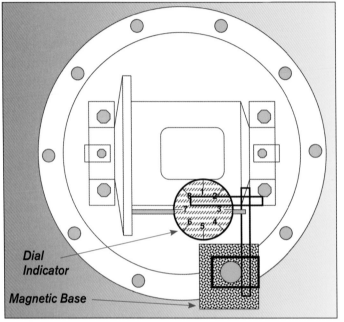

Dial Indicator

Magnetic Base

*In an earlier step, if the ring gear runout was more than .005 inch, the differential case flange runout should be measured again. Install the differential case and its respective bearing cups and adjusters in the housing.*

*Attach a dial indicator to the carrier housing, so that the pointer is perpendicular to the ring gear surface of the differential case flange. Place it between the outer edge and the ring gear attaching bolt holes. Rotate the differential case several complete revolutions while noting the total indicator reading. This reading must not exceed .003-inch runout. If the runout is more than .003 inch, the differential case must be replaced.*

out of the axle housing and take into account that the differential case is quite heavy.

**42** A lock screw keeps the pinion shaft secure inside the differential

case. Use a socket and ratchet to remove the lock screw from the differential housing. Once the lock screw has been unscrewed and removed, use a brass drift and hammer to drive the pinion shaft out of the case.

43 Remove the pinion gears from the differential case. Rotate the differential housing side gears until the differential pinions appear at the case window opening. Once aligned or centered in the window, lift the pinions and washers out of the differential case by hand. Take the opposite one out the opposite window or rotate the side gear to move the second pinion into the window.

44 Once the pinion gears have been removed, you can remove the side gears. By hand, lift the differential side gears and thrust washers from the case.

45 Use a bearing puller to remove the differential bearing cones from the differential case.

*Remove bearings from the differential assembly and ring gear. This is done using a special differential bearing remover. There are several pieces to the tool. This view is fully assembled into the differential bearing and ready to remove it. There are two pieces that fit around the differential bearing and the end of the case. The tall, threaded adjuster fits on top of the end of the case. Once the two halves have been fitted around the bearing, the outer sleeve is dropped over it and the bearing removal can begin. An air impact gun or large socket/ratchet is applied to the top of the threaded adjuster to actually remove the bearing (see page 26 for partial assembly of this tool).*

46 Thoroughly clean and inspect all parts. Dirt is the enemy of any moving part. Cleaning allows you to see cracks, especially small cracks in your hardware. It also allows you to observe surface for scuffing and any discoloration.

## Chrysler Carrier-Tube Cleaning and Inspection

With the differential completely disassembled, it is time to check all the parts and see what you have. Obviously wearable parts, such as bearings, that are replaced do not need to be checked

1 Clean all parts with mineral spirits or a dry cleaning solvent. Use compressed air to dry the axle shaft bearings.

2 To clean the axle housing tubes, insert a long, stiff wire into the axle tube from the outer end. Attach a clean cloth

*Scrape the gasket surfaces on both the housing and the cover. Remove all gasket material.*

to the wire in the center housing and pull the cloth from the center outward. Scrape gasket surfaces of carrier and cover to remove old gasket material.

3 Inspect the axle splines. They should be smooth, uniform, and without signs of excessive wear. On a worn shaft, the spline edges is rounded, chipped, and in some cases, sheared off. Splines might not be straight or might show signs of wear or scuffing.

4 Clean and inspect the axle shaft bearings. Replace as required. While you can replace the used bearing with a new one, many rebuilders choose to reuse the bearing if it is in good condition. Often, an axle is rebuilt because it has high miles, suffered a failure, or been raced or put under demanding use. In those cases, the bearings should be replaced. On the other hand, many owners of drag racers

and street dual-purpose vehicles change to a new axle because they want a different ratio.

5 Check the axle housing and differential bearing caps for sharp edges. Use emory cloth or fine sandpaper to remove sharp edges. Both should be smooth with no raised edges.

6 Use mineral spirits or a degreaser to clean the axle shaft oil seal bores at both ends of the housing tubes. Check for damage or wear. The area should be free of rust or corrosion. This also applies to the brake support plate and housing flange face surfaces.

7 Inspect the differential bearing cones, cups, and rollers for pitting or other damage. Also look for any discoloration or burned/blackened appearance, damage to flat-sided rollers, and scuffed cups,

cones, and rollers. If replacement is necessary, remove the bearing cones from the case using a bearing puller.

**8** Inspect the differential case for an elongated or enlarged pinion shaft hole. If the case has an elongated hole, the pinion is not be fully supported, so the differential needs to be replaced. The machined thrust washer surface areas and counterbores must be smooth. Inspect the case for cracks or other damage.

**9** Inspect the differential pinion shaft for excessive wear in the contact area of the differential pinions. The shaft should be smooth and round with no scoring.

**10** Inspect the differential pinion shaft lock pin for damage or looseness in the case. If the threads in the differential case are damaged, you have to retap the bolt hole. Likewise, if the threads are damaged on the bolt, the bolt should be replaced. It is a special pin, not a hardware store bolt. Therefore, you have to throw away the bolt and get a new one with clean threads.

**11** Inspect the ring gear and pinion for worn or chipped teeth or damaged

*This is a side gear with splines on the inner diameter. Inspect the differential side gears and pinions. They should have smooth teeth with a uniform contact pattern. The tooth edges of the side gears should be square. No chips or nicks should be present.*

attaching bolt threads. In some cases, the profile of the tooth is worn or the top of the tooth is wavy or damaged. You can often see the point where the tooth's surface has been worn away because it's a different color than the rest of the teeth. In extreme cases of damage or wear, the teeth are severely chipped, cracked, or the actual tooth has been broken. You've gone to the trouble of rebuilding the differential, so if there's any doubt about the condition of the ring gear, you should replace it. Always replace as sets.

**12** Inspect the drive pinion bearing cones, cups, and rollers for excessive wear or damage. Replace as sets if required.

**13** Inspect the differential carrier housing for cracks or other damage. Check the machined thrust washer surfaces inside the differential case for scuffing and/or cracks mainly.

**14** Inspect the drive pinion for damaged bearing journals or excessively worn splines.

**15** Inspect the yoke for cracks or worn splines. Replace if required.

**16** Inspect the drive pinion bearing shim pack for broken, damaged, or distorted shims. Replace if necessary during the adjustment of the pinion bearing preload.

**17** Inspect the axle shaft C-clip lock for signs of cracks or wear. Replace if required.

**18** Check each adjuster to determine that it rotates freely. If the adjuster binds, repair damaged threads or replace the adjuster. Adjusters should turn freely.

## Chrysler Carrier-Tube Assembly

Here I focus here on the assembly of the 8¼-inch axle, but tips for the 7¼- and 9¼-inch axles are also included. The 8¼-inch axle was used in popular performance cars in the late 1960s and early 1970s.

**1** Count the teeth on the ring gear and pinion to verify that you have received the correct parts. Divide the number of ring gear teeth by the number of pinion teeth to determine the ratio. For example, if the ring gear teeth count

### Chrysler Carrier-Tube Axle Torque Specifications

| | Chrysler 7¼ (ft-lbs) | Chrysler 8¼ (ft-lbs) | Chrysler 9¼ (ft-lbs) |
|---|---|---|---|
| Differential Bearing Cap Bolts | 45 | 100 | 100 |
| Ring Gear to Differential Case Bolts | 70 | 70 | 70 |
| Drive Pinion Flange Nut | 210 min. | 210 min. | 210 min. |
| Carrier Cover Bolts | 35 | 21 | 21 |
| Brake Support Plate Retaining Nuts | 35 | 35 | 35 |
| Driveshaft Bolts (Rear) | 15 | 15 | 15 |
| Spring Clip (U-bolt) Nuts | 45 max. | 45 max. | 45 max. |
| Wheel Stud Nuts | 85 | 85 | 65 |
| Shock Absorber Stud Nuts (Lower) | 50 | 50 | 50 |

is 43 and the pinion gear teeth count is 11, the ratio is 3.91:1 (43 ÷ 11 = 3.91).

For street use, use ratios in the range of 2.5 to 3.5:1. For dual-purpose applications, use ratios in the range of 3.5 to 4.1:1. For drag racing, use ratios of 4.10:1 and higher (numerically lower). Overdrive transmissions and/or add-on units change these basic numbers. The blueprinting clearances and specifications are listed in an earlier section.

**2** Clean all parts thoroughly and dry-wipe (or air dry) and inspect. Check all new parts for damage.

**3** Lubricate all components with rear axle lubricant.

**4** Re-tap the threads and blow out the holes. The main caps were marked at disassembly; they must be reinstalled in their original locations.

**5** Remember to make the adjustments to pinion depth, pinion bearing preload, backlash, and carrier bearing preload.

### TECH TIP
### Techniques for Setting Pinion Depth

There is more than one way to set the pinion depth. The basic pinion depth is based on the plus/minus numbers that are found on the old pinion and on the new pinion. This approach is fine if you are using a good original axle. However, if you have a brand-new axle housing or one that was broken or severely damaged, you must go through a more detailed measuring process.

You need to go through this more detailed process if you didn't have the plus/minus numbers from one or both of the pinions. (See sidebar "How to Set Pinion Gear Depth" on page 49.) ■

**6** With two-piece differentials, including some limited-slip units, the two halves were marked at disassembly. Reassemble them in the same relationship, so the case halves correctly align. Torque the differential case bolts to 45 ft-lbs. Use a criss-cross torque pattern. Note that while the 1970-and-newer production Sure-Grip assemblies are two-piece units, they are serviced as assemblies. There are no clutches or discs inside the newer units similar to the clutches in the older units. Aftermarket Sure-Grips or lockers may be one- or two-piece units and tend to come fully assembled, ready to install. (See Chapter 7 for more information on Sure-Grips.) Note that 1970 through approximately 1985, these Sure-Grip dif-

*The Chrysler 8¼- and 9¼-inch axles use a two-piece limited-slip differential similar to the newer 8¾-inch axles. (See Chapter 7 for details.) The standard (open) differential is also a one-piece design.*

*Several two-piece differentials include some limited-slip units and most lockers. The two halves should be marked at disassembly. Reassemble them in the same relationship. Torque the differential case bolts to 45 ft-lbs. Aftermarket limited-slips or lockers may be one- or two-piece units and tend to come fully assembled, ready to install. Note the two separate bolt circles; a smaller one inside the basic ring gear bolts. Newer, two-piece Sure-Grip units thread in the differential bolts from the ring gear side. (See Chapter 7 for more information on limited-slip differentials.)*

ferentials were cone-design friction units and were not generally re-buildable.

**7** Install the thrust washers on the differential side gears and position the gears in the counterbores inside the case. See later section on Adjustment. The ring gear flange runout was checked at disassembly using a dial indicator with .003-inch maximum reading. If this step was skipped, perform it before reassembly. (See bottom photo on page 86.)

**8** Position the thrust washers on both differential pinion gears and mesh the pinion gears with the side gears keeping the two pinion gears exactly 180 degrees apart. Rotate the side gears to bring the pinions inside the differential case, one at a time.

*As you begin to put the differential back together, place the thrust washer onto the back side of the side gear.*

**9** Use your fingers to rotate the side gears and washers so that they align with the differential pinion shaft holes in the case. You can insert an axle shaft into the side gear and use it to help rotate the gear. In order to install the pinion shaft through the different case and into the pinion gears, all parts must be properly aligned.

**10** Install the pinion shaft and the lock screw (from the ring gear side) after the axle shafts and C-clips are installed. Insert the pin once the pin hole in the case and cross-shaft are lined up.

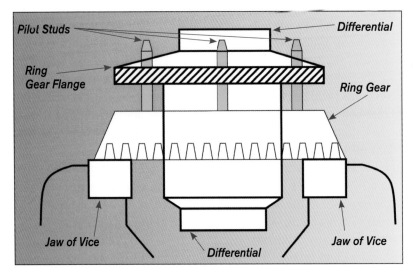

Pilot Studs

Ring Gear Flange

Jaw of Vice

Differential

Ring Gear

Differential

Jaw of Vice

Heat the ring gear with a heat lamp or by placing the gear in hot fluid (water or oil). Do not use a torch. The temperature should not exceed 300 degrees F. Use three pilot studs that are equally spaced to align the gear to the case. In most cases, you can fit the ring without using heat.

**11** Examine the ring gear mounting surface for nicks and burrs. De-burr as required. Use an Arkansas stone or a large, round file to remove the sharp edge on the chamfer on the inside diameter of the ring gear.

**12** Reference the Pinion Depth illustration on page 71. Check the original pinion for its number and check the new matched ring-and-pinion set for their number(s). Record all numbers on your build sheet in a notebook. The key number for reassembly is the one marked on the pinion gear face. It is a zero (0), minus 1 (–1), plus 2 (+2). You combine these numbers with the existing shim numbers to find the proper shim thickness. See chart on page 49.

**13** Place the ring gear over the three pilot studs, which are on the flange of the differential case. This correctly orients the ring gear for installation on the differential housing.

**14** Insert new ring gear screws (left-hand threads) through the case flange and into the ring gear. Tighten each screw to 55 ft-lbs (on the 7¼-inch axle) or 70 ft-lbs (on the 8¼- and 9¼-inch axles) using an alternating tightening pattern. When fitting a new ring gear to a differential case, torque the bolts in a cross-over pattern, using new bolts, in increments of 25 ft-lbs. Use steps of 25, 50, and 70 ft-lbs to reach the final torque specification. This allows the ring gear to sit correctly on the case and prevents cocking the ring gear.

**15** Position each new differential bearing cone on the hub of the differential case (cone taper away from the ring gear) and carefully press on the bearing cones. An arbor press may be used with a bearing installation tool. Use only new bearings, seals, and a new crush sleeve. Many of these parts are provided in a complete rebuild kit. To press on the bearing cones, you use a flat metal block and a hammer.

## Chrysler Carrier-Tube Housing Prep

**1** Use a special tool to install the front and rear pinion bearings. The tool is selected based on bearing size. (See the photo on page 75.)

**2** Place the pinion bearing cups squarely in the bores in the carrier housing, making sure they are not cracked. One is placed in front while the other is installed in the rear.

**3** Use the special bearing installer to press the pinion bearing cups (races) into position. Install one race at a time with a bearing installer and hammer. The front pinion bearing cone, rear bearing cone, and compression sleeve are also installed at this time using the same tool.

**4** The various adapters used with this special tool change with the axle design—7¼-, 8¼-, or 9¼-inch. The size (diameter) of the tool is based on the seal/bearing size (diameter).

## Chrysler Carrier-Tube Depth of Mesh

This section is not required for most axle rebuilds. In most cases you have shim thickness numbers, both on the the new gear set and the old gear set. If this is the case, you can skip to the marking pattern step.

However, if you have no numbers (old gear can't be read), any number is not available, you have a brand-new housing, or you have a broken housing (welded on to repair, etc.), you need to refer to sidebar "How to Set Pinion Gear Depth" on page 49.

The position of the pinion with respect to the ring gear (depth of mesh

*A gauge arbor (the cross-bar in the photo) has three basic pieces, not counting the dial indicator/measuring hardware. The two metal discs are inserted into the differential case's main bearing bores. (They are sized to fit exactly.) Then the main caps are installed. The disc in the right-side main can be seen here. Then the cross-arbor is slid across between the two discs in the sized holes in their centers. From this basic setup, the gauge block and indicators are used to measure from the across-arbor (the rod) down to the pinion head.*

or pinion depth) is determined by the location of the bearing cup shoulders in the carrier housing and by the amount of the pinion that is in back of the rear pinion bearing.

On the 7¼-and 9¼-inch axles, the shim is located between the rear pinion bearing cone and the head of the pinion.

On the 8¼-inch axle, the shim is located between the rear pinion bearing cup and the housing.

## Chrysler Carrier-Tube Pinion Prep and Installation

Here I focus on the 8¼-inch axle. Use a gauge block and cross-arbor to determine the thickness of the rear pinion bearing mounting shim suitable for the carrier can be determined.

1 Wear nitrile gloves to lubricate the front and rear pinion bearings with rear axle lubricant. Thoroughly coat the gears so bearings don't overheat during initial operation. Also rotate the pinion gears several complete revolutions to help set the bearing rollers.

2 The cross-arbor fits into the mains and should be bolted securely in place. On the 9¼-inch axle, insert a piece of .002-inch shim stock between the arbor and each cap. Tighten the main cap bolts to 10 ft-lbs.

3 The selection of the rear pinion bearing mounting shim is based on the thickness of shim that will fit between the crossbore arbor. (Refer to "Techniques for Setting Pinion Depth" on page 89.)

4 The ring gear and pinion are manufactured and lapped in matching sets. These components are sold in matching sets only, so you must make sure to install them as a set. *Do not install one without the other.* In other words, don't use a new pinion with an old ring gear and vice versa.

On the end of the pinion head, you find the adjustment position for the best tooth contact pattern. To obtain the correct pinion setting in relation to the ring gear, you must determine the ideal thickness of the mounting shim before the drive pinion is installed in the carrier. (See sidebar "How to Set Pinion Gear Depth" on page 49.)

5 On 7¼- and 9¼-inch axles, position the shim and then the rear pinion bearing cone onto the pinion. Press the bearing onto the pinion stem. Using a long sleeve to extend over the pinion stem, press the bearing on with an arbor press.

On the 8¼-inch axles, position the selected shim in the axle housing rear pinion bearing cup bore and install the rear bearing cup. Then position the rear pinion bearing cone on the pinion and press the bearing onto the pinion stem.

Each of the three axles requires a different sleeve.

6 Lubricate the front and rear pinion bearing cones with rear axle lubricant.

7 Insert the pinion and bearing assembly through the axle housing. Install a new collapsible spacer over the pinion stem. Position the front pinion bearing cone over the pinion stem. Install the yoke (companion flange).

8 Hold the yoke using a special tool and install the front pinion bearing cone. (See Step 33 on page 85.)

9 Remove the special tool and yoke.

10 Install the drive pinion oil seal. It is properly installed when the seal flange contacts the housing flange face.

11 While supporting the pinion in the carrier, reinstall the yoke using the yoke holding tool. Tap the yoke using a wood or plastic mallet and install the yoke holder. Using a wood or plastic mallet does not mar or damage the yoke.

12 Remove the tools and install the Belleville washer (convex side facing outward) and the pinion nut.

13 Hold the yoke with the holding tool and tighten the pinion nut to remove endplay in the pinion, while rotating the pinion to ensure proper seating of the bearing rollers.

14 Remove the holding tool and rotate the pinion several full revolutions in both directions to allow the rollers in the bearings to seat properly.

## Chrysler Carrier-Tube Pinion Bearing Preload

1 Using the yoke holding tool, torque the pinion nut to 210 ft-lbs. Measure the pinion bearing preload by rotating the pinion using an inch-pound torque wrench. The correct bearing preload specifications are 15 to 30 inch-pounds for a 7¼-inch axle and 20 to 35 inch-pounds for 8¼-and 9¼-inch axles with new bearings.

2 If the correct bearing preload cannot be obtained at 210 ft-lbs, continue tightening the pinion nut in small increments and checking the preload reading until the proper amount of preload has been reached. Torque the pinion nut to 210 ft-lbs first, then rotate the pinion and measure the preload in inch-pounds. Now the torque has settled slightly so re-torque to 210 ft-lbs and re-measure the preload. If it is not at 20 to 35 inch-pounds at that point, re-torque the pinion nut in small increments to a torque reading higher than 210 ft-lbs until you find the correct preload. The key words here are "small increments."

3 Pinion bearing preload should be uniform during the complete revolution. A preload reading that varies during a complete revolution indicates a binding condition, which must be corrected.

4 Do not—under any circumstances—loosen the pinion nut and reduce the preload. If you do, a new pinion bearing collapsible spacer must be installed and the nut re-tightened until the proper preload is obtained.

## Chrysler Carrier-Tube Differential and Ring Gear Installation into Carrier

1 Coat the differential bearing cones, caps, and adjusters with axle lubricant.

2 Install the bearing cones onto the differential case assembly. Use an arbor press and sized spacers/adapters. See photo on page 74, upper right.

3 Carefully install the differential assembly with bearing cups into the housing. Assemble the differential unit taking care that the bearings (especially the side bearings) are sitting correctly in the bearing housing, not off center or sitting at a slight angle.

4 Install the differential bearing main caps on their respective sides, using the marks made at disassembly. Line up the identification marks, added at disassembly, on the cap and the carrier housing pedestals.

5 Install the bearing cap bolts. Tighten the top bolts to 10 ft-lbs. Finger tighten the bottom bolts until the bolt head is seated on the bearing cap.

## Chrysler Carrier-Tube Differential Bearing Preload and Ring Gear Backlash

1 Two precautions must be observed when adjusting differential bearing preload and ring gear backlash. First, the permissible backlash variation is .003 inch. For example, if the backlash is .006 inch at the minimum point, it may be .009 inch at the maximum point. This variation would be a permissible run-out. Therefore it's important to index the gears so that the same teeth are engaged during all backlash measurements.

Second, it is important to maintain specified adjuster torque to obtain accurate differential bearing preload and ring gear backlash settings. Excessive torque introduces high bearing loads and causes premature bearing failures. Inadequate

*Install a dial indicator to the housing and position the indicator point on the drive side of the gear tooth. To find the point of minimum backlash, check the backlash at four positions at approximately 90-degree intervals around the ring gear. Rotate the gear to the position of least backlash. Mark the index so that all backlash readings are taken with the same teeth in mesh.*

*The differential bearing cups do not always move directly with the adjusters; therefore, to ensure accurate adjustment changes and to maintain the gear mesh index, bearings must be seated by oscillating the drive pinion a half-turn in each direction 5 to 10 times each time the adjusters are moved.*

torque does not support the ring gear properly and may lead to free play of the differential assembly and excessive gear noise.

2 Loosen the right adjuster and tighten the left adjuster until the backlash is .003 to .004 inch with each adjuster tightened to 10 ft-lbs. Seat the bearing according to the oscillating tip on page 92.

3 Tighten the bearing cap bolts to 100 ft-lbs (45 ft-lbs on a 7¼-inch axle).

4 Use the long, special tool to tighten the right hex adjuster to 70 ft-lbs (75 ft-lbs on a 9¼-inch axle). Repeat the bearing seating procedure in Step 1.

5 Continue to tighten the right adjuster and seat the bearing rollers until the torque remains constant. Measure the backlash. If the backlash does not measure between .004 and .006 inch (on a 7¼-inch) or .006 inch to .008 inch (on 8¼- and 9¼-inch), increase torque on the

*Use the long special tool shown on page 85 to turn the hex bearing adjuster until the bearing free-play is eliminated with some ring gear backlash (approximately .010 inch) existing between the ring gear and the pinion.*

right adjuster and seat the bearings until you obtain the correct backlash.

6 Tighten the left adjuster to 70 ft-lbs and seat the bearings until the torque remains constant. If all previous steps have been properly performed, initial reading on the left adjuster is approximately 70 ft-lbs. If it is substantially less, the complete procedure must be repeated.

7 Install the adjuster locks on the differential main caps. Be sure that the lock finger is engaged in the adjuster hole (8¼-inch) or that the lock teeth are engaged in the adjuster threads. Tighten the lock screws to 90 in-lbs.

8 Install axle shafts by pushing in one at a time and installing the C-clips (cross-shaft not installed or rotate notched shaft toward axle being installed) inside the differential case. Use a flathead screwdriver to push the C-clip into slot on the end of the axle shaft. Once the C-clip is installed, pull the axle outward to seat the C-clip inside the side gear.

## Differential Side Gear Clearance Checking and Adjustment

1 Select the correct thickness of the side gear thrust washer to get the correct differential side gear clearance. (Auto parts suppliers sell side gear thrust washer packages to fit.) When measuring side gear clearance, treat each gear independently. It is possible for one side to have an acceptable clearance and for the other side to require servicing. Always install side gears in matched sets, if required.

2 With the axle shafts and C-clips in place, measure the clearances behind each side gear by inserting a matched pair of feeler gauges on opposite sides of the hub.

If you have .005-inch clearance or less, be sure the axle shaft on that side is contacting the pinion shaft. Do this with the gauges still in place behind the side gear. If the axle shaft does not contact the pinion shaft, the side gear clearance is acceptable (on that side).

If you have more than .005-inch clearance and the axle shaft does not contact the differential pinion shaft, the side gear clearance is not acceptable.

Remove the thrust washer and measure its thickness with a micrometer. Add or subtract that washer thickness number to the side gear clearance number. The total tells you which replacement washer to install.

For example, if you have .007-inch side gear clearance and the thrust washer thickness is measured at .032 inch, the total thickness is .039 inch. Install the thickest thrust washer from the service package that does not exceed this total thickness. In the example, you would install the .037-inch washer since the next larger size is .042 inch, which would be too large. When reassembled, the side clearance should now be .002 inch.

3 Repeat these steps for the other side.

## Chrysler Carrier-Tube Gear Tooth Contact Pattern

At this stage, you need to set the pinion gear and the ring gear contact pattern. This is a crucial step in the rebuild process and it must be closely followed to achieve the ideal contact pattern. If the ideal contact pattern is not achieved, performance and reliability will suffer. Follow the contact pattern procedure on page 78. After taking all the detailed measurements, you may feel that establishing the contact pattern is not required, but this step is very important.

The gear tooth contact pattern discloses whether the correct rear pinion bearing mounting shim has been installed and the drive gear backlash set properly—the final setup test.

The correct pattern is the key to low noise and long wear, which directly correlates to durability and your satisfaction.

Running the contact pattern determines the axle has been properly set up. Basically you adjust the depth of the pinion and the left to right location of the differential case. The shape and general location of the contact pattern tells you which way to adjust these items.

To obtain the tooth contact pattern, apply a thin film of hydrated ferric oxide, commonly known as yellow oxide of iron, on both the drive and coast side of the ring gear teeth. Using a round bar or large screwdriver (between the carrier housing and the differential case flange), apply a load against the backside of the ring gear and rotate the pinion several 360-degree revolutions in both directions. This procedure leaves a distinct contact pattern on both the drive and the coast side of the ring gear teeth.

Maintain backlash between the ring gear and the pinion within the specified limits until the correct pattern is obtained.

Compare your observed contact pattern to the patterns shown in Chapter 2 on pages 21–25 to determine if all adjustments have been made properly. The correct contact pattern is very well centered on both the drive and coast sides of the teeth. When the tooth contact patterns are obtained by hand, the actual contact area tends to be small. Under actual operating loads, the contact area increases while centered on the smaller area.

## Chrysler Carrier-Tube Axle Shaft Assembly and Installation

1 Inspect the axle shaft seal journal for scratches and polish with 600-grade crocus cloth if necessary.

2 Clean the axle housing flange face thoroughly and install a new gasket followed by the brake support plate assembly on the driver's side of the axle housing.

3 The seal installation tool is made of steel and features a round face; the seal rests on the lip. Place the seal on the end of the axle and squarely align the tool with the seal. Use a mallet to gently drive the seal into place in the axle housing.

4 Lubricate the wheel bearings with multi-purpose grease (if required).

5 Place a new gasket over the studs on the studs of the axle housing.

6 Install new axle shaft seals (on the 7¼). Position new gaskets on the brake

*In the Chrysler rear axle family, Sure-Grip differentials are the most popular name for the special limited-slip differentials. The clutch-type sure-grip has maintained service parts and general availability. The newer cone-type Sure-Grip was only serviced as an assembly because no clutches or discs needed to be replaced. These basic cone-style Sure-Grip differentials are still available. There are also a whole group of new Sure-Grip differentials or lockers. Some function as air lockers and some as electric. There are many different styles and technologies. This is a side-view of a Detroit Locker.*

support plates and carefully slide the axle shafts into the housing and engage the splines in the differential side gear.

7 Install and tighten the retainer plate nuts to 35 ft-lbs (newer models) or install C-clips (older models) on the end of the axle shafts inside the differential.

8 Carefully slide the axle shafts into place and engage the splines in the differential side gear (on 8¼- and 9¼-inch axles).

9 Lightly tap the end of the axle shaft with a non-metallic mallet to position the axle shaft bearing in the housing bearing bore.

10 Install the C-clips in the recessed grooves in the ends of the axle shafts. After C-clip is in place, pull outward on each axle shaft so the C-clip seats in the counterbore of the differential side gear.

11 Install the differential pinion shaft through the case and pinions, aligning the hole in the shaft with the lock screw hole in the case.

12 Install the lock screw and tighten to 100 inch-pounds.

13 Lightly tap the end of the axle shaft with a non-metallic mallet to position axle shaft bearing in the housing bearing bore. Position the retainer plate over the axle housing studs.

14 Install the retainer nuts and tighten to 30 to 35 ft-lbs. Begin with the bottom nut.

15 Install a new gasket (or RTV). To assist in holding the gasket in place, apply a thin coat of gasket sealer to both sides of the gasket. Install the cover assembly into the axle housing. Tighten the carrier to axle housing screws to 25 ft-lbs.

Optional: Install the ratio identification tag on one of the cover attaching screws. The aftermarket services gaskets for the axle covers while the factory often recommends a bead of RTV.

Thoroughly clean the gasket surfaces of the cover and the rear axle housing with a degreaser.

## Chrysler Carrier-Tube Driveshaft

1 Install the driveshaft into the transmission (if removed). Remove the cup seal to keep it from leaking and Insert the forward split yoke into the end of the transmission. Slide it forward as far as possible and lift the driveshaft to fit the U-joint into the saddles of the yoke. Hold in place while you install the straps and thread in two bolts per side. Once bolts have been threaded, tighten screws.

2 Install the rear U-joint of the driveshaft into the saddle of the yoke. Make sure to align the marks on the U-joint and driveshaft. The U-joint slips over the splines and you may have to tap it into place with a plastic or wood mallet. Once seated on the spline, tighten the clamp screws to 15 ft-lbs.

3 Install the brake drums. Once the axle is in place, the brake shoes should still be backed-off so you just align the bolt pattern and slip the drum over the studs. Insert the retaining clips. Re-attach the parking brake cable(s). Adjust the rear brake shoes for proper operation.

4 Install the rear wheels and tighten to 55 ft-lbs.

5 It is very important to fill the unit with oil! Use the lube recommended by the ring-and-pinion or Sure-Grip manufacturer. Use a syringe to fill the axle because typically there is limited room for other oil-fill approaches. The general lube recommendation is 90W for street and 140W for race. (There are also synthetic oils, such as 75-140 synthetic, that may offer wider coverage.) The 8¾ production Sure-Grip units required a special Sure-Grip oil be added to the standard rear axle lube. This special Sure-Grip additive comes in a small can (1 pint or less). It should be added at half full or after 2 pints of standard axle lube.

6 On 7¼-inch axles, remove the fill plug and fill the axle with two pints of rear axle lubricant or until the lubricant is between the bottom of the plug opening and a point 1/2 inch below the plug opening. Replace the plug and tighten.

On 8¼-inch axles, remove the fill plug and fill the axle with 4.4 pints or until the lubricant is between the bottom of the plug opening and a point 1/4 inch below the plug opening. Replace the plug and tighten.

On 9¼-inch axles, remove the fill plug and fill the axle with 4½ pints or until the lubricant is between the bottom of the plug opening and a point 1/2 inch below the plug opening. Replace the plug and tighten.

7 Keep the unit free from dirt and moisture before filling. Otherwise, this can lead to failure because it prevents lubrication from entering critical load areas.

### Break-In Procedure for New Rear Axle Gear Set

On any new ring-and-pinion set with new bearings, especially the higher numerical ratios, excessive heat can build up in the rear end. This over-heating situation can cause durability problems, such as softening, with the gear teeth and bearings. Avoid over-heating by performing the proper break-in procedure. All new axle gear sets require a break-in period.

Be sure that the axle has been filled to the correct fluid level with the proper axle lubricant before driving the vehicle. The oil rating must be GL5 or higher; follow the ring-and-pinion manufacturer's suggestions.

*Street Vehicles*

On basic street vehicles, bring the axle to normal operating temperature by driving it (unloaded) for approximately 10 to 20 miles. Do not run full-throttle (heavy) accelerations or create any shock loads (hard launch). Stop and let the vehicle cool completely (about 30 minutes). Repeat this procedure two or three times.

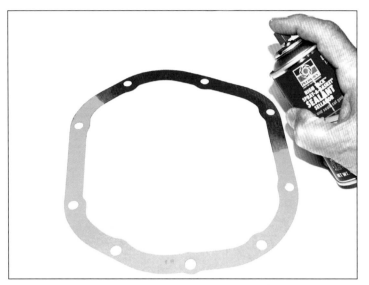

Spraying gasket sealer onto the gasket surfaces (both sides) helps gasket stay in place while you are assembling the cover/ housing until you can get a couple screws started.

*Rear axle covers are used on all carrier-tube axles and can be seen installed on the vehicle if you look at the rear of the axle. The location and visibility mean that it is a good place to customize your vehicle. Covers come in all shapes and styling themes from painted stamped steel (stock), to chrome, to cast aluminum and special cast aluminum with logos.*

As an option, you can also drive gently for 100 to 200 miles with no heavy loads.

### Off-Road and Trail Vehicles

Drive the vehicle (unloaded) off-road or on-trail for approximately 15 minutes. Do not use full-throttle accelerations. Stop and let it cool for about 30 minutes. Repeat this procedure two or three times.

### Circle Track Race Vehicles

Run approximately six to eight laps at slow speed and then let the vehicle cool for 30 minutes. Repeat for six to eight laps, then two or three laps at full speed, and then cool again for 30 minutes.

### Drag Race Vehicles

Perform an initial run-in, such as a one part-throttle run down the drag strip and then let the vehicle cool for about 20 minutes. Drag strip race cars are only driven short distances and heat is not typically a problem with the proper lube and backlash installation.

### Trailer Towing

If trailer towing is intended, an additional break-in of 200 to 300 miles is required without the trailer. This is very important! To properly break in a new gear set, a minimum of 500 miles (general street break-in of 200 miles plus the additional 300 for trailer towing use) of driving is essential before towing. On the first actual trailer tow, drive 15 miles then stop. Repeat two more times (45 miles total) to fully break in the gears.

### Optional Additional Step

It is optional to change oil after first 500 miles (consult your ring gear manufacturer). Remember, there are acceptable noise levels that may vary from manufacturer to manufacturer. Break-in of gears is paramount to gear life. The initial run-in should be at low speeds. This enables gears to run-in without overheating.

## Chrysler Banjo Upgrades

The Chrysler 8¾ banjo rear axle was installed in the vast majority of the Chrysler performance cars in the muscle car era. In the 1980s and early 1990s, there wasn't much new hardware available for rear axles for upgrades past basic ratio options and Sure-Grips and service items. This situation has drastically changed over the past 10 to 20 years.

### Ratios

The one aspect of rear axles that seems to have been a constant is the availability of ratios. They are available into the 5s. The other end of the scale (low numbers such as 2.5 and 3.0) is handled by overdrive ratios or add-ons in the transmission area.

### Bearings

Rear axles wear out pinion, differential, and axle shaft bearings. Since they are commonly replaced, they maintain their availability along with other service items. While they may not always be available individually, they are readily available in service or repair kits. For rear axles, always replace parts as sets.

### 4-Wheel Disc Brakes

Brakes may not be considered a rear axle part, but they bolt directly to the axle housing, and in many cases must be removed to allow the rear axle to be rebuilt. All original 8¾-inch axles used

The is a nodular iron housing for the 8¾-inch banjo axles, and it is often identified by the last 3 digits of their case number. The tapered pinion version is identified as the 489 case, which was introduced in 1969 and produced through 1974. A few years ago, the center section was remanufactured according to the original design, and it still uses the 489 casting number for identification. While the original case was cast iron, this new case is made of stronger nodular iron.

This is a top view of a Detroit Locker shows the 8 bolts the hold it together. These lockers are two-piece designs.

drum brakes. Many of the 8¼-and 9¼-inch axle also used drum brakes. Starting in the mid 1990s, manufacturers began offering disc-brake conversion kits for these axles. This allows owners of many of these older cars to upgrade their braking systems to 4-wheel disc brake systems. Manufacturers now also offer better drum brakes, such as upgrading production 9-inch drums to 10-inch drums.

### Aluminum 8¾-Inch Housing

In the late 1990s, Mopar Performance designed a lighter and stronger 8¾-inch aluminum housing. It does not look like the earlier cast-iron cases. It uses the large-stem, pinion and standard components of the 742-case design. It is made of aluminum that offers a 44-percent weight reduction for the case, from 25 to 14 pounds. Mopar Performance

used a CAD (computer-aided design) program based on an FEA (finite element analysis) to add stiffening ribs in locations that offered the maximum strength increase for the least amount of weight added. The result is that this lighter aluminum case is about 10 percent stiffer than the cast-iron 742 case, which is based on pinion deflection under high load.

A few years ago, Moser started building a fabricated 8¾-inch banjo axle housing. These fabricated housings are made from 1/8-inch thick laser cut mild steel. This is combined with a 3/8-inch thick face place. These axle housings are often used in high horsepower racing application.

# REBUILDING DANA REAR ENDS

Chrysler, Jeep, and AMC products were equipped with various Dana axles. Chrysler and AMC axles were also used on the same cars, trucks, and Jeeps. Many styles of Dana axles were used over the years, including the Dana 30, Dana 35, Dana 44, and Dana 60. This chapter focuses on the Dana 44 and the Dana 60.

The two key ways of telling one axle from another are the number of bolts used to attach the cover or center section, and the shape of the bolt pattern. This shape can also be considered the gasket surface. In Chapter 4 the method for identifying the AMC 20 is detailed, and Chapter 5 covers the various Chrysler axles. Most people find it easier to tell the difference between those groups and the Dana group than it is to tell which Dana you have, especially the Dana 44 versus the Dana 60.

AMC used the AMC 20 axle plus several Dana axles while various Jeep models used the AMC axle and many Dana axles and some Chrysler axles, such as the 8¼-inch. Plus, Chrysler has used five different axle assemblies since 1960 in RWD vehicles: 7¼-, 8¼-, 8¾-, 9¼- and 9¾-inch Dana. If you count the trucks, a couple more differentials were offered, such as the Dana 44. These axles are either banjo or carrier-tube types. Chrysler built the first four axles previously mentioned while Dana built the last two the Dana 44 (8½-inch) and the Dana 60 (9¾-inch). Dodge, Plymouth and Chrysler all used Dana axles so knowing the model of the vehicle does not always tell you the brand of the axle.

All of these axles fall into two basic groups: banjo and carrier-tube. Banjo axles feature a one-piece main housing, shaped like a banjo, with a center section that is removed OTF. Carrier-tube axles have a definite center housing with the axle tubes pressed into this housing and a cover bolted onto the rear of the housing. In carrier-tube axles the ring and pinion are removed OTB. All of the Dana axles being discussed are carrier-tube axles. In summary, the axle is a banjo if the ring-and-pinion assembly is removed OTF

*All Dana axles use 10 bolts to attach the rear cover. The Dana 30 and 35 have unique shape; the Dana 44 and 60 have this non-symmetrical six-sided shape.*

The Chrysler 8¾-inch axle is the only one of this group that is a banjo design. The axle is a carrier-tube if the ring and pinion remove individually OTB.

Another way of looking at this is to determine which side the bolts are on; front side holding the center section in place indicates banjo, while rear side holding the rear cover in place indicates carrier-tube. All the Dana axles discussed in this book are carrier-tube designs.

Most Chrysler vehicles discussed in this book are rear-wheel-drive (RWD) vehicles, which use leaf-spring rear suspensions. This is true of both passenger cars and trucks. However, Jeeps have used both leaf-spring suspensions and coil-spring suspensions. A leaf-spring rear suspension uses a solid rear axle and two leaf springs. With this style of rear suspension the rear axle hardware is pretty straightforward—a left and right spring seat welded to the axle tubes. With coil-spring suspensions, you have more brackets welded to the axle in addition to the two spring seats.

The 9¾-inch Dana 60 used in the 1966–1972 426 Hemi and 440 high-performance cars with 4-speed manual transmissions was one of the most well-known production applications of the Dana axles. There were other heavy-duty applications during this period but the large-displacement muscle cars were the ones that everyone talked about. These production cars would have come with a 3.31 or 3.54:1 ratio up to a 4.10:1.

Sure-Grips were also very popular in these vehicles. The Dana 60 9¾-inch axle used two types of Sure-Grip units. The 1970-and-newer unit is called Trac-Loc (cone design). The 1966–1969 unit is called Power-Lok (disc design). The two Sure-Grip units are interchangeable as assemblies.

The 1966–1970 Belvedere and Coronet (B-Body) Dana 60 axles are narrower than the 1970–1971 Barracuda/Challenger

(E-Body) Dana 60 axles. The 1971–1972 Coronet and Satellite (both B-Body) Dana 60 axles are the same width as the Barracuda/Challenger axles. The 1966–1970 B-Body Dana 60 axles use 23-tooth splines on the axle shaft and side gears, while the newer and wider 1970–1972 E-Body design and the 1971-and-newer B-Body use 35-spline axle shafts and side gears. The Dana 60 is also used in heavy-duty Dodge trucks from 1969 through 2003.

The Dana 60 has a rich racing history. The first high-performance use of the Dana 60 was in 1966, and it quickly became the standard for use with 4-speed manual transmissions in drag racing. The Chrysler 10½-inch clutch, Chrysler A833 4-speed manual transmission, and the Dana 60 rear axle became the standard for drag racing's fastest and quickest cars. In production the Dana 60 was used behind the big, high-horsepower engines, such as the 440 and the 426 Hemi, so it naturally followed them into racing. The 426 Hemi became the leader.

In 1968, Chrysler built the quickest production car—the 1968 426 Hemi Dart/Barracuda. Half of these cars were built with manual transmissions, which meant Dana 60 axles. These Super Stock cars went match-racing, which led to a

new class in 1970 called Pro Stock. The stock-bodied cars were getting quicker and faster and the tires were getting bigger, which created a demand for narrower axles.

The first version was the 52½-inch-wide Dana 60 in 1970–1971. The second version followed some rules changes and was 44½-inches wide and built in 1972–1974. While these specific axles are no longer offered through Mopar Performance, their use created a demand for narrowed axles and shorter, stronger axle shafts in racing and several manufacturers became leaders in making special racing axles and axle hardware such as axle shafts. This market was started based on the Dana 60 but has expanded over the past 20 to 30 years to cover many other axles.

## Identification of Dana Rear Ends

The trick to axle identification is not to confuse the two Dana axles with the AMC and Chrysler units. The banjo axle is a one-piece unit when viewed from the rear. The center section with the ring and pinion is unbolted and removed OTF. The 8¾-inch axle is the only Chrysler banjo axle.

*This is a Jeep rear suspension with a Dana axle. Note the coil springs that sit on top of each axle tube and the track bar that runs from the upper right to the left side in the photo.*

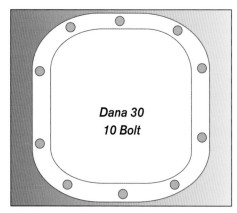

The Dana 30 uses a 10-bolt pattern in the basic shape of a square. It has a 7.20-inch ring gear and was introduced in 1967.

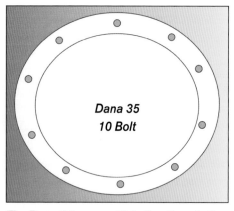

The Dana 35 uses a 10-bolt pattern in the basic shape of an oval so it is wider than it is tall. It has a 7.562-inch ring gear and was introduced in 1984.

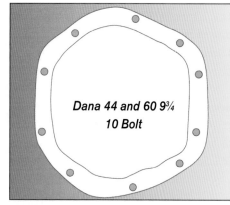

The Dana 44 and the Dana 60 share the similar 10-bolt non-symmetrical six-sided (hexagon) gasket shape. The 60 is about 1.5 inches wider (10.5 to 9 inches) measured on bolt-centers. Both were introduced in the early 1960s.

With the shape being the same, the only way for a novice to tell one from the other is by measuring them across (width). The bolt-center width on the 44 is about 9 inches while the Dana 60 is about 10.5 inches or 1½ inches wider.

## Dana Axle Cover Identification

| Axle | Ring Gear Diameter (inches) | Fastening Bolts (rear) |
|------|------------------------------|-------------------------|
| Dana 30 | 7.20 | 10 (symmetrical left to right) |
| Dana 35 | 7.56 | 10 (round/oval) |
| Dana 44 | 8.50 | 10* |
| Dana 60 | 9.75 | 10* |
| 8-1/4 | 8.25 | 10** |

\* The Dana 44 (8½) also has 10 in the same shape as the Dana 60 (9¾)
\*\* For reference; 10 not enough to separate from Dana models

Counting bolts doesn't help you identify a Dana axle. Instead, you have to rely on the shape and the size (width) of the bolts. Number of bolts and the basic gasket shape defines most Dana axles but measuring the cover width is the only way to distinguish the Dana 44 from the Dana 60.

All the rest of the axles being discussed are carrier-tube designs. The carrier-tube group has six different axles (three Chrysler, two Dana, and one AMC) that are semi-floating, hypoid gear designs. The number of bolts that hold the rear cover on and the shape of the cover gasket can be used to identify the axle.

The Dana 60, 44, 30, and 35 axles use a 10-bolt pattern. The Dana 30 and Dana 35 have unique shapes, while the Dana 44 and Dana 60 share a similar offset, six-sided pattern. For the Dana axles, the shape of the bolt pattern is the most important aspect.

The AMC design is easy to distinguish, with its 12 attaching bolts. The 7¼-inch (9 bolts) and 9¼-inch (12 bolts) Chrysler designs can also be distinguished by counting the bolts. The 8¼-inch carrier-tube axle has a symmetrical (almost round) 10-bolt cover.

Obviously knowing your axle has 10 bolts doesn't narrow down the field much. Knowing the size of the Dana 44 (9½-inch) and the Dana 60 (11-inch) helps, but they are the same shape. Once the basic axle has been identified, specific details, such as model, model number, and build date, can be useful. Some of this information may be stamped on the rear of the right axle tube (manufacturing date and part number) or on the rear of the center carrier housing (lower right side).

The most useful piece of information is the ratio. It is typically found (in the form of an actual teeth count) or a small metal tag under on the attaching bolts (lower left side on Dana axles

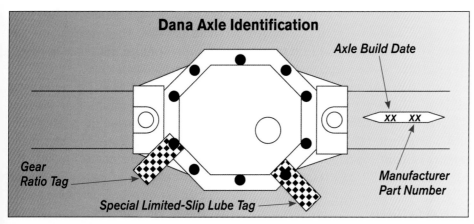

**Dana Axle Identification**

Axle Build Date

XX   XX

Manufacturer Part Number

Gear Ratio Tag

Special Limited-Slip Lube Tag

*Once you know the make and model of your axle, the next piece of information that you need is the axle ratio. Most Chrysler axles have the ratio stamped on a metal tag attached to one of the bolts that hold the cover onto the center section. It is common for the original tags to be lost. The limited-slip information is shown in the same way if that option was included in the original production. While it is helpful information, never trust it. The axle ratio could easily have been changed several times after the vehicle was originally produced.*

looking at rear of housing). If the axle has been worked on, this tag may be gone or it may no longer represent the ratio currently installed. It may be helpful but double-check. Adding the limited-slip info to a separate tag, on lower right side identifies it as a production limited-slip

Another piece of valuable axle information is the axle's bolt circle. Some early Chrysler A-Body cars used 4-inch bolt circle wheels/axle shafts, while most vehicles used the standard 4½-inch bolt

circle. Jeeps also use the 5-on-4½-inch bolt circle, but other bolt circles are also used in Jeeps and Dodge trucks. Some Dodge trucks used a bigger bolt circle, but most light duty trucks also use the 4½ bolt circle. (See Chapter 1 to learn how to measure the bolt circle.)

### Ratios

The best way to determine the axle ratio is to count the teeth on the ring gear and on the pinion. Then divide the

pinion number into the ring number. For example, if there are 41 teeth on the ring gear and 10 teeth on the pinion, the ratio is 4.10:1 (41 ÷ 10 = 4.10).

### Gasket/Cover Shape

All Dana axles use 10 attaching bolts. The Dana 30 and 35 have unique gasket shapes; the 44 and 60 have similar shapes but the 60 is larger by about 1 inch.

### Width

Refer to the track drawing on the top of page 36. With the wheels off, it is much easier to measure the axle's total width, wheel-mounting face to wheel-mounting face. On vehicles with leaf-spring suspension the spring seats are welded to the outer ends of the axle tubes. All Dana axles use 3-inch tubes. There is a small hole in the flat of the spring seat that locates the axle on the leaf spring rear suspension. The distance from the center of one spring seat to the center of the other spring seat is an important width for mounting the axle in the car.

The ends of each axle tube have a flange and a mounting face and bolt pattern that holds the brake hardware. (See Chapter 9 for more details on axle shafts and housings.)

*There can be a lot of information located on the ring and pinion. On the outside of the ring gear, the manufacturer will stamp/etch all kinds of data such as part numbers, gear ratios, dates, etc. It should all be written down in your assembly sheet.*

*You should always count the teeth on your ring and pinion. The Dana 44 and 60 uses 7 to 14 pinion teeth; this one has 11.*

*To determine the actual ratio, you also need to count the teeth on the ring gear. The two Danas use 39 to 53 teeth; this one has 43.*

*The size (width) of the yoke or U-joint should be measured across the saddles of the U-joint—straps and two bolts per side or a small U-bolt with two nuts per side. (See Chapter 9 for more details.) The typical passenger car rear U-joint uses a strap and two bolts per side, except for the early Dana 60 in the mid 1960s Chrysler B-Body 4-speed cars, which used U-bolts and nuts. To determine the difference between U-joints, such as the 7260 and 7290, the easiest method is to measure the width.*

### Yoke/Flange

The rear yoke or flange of the driveshaft attaches to the axle's yoke through a single or double U-joint.

The style of U-joint cap varies between attaching methods (straps and U-bolts). The straps or U-bolts are only used in the rear U-joint. The 1310 and 1330 numbers are from Spicer while the 7260 and 7290 numbers are from Chrysler. The aftermarket offers U-joints that can adapt various driveshafts to various rear axles by having two styles of U-joint in the same part: two vertical caps and two horizontal caps.

### Splines

The yoke is designed to slide over the pinion's splines so the number of splines is an important factor. The two popular ones are 10 (coarse) and 29 (fine), which were used on the pre-1969 Dana 60 (10 spline) and the 1970-and-later Dana 60 (29 spline).

If the axle housing or complete assembly is being swapped or changed, the length of the axle housing in the side view has to be checked. Each axle design's length is different. (See Chapter 1.) If a swap is being performed and there is a difference in side-view lengths, the driveshaft's length must be revised to compensate or a new driveshaft must be fabricated to take this length into account.

### Reverse-Cut Gears

When an axle is installed in the front for a 4WD application, the actual gears are reverse cut. The ratio stays the same and the number of teeth stays the same for each ratio. The aftermarket labels these gears as reverse-cut gears.

### Wheels

The bolt circle drilled into the axle shafts dictates the bolt circle of the wheels. The 5-on-4½-inch bolt circle is the most common. The way the axle sits under the car (widths and wheel well location and size) determines the best wheel offset and tire clearances. (See Chapter 1.)

### Axle Tube Size

Most Chrysler rear axles use 3-inch axle tubes. Racing manufacturers sometimes use larger ones for special requirements.

### Basic Features

The vast majority of RWD Chrysler products built prior to 1994 (the introduction of the Ram pickup truck) used a leaf-spring rear suspension. Leaf springs are also used in Jeep and AMC models. The head of the center bolt of the leaf-spring center-bolt pilots into the center hole in the bottom of the spring seat to locate the rear suspension and, therefore, the axle.

The spring seat is welded to the outer ends of the axle tubes and the spring is held onto the spring seat by two large U-bolts per side. The orientation of the two spring seats on the axle tubes determines the driveshaft angle.

If the driveshaft angle needs to be corrected for any reason after the seats are welded on, angled shims are placed under the spring seat. Any shim found there should be maintained to keep the driveshaft angle at its current number. If you plan on installing new spring seats, try to take the shim angle into account so the shims are not required while the vehicle's driveshaft angle is maintained

The driveshaft angle is basically determined by the relationship between the pinion centerline and the bottom surface of the spring seat. Because the seat is welded to the axle tube, any adjustment to the driveshaft axle is done by adding thin, angled shims (1, 2, or 3 degrees) between the spring and the seat, which adds complications.

On most Chrysler RWD passenger cars that used leaf springs, a pinion snubber is located on top of the axle housing, just above the rear U-joint. The pinion snubber is bolted to the top of the

*The driveshaft angle is basically determined by the by the relationship between the pinion centerline and the bottom surface of the spring seat. Since the seat is welded to the axle tube, any adjustment to the driveshaft axle is done by added thin angled shims (1, 2, or 3 degrees) between the spring and the seat, which adds complications.*

housing with two or three bolts. There's a boss for a fourth bolt but it is not machined. Pinion snubbers are not used on trucks, or might be considered optional. They actually function as part of the rear suspension but do bolt directly to the axle. Pinion snubbers do not have to be removed to rebuild the axle.

Many Dana 44 and 60 axles that were originally built for other non-Chrysler or non-passenger car applications may not have the pads machined for the pinion snubber.

## Other Things to Check

The complete axle assembly does not have to be removed on the typical rebuild. With carrier-tube axles, if time allows, remove the assembly and set it up on an axle fixture. This helps with the build-up process.

### Tapered/Flanged Axle Shaft

All Dana axles use flanged axle shaft ends.

*This is the general appearance of a flanged axle shaft without the studs. There are five threaded holes for the wheel studs, five (larger) lightening holes, and one (closest to the center hole) that is used to access the inner retainer nuts. The wheels and brake assemblies pilot on the lip or flange toward the center of the axle.*

*This is a speed sensor from the newer cars, Jeeps, and mid-1980s-and-newer trucks. The outer edge of the Dana differential is machined and the ring gear for the speed sensor is pressed on. There also could be a speed sensor attached to the rear axle housing, which is used with anti-lock brakes. If the axle is not being removed, it can remain attached. There may also be an electric line or an air line for an electric or air-controlled Sure-Grip/locker assembly. It can remain attached if the axle is not being removed.*

Tapered axle shafts were only used in 1964-and-earlier Chrysler 8¾-inch axles and the AMC 20 axle.

### 4WD

Typical 4WD vehicles do not always use the same axle design in the front and rear locations. It is very common for the front axle in 4WD applications to be a Dana. With a Dana 44 in either front or rear location, the differential, ring, and pinion rebuild in the same way, except for the reverse-cut gears. (See Chapter 8.)

### Brake Lines

The brake lines can stay attached if the axle assembly is not being removed.

*The conventional (open) differential has two side gears (top and bottom inside the differential window), two pinion gears (left and ring inside the window), and the cross-shaft (runs left to right). The case is a one-piece design and everything inside has to come out through this window.*

However, it might be helpful if the parking brake cable is disconnected.

### Differential Case

Does the axle have a limited-slip differential? Is one going to be added? A limited-slip or locker assembly usually comes with its own differential case. In some cases, when switching ratios from a high ratio (numerically low, such as 2.45:1) to a lower ratio (numerically

*Typically, Dana axles used in passenger cars do not have C-clips to retain the axle shafts. But some versions may have C-clips. The aftermarket offers C-clip conversion packages for axles. An axle designed for use with C-clips has a groove cut around the end of the shaft (top).*

*Chrysler 8¼- and 9¼-inch carrier-tube axles do use C-clips to retain the axle shafts, so the rear cover must be removed first, then the C-clips, one off each axle, and then the axle shafts. (See Chapter 5 for details.)*

From 1966 through 1969, Dana passenger car axles used a clutch disc style of Sure-Grip. It used a two-piece differential with the differential bolts coming in from the side opposite the ring gear. In 1969 through 1974, a cone-style unit replaced these Sure-Grip units. The cone-style unit also has a two-piece case, but the bolts come in from the same side as the ring gear and are located inside the bolt circle for the ring gear.

The Dana 44 and 60 gaskets look the same, but the 60 is more than an inch wider. Four bearings are included in the kit. There are two for the differential and two for the pinion; one front, and one rear (largest in diameter).

high, such as 4.10:1), the differential case has to be changed.

### Gaskets

Have new cover gaskets or RTV sealant, bearings, and rebuild kit hardware gathered together *before* starting your rebuild project. Also remember to get fresh rear axle oil (Sure-Grip fluid, if required). Note that the Dana 44 and 60 gaskets look the same, but the 60 is more than 1 inch wider.

### Dana OTB Carrier-Tube

All Dana axles are carrier-tube designs. Several features identify the typical carrier-tube axle. First, the axle has a center housing with two tubes pressed into it. An inspection plate or cover is also bolted to the rear of the center housing. The carrier-tube axle requires the ring-and-pinion to be removed OTB, one at a time, ring and differential assembly first. The Dana 44 has been installed in numerous applications. It comes in both front and rear axle models. The Dana 60 is big and strong and also has many applications.

All these Dana axles remove the ring-and-pinion OTB. Having two tubes pressed into a center housing was the key to the early narrowed axles (called the 52½ and the 44½ axles for the approximate width) that were used in Super Stock and Pro Stock drag racing classes.

All early high-performance drag racing hardware focused on the Dana 60.

The early-style axles (late 1960s and early 1970s) made for racing by Dana and distributed through Chrysler/Mopar Performance/Direct Connection outlets started a market that just kept growing. Aftermarket manufacturers, such as Strange, Mark Williams, and Moser, soon took over the leadership roles. Sanctioning bodies also changed the rear axle rules to allow spools. Spools created a demand for stronger and stiffer axle shafts.

A spool is a solid or locked differential. They are a solid, one-piece unit designed for light weight and equal torque distribution. The spool itself is

The "carrier" of a carrier-tube axle is simply the center housing. Once all the parts are removed, the only things left are the housing and the left and right bearing caps.

generally very strong but puts a large amount of load into the axle shaft so sanctioning bodies for various competitions require XHD axles with their use.

### The Dana 30 and Dana 35 Carrier-Tube Axles

The Dana 30 axle was introduced in the late 1960s; the Dana 35 was introduced in the late 1980s. The 30 has a stem diameter of 1.375 inches and the 35 has a stem diameter of 1.406 inches. Both are commonly used for front axle and rear axle applications. The ring gear diameter on the Dana 30 is 7.20 inches and the ring gear diameter on the Dana 35 is 7.56 inches.

### The Dana 44 Carrier-Tube Axle

The Dana 44 carrier-tube axle design was introduced in the early 1960s. The axle tubes are the standard 3-inch-diameter versions so that the commonly available 3-inch spring seats can be used. It is also used in both front axle and rear axle applications. The Dana 44 has a pinion diameter of 1.375 inches and the ring gear diameter is 8.50 inches.

The Dana 44 has been installed in almost all kinds of Dodge trucks and Jeeps of every size and shape. It was not used in any regular Chrysler passenger

You can easily stick the axle shaft into a bare housing. However, if the assembled differential is bolted between the two main caps, the splines on the axle shaft have to be fitted into the splines in the side gears. This may take a little patience.

cars except, oddly enough, in V-10 Dodge Vipers.

Special differential cases are dictated when ratio changes from 3.73 and 3.92:1 axle ratios.

### The Dana 60 Carrier-Tube Axle

The 9¾-inch Dana 60 axle is the biggest and strongest axle that has been used in passenger cars in production applications. Introduced in the mid 1960s, its first appearance in a production car was in the 1966 Chrysler 426 Hemi B-Body with a manual transmission.

These cars were subjected to enormous loads and put under the highest stress of any Chrysler in the muscle car era. Dana 60 axle has also been used in heavy-duty Dodge trucks since the late 1960s. It is also been used in heavy-duty Jeeps. The Dana 60 has a stem diameter of 1.625 inches and a ring gear diameter of 9.75 inches.

The special differential cases are dictated when ratios change from 4.10 and 4.56:1 axle ratios.

## Dana Carrier-Tube Axle

The following process applies to standard passenger vehicles with a semi-floating rear axle. It does not apply to the full-floating axle design used in extra-heavy-duty trucks.

### Full-Floating Axles

Full-floating axles are only used in heavy-duty applications. Aftermarket companies make kits to convert C-clip axles to non-C-clip axles; conversions are also offered for flanged axles. Whether a limited production option or an aftermarket conversion, this rebuilding process primarily uses standard production hardware. Since these axles are more than 25 years old, many changes may have occurred. ■

## Dana Carrier-Tube Axle Disassembly

There are four main styles of Dana carrier-tube axles: 30, 35, 44, and 60. This rebuild process focuses on the Dana 60. The design of the 44 and 60 is very similar, while the 30 and 35 have some detail differences.

1 Before you start to disassemble the axle assembly, be certain you have all the tools, replacement parts, gaskets, cleaners, and sealers required to complete the job.

2 Place jack stands under the frame rails next to the wheels so both rear wheels off the ground. It is not necessary to remove the complete axle assembly to rebuild/recondition the differential or change the axle ratio.

3 Disconnect the parking brake. With parking brake cables, it is generally best to release the forward cable adjustment before working on the parking brake at the rear.

4 Remove the lug nuts that retain both rear wheels and then remove the wheels. Store the wheels in area away from the car, so you have plenty of room to work on the rear axle.

5 If used, remove the retaining clips on axle studs and then the brake drum assemblies, which allows access to the flanged axle shaft ends. Note that axle shaft endplay should be .005 to .012 inch. With drum brake removal, loosen the brake shoe adjustment first. With the wheel removed, remove the small retaining clip on several of the wheel studs, if they are used or still installed. Then slip the brake drum off over the wheel studs and set aside.

6 Clean all dirt from the area around the housing cover.

7 Rotate the axle shaft flange to allow access to the brake retainer plate nuts. Use a ratchet and socket to remove the nuts and then discard the nuts. Remove the backing plates. On the right axle shaft, the endplay adjuster lock is under one of the studs. Locate and remove it and the threaded adjuster.

### Disc Brakes

Disc brakes were commonly installed in the front and rarely used in production on the rear. Therefore, in this axle build procedure includes a drum brake setup. While the disc brake rotors remove somewhat similarly, you must remove the disc brake caliper first. Today, there are many manufacturers that build disc brake conversion kits for these vehicles originally fitted with drum brake. ■

8 Remove the axle shaft using a slide-hammer puller. Place the base of the puller over 3 axle shaft studs and install wheel nuts, center on axle shaft and tighten. Slide the heavy hammer slide away from the axle shaft and up to the bump-stop, which stops the slide and applies force toward pulling the axle out of the housing. Repeat using more force/speed on the slide as required. Once shaft is free, remove puller and carefully slide shaft the rest of the way out of the housing.

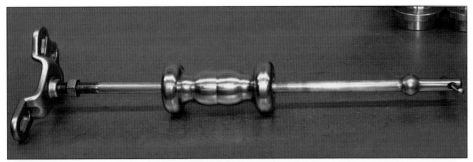

*A slide hammer is used to remove flanged axle shafts. The bracket on left end attaches to the axle shaft's flange by three wheel studs using wheel nuts. The long bar fits into the center. The right end of the shaft has a bulge so that the slide cannot pass. Once attached, the slide is moved from the left side to the right side and stops at the bump, which applies force to the axle shaft, pulling it out. Several strikes are often required.*

9 Mark the driveshaft at the U-joint and pinion flange with a scribe or Sharpie. Mark the flat area on the yoke below the U-joint cup and then on the tube.

10 By hand or using a block of wood, push the prop-shaft forward and support it in near-horizontal position, disconnect it, and move it out of your way. Use a small box-end wrench to remove the four screws. In some cases, two small U-bolts hold on the U-joint, so the four nuts must be removed with com-

*Once the driveshaft has been disconnected, find a place to safely store it so it's handy when you reinstall the axle. If you slide the driveshaft out of the end of the transmission, the transmission case is open and will leak onto the garage floor. Insert a plastic cap into the end of the transmission to solve this problem. Caps are available for most transmissions.*

mon tools. Then you may need a large flat-blade screwdriver to insert between the nose of the pinion and the U-joint to provide leverage to push the driveshaft forward. Caution: You need to hold rear of the driveshaft up as soon as it is loose from the yoke. If you remove the driveshaft from the transmission, the transmission may leak. Insert a plastic plug in the tail section of the transmission, so transmission fluid does not leak all over the floor.

11 Tape the U-joint to hold the caps together so they are kept together for correct reassembly.

12 Now it's time to prepare to drain the differential fluid out of the rear axle assembly. To effectively drain the axle assembly, you must remove the axle cover. Start by placing an oil drain pan below the axle cover.

13 The oil fill plug is only used to fill and is too high to function as a drain. It is required to be open at assembly to allow oil to be added. If there is no actual drain plug, follow the procedure below.

14 Use a wrench or socket and ratchet to remove the housing cover bolts

but leave one bolt in the housing but loose. Pry the cover loose at the bottom.

15 Let the oil flow out of the differential from the bottom of the cover and housing.

16 Remove and clean the rear cover. Remove gasket material with a scraper. Use a cover gasket at reassembly.

17 Inside the axle housing, you see the differential, axle ends, side gears, pinion gears, and other hardware. At this stage, you should verify whether you have an open versus limited-slip differential. The Sure-Grip test (see Chapter 7, page

*Once the rear cover has been removed, you can check the differential to see if it is an open or limited-slip style. This is an open differential; there are no C-clips. The main cap is loose in preparation for removing the ring gear and differential assembly.*

*The C-clip fits over the notch in the end of the axle shaft and holds the axles in place. They must be removed before the axle shaft can be removed on C-clip designs. Most Dana axles do not use C-clips.*

*The axles shaft ends have a cut groove and use a flathead screwdriver to slip the C-clip into the groove and over the axle. There is also a relief cut in the side gears into which the C-clip fits so it doesn't fall out once installed.*

131) should have been done earlier. Now look inside the differential.

**18** On C-clip axles only: Turn the differential and check the C-clips on the axle shaft ends; there is one clip on each axle shaft. If the axle has C-clips, they must be removed to allow the axles to be removed.

*The arrow points to the C-clip. It sits in a recess in the side gear, over a 360-degree slot on the end of the axle shaft. (C-clips are only used on some Dana axles.)*

On C-clip axles only follow these steps:

A. Rotate the differential by hand so you gain access to the pinion shaft lock pin. Once accessible, remove the lock pin. Often, you must use a hammer and brass drift to drive it out of the differential. The pin lock should be replaced with a new one.

B. Drive out the differential pinion shaft using a hammer and a brass drift.

The cross-pin may need to be driven out as well, so use a brass drift if required.

C. Push the axle shaft inward by hand so it moves toward the center of the vehicle.

D. Remove the C-clips/locks inside the differential housing, from the recessed groove in the end of each axle shaft. Do one side at a time.

**19** Remove the axle shafts and be careful not to damage the axle shaft seal and bearing. Remove a normal axle shaft using an axle puller.

**20** On C-clip axles only, reinstall the pinion shaft and lock screw but do not fully tighten.

*This one-piece case has been rotated 90 degrees so the windows are to the sides. The cross-shaft is the large round hole (end of the shaft actually) in the center, just above the ring gear. The lock-pin hole is vertical and located in the recess just above the end of the cross-shaft. This hole extends through to the other side.*

**21** Inspect the axle shafts, especially in the bearing and seal areas for any cracks, scuffing, or other damage.

*Bearing pullers/installers come in all sizes because of the many sizes of bearings involved in an axle. The puller/installer is selected based on the size of the bearing and it location (length of handle). However, a brass drift or punch and a hammer may be used in a pinch. The bearing race (on the left) is what selects the installer/remover (on the right).*

**22** Remove the axle shaft seal from the housing bore. The fingers of the seal puller fit inside the seal itself and then the slide hammer pulls the seal out. Smaller seal pullers may use a separate hammer and have only one finger and a fixed two-finger.

**23** Runout checks taken during disassembly are optional but are essential at reassembly.

**24** Optional: To measure the differential side play, place a flat-blade screwdriver or small pry bar between the left side of the axle housing and the differential case flange. Next, use a prying motion to determine if there is side play. No side play should be present. If side play is found, use a threaded adjuster

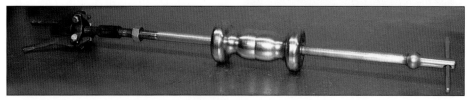

*The fingers of the seal puller fit inside the seal itself and then the slide hammer pulls the seal out. Smaller seal pullers may use a separate hammer and have only one finger and a fixed two-finger.*

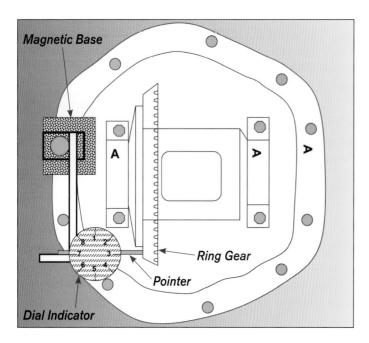

Magnetic Base

A

A A

Ring Gear

Pointer

Dial Indicator

To measure the differential side play, place a flat-blade screwdriver or small pry bar between the left side of the axle housing and the differential case flange. Next, use a prying motion to determine if there is side play. No side play should be present. If side play is found, use a threaded adjuster and special tool to remove the side play. Note: The setup to measure side play is the same as the setup for measuring flange runout.

Measure ring gear runout on the differential case: Mount a dial indicator onto the flat surface of the carrier housing left side. Place the stem of the indicator slightly when the plunger is at right angles to the back of the ring gear. The measurement: to measure ring gear runout, turn the ring gear several full revolutions and read the dial indicator. Mark the ring gear and differential case at the point of maximum runout. This marking will be very important later in checking the differential case runout. Total indicator reading should be no more than .006 inch. If runout exceeds .006 inch, the differential case may be damaged.

and special tool to remove the side play. Note: The setup to measure side play is the same as the setup for measuring flange runout.

If side play is present, use a threaded adjuster and a long, special tool to reach in through the axle tube to remove the side play.

## 25
At this stage in the rebuild process, you don't have to measure ring gear runout, but many rebuilders do so they have a benchmark measurement for runout. That way, you know what runout should be when you take final measurements. In addition, measuring runout can help you identify serious problems. Mount a dial indicator onto the flat surface of the carrier housing left side. Place the stem of the indicator slightly when the plunger is at right angles to the back of the ring gear.

## 26
To measure ring gear runout, turn the ring gear several full revolutions and read the dial indicator. Mark the ring gear and differential case at the point of maximum runout. This marking will be very important later in checking the differential case runout. Total indicator reading should be no more than .006 inch. If runout exceeds .006 inch, the differential case may be damaged.

One of the unique features of Dana axles is that the factory has labeled the main caps, so you can't get them switched or installed reversed: a vertical F and a horizontal F. There is a matching letter for alignment on each main cap.

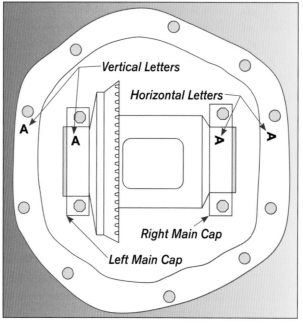

Vertical Letters

Horizontal Letters

A

A

A A

Right Main Cap

Left Main Cap

Use a punch to mark the carrier housing and the main caps for re-installation. Place one mark on the left and two marks on the right. Note the stamped letters used for identification on the bearing caps and the face of the carrier housing gasket surface. Letters stamped on the left side are horizontal while on the right side the letters are vertical. Match them up at reassembly. If there is no factory identification on the caps, you must stamp-in your own. (The letter A is just an example here.)

**27** Insert a .003-inch feeler gauge between the differential bearing cap and the bearing cup to check the clearance. It should not fit. If the clearance is more than .003 inch, the bearing cup may have turned in the carrier, causing excessive wear.

**28** Mark each half of the differential case, if it is a two-piece (a Sure-Grip), for reinstallation. This is especially important if you plan to disassemble the two-piece differential. You need to be sure that the case properly aligns. A good place to make the alignment marks is on the flat surface near the parting line.

**29** Use a socket and ratchet to loosen the four main cap bolts, but do not remove the bearing caps.

**30** Remove the dial indicator. Use a heavy-duty screwdriver and a pry bar (or two pry bars) to remove the differential and ring gear assembly. Use caution.

*Remove the dial indicator. Use a heavy-duty screwdriver and a pry bar (or two pry bars) to remove the differential and ring gear assembly. Use caution. Pry against the outer housing.*

**31** Attach a spreader tool to the carrier housing. Place the spreader tool's dowel pins into the locating holes on the left and right sides of the axle central housing. Install a dial indicator on the left side of the axle housing. Tighten the spreader tool nut to obtain .015-inch movement. Do not go over .020 inch. Generally the spreader is not required on the Dana axle. Two pry bars can be used to remove the differential assembly.

**32** Use a socket and ratchet to remove the four cap bolts while holding the assembly in place. Carefully remove the two main bearing caps. The bearing caps must be kept with their respective bearing cones.

*There are two different techniques for removing the pinion nut and its washer. If you use an air impact gun on the pinion nut, the yoke holder can be a large pair of channel locks. If you are using a socket and manual ratchet/breaker bar, you need to hold it more securely, which requires a yoke holder similar to the one shown on page 25 in Chapter 2. Two bolts are used to attach the yoke holder on the yoke saddles, which are diagonally opposite each other. The trick with various yoke holders is that the torque wrench, breaker bar, or air impact gun has to pass through the center of the tool to apply torque to the pinion nut.*

**33** Use a yoke holder to hold the assembly and remove the drive pinion nut and washer. If you use an air impact gun on the pinion nut, the yoke holder can be a large pair of channel locks but if you are using a socket and manual ratchet/breaker bar, you need to securely hold it, which requires a yoke holder similar to the one shown in Chapter 2 on page 25. The torque wrench, breaker bar, or air impact gun has to pass through the center of the tool to apply torque to the pinion nut.

*The yoke remover has a smaller puller with two fingers and a center adjusting screw. The fingers generally go over the outside of the yoke saddles and the center adjuster pushes on the pinion stem. Once set up, a small socket and ratchet is all that is required to removed the yoke.*

**34** Remove the drive pinion flange (yoke) using a flange puller tool and a holding tool.

**35** Remove the drive pinion oil seal and slinger, gasket, front pinion cone, and preload shim. Record shim thickness.

*To remove the pinion, use a non-metalic, plastic, rubber, or rawhide hammer to push/tap/drive the pinion stem rearward and out of the bearing in the housing. Cushion the assembly fall into the housing with towels or your hand, if the rear cover isn't re-installed.*

**36** Remove the front and rear bearing cups from the housing using a bearing puller. Note that bearing pullers come in all sizes to fit bearings of a particular size. The puller is selected based on the size of the bearing and its location (length of handle). However, a brass drift or punch and a hammer may be used if a puller is unavailable. Use a hydraulic press to remove the press-off pinion bearing from the pinion stem. The shims are located between the bearing and the head of the pinion.

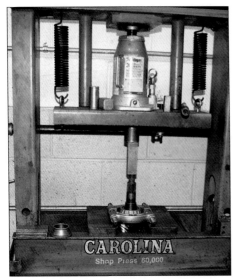

*Bearing pullers come in all sizes because of the many sizes of bearings in an axle. The puller is selected based on the size of the bearing and its location (length of handle). However, a brass drift or punch and a hammer may be used in a pinch. The bearing race (on the left) is what selects the installer/remover (on the right).*

**37** Use a caliper micrometer to measure and record shim thickness on either side of the bearings. Replace the pinion bearings in both locations. There may only be one shim location per bearing. You can hang the shims in order on a wire or spare coat hanger or place a tie-rap around each pack and place in a zip-lock bag.

**38** Mark all shim thicknesses and locations. Thread a piece of wire through the shims in a particular order, so that you keep all the shims together and in the correct order.

**39** Use a socket and ratchet to remove the ring gear screws that secure the ring gear to the differential housing only if the ring gear is being replaced. Replace the ring gear only if it's worn or damaged. If it is not being replaced, then it stays on and gets inspected and should pass checks.

**40** Remove and discard the ring gear screws. Note that they are right-hand threads.

*If the ring gear is being replaced, use a non-metallic hammer and brass drift to tap the ring gear loose. Cushion the ring gears fall from the case flange to the workbench with shop towels.*

**41** If the ring gear runout was more than .006 inch, remeasure the differential case flange runout. Install the differential case and respective bearing cups in the housing.

**42** Loosen the spreader tool and remove (if used).

**43** Use a socket and ratchet or wrench to install the bearing caps and bolts and lightly tighten the bearing cap bolts.

**44** Attach a dial indicator to the carrier housing so that the pointer is perpendicular to the ring gear surface of the differential case flange (between the outer edge and the ring gear attaching bolts holes).

**45** Rotate the differential case several complete revolutions while noting the total indicator reading. The indicator reading must not exceed .003-inch runout. The differential case must be replaced if the runout is over .003 inch.

**46** Loosen and remove the bearing cap bolts and remove the differential case assembly from the housing.

*Remove the lock screw and the pinion shaft from the differential housing. Note: A lock-pin may be used on some models. Use a thin, long punch and a hammer to tap out the lock-pin. The lock-pin hole (on the left side) is above the ring gear.*

**47** Rotate the differential housing side gears until the pinions appear at the case window opening. The cross-shaft runs left to right in the center of the differential case. It must be removed first. Then the pinion gears can be removed (one at a time) from the left and right window. Once the pinions are out, the side gears can be removed from the top and bottom.

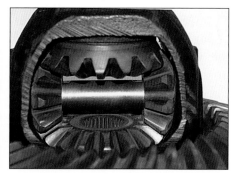

*Here's how the differential housing side gears appear in the case window opening.*

**48** Remove the pinion gears. Once the cross-shaft has been removed, rotate the side gear to move the pinions into position. If required, insert an axle shaft into the side gear and use it to turn the gear itself. You only need to turn one side gear to get the pinion gears to move into position.

**49** Remove the differential side gears and thrust washers. Once the pinion gears have been removed, you can pick up these gears and thrust washers by hand.

*Use a special differential bearing removal tool to remove the differential assembly and the ring gear. There are several pieces to the tool. This view shows it fully assembled into the differential bearing and ready to remove it. Two pieces fit around the differential bearing and the end of the case. The tall, threaded adjuster fits on top of the case end. Once the two halves have been fitted around the bearing, the outer sleeve is dropped over and the bearing removal can begin. An air impact gun or large socket/ratchet is applied to the top of the threaded adjuster to actually remove the bearing. (See Chapter 2 for partial assembly of this multi-piece tool.)*

**50** Remove differential bearings cones from the differential case using a bearing puller.

**51** Remove the shims and record the thickness.

**52** Thoroughly clean and inspect all parts. Dirt is the enemy of any moving part. Cleaning allows you to see cracks, especially small cracks in your hardware. It also allows you to observe the surface for scuffing and any discoloration.

## Dana Carrier-Tube Cleaning and Inspection

With the differential completely disassembled, it is time to check all the parts and see what you have. Obviously, wearable parts, such as bearings, that are replaced do not need to be checked.

**1** Clean all parts with mineral spirits or a dry cleaning solvent (except for bearing cones). And dry with compressed air. Clean bearing cones with a clean soft cloth.

**2** To clean the axle housing tubes, insert a long, stiff wire into the axle tube from the outer end. Attach a clean, lint-free cloth to the wire in the center housing and pull the cloth from the center outward.

**3** Clean and inspect the axle shaft bearings. On a high-mileage axle, bearing are just replaced. Inspect the bearing races for cracks or deformations and then inspect the roller pins for any flat spots. If any significant wear or damage is found, replace them.

**4** Check the axle housing and differential bearing caps for sharp edges. Both should be smooth with no raised edges. If any sharp edges are found, use a deburring tool to remove the sharp edges.

**5** Clean and inspect the axle shaft oil seal bores at both ends of the housing tubes for damage or wear. They should be free of rust or corrosion. This applies to the brake support plate and housing flange face surfaces.

*Inspect the differential bearing cones (shown), cups, and rollers for pitting or other damage. If replacement is necessary, remove the cones from the case using a bearing puller. Replace cup and cone as a set only.*

*The axle shaft splines are parallel and should be smooth and straight, without any sign of excessive wear. To remove flaws and rough spots, polish the area with 600-grade crocus cloth.*

6 Inspect the differential case for an elongated or enlarged pinion shaft hole. Inspect the case for cracks or other damage.

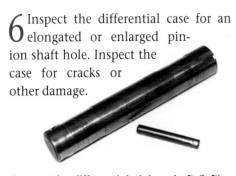

*Inspect the differential pinion shaft (left) for excessive wear in the contact area of the differential pinions (right). The shaft should be smooth and round with no scoring. This shaft shows wear and scuffing and should be replaced.*

*Inspect the differential side gears and pinions. They should have smooth teeth with a uniform contact pattern. This is a pinion gear with its cone-shaped thrust washer. (See Chapter 7 for details on limited-slip differentials.)*

*On the left is a side gear with splines on the inner diameter. On the right is the backside where the flat thrust washer sits.*

7 Inspect the ring gear and pinion for worn or chipped teeth or damaged attaching bolt threads. The ring gear's teeth should have an even profile and the top should be square. No signs of excessive wear should be evident from heel to toe. In extreme cases of ring failure, the teeth on the ring gear are sheared off, but in other cases of less extreme wear, the top of the teeth are deformed. Always replace as sets. Be sure the mounting face of the ring gear is flat. Slide a large, flat file over the rear mounting face to remove nicks and sharp edges.

8 Inspect the drive pinion bearing cones, cups, and rollers. Examine parts for cracks, chips, marring, and other readily apparent signs of excessive wear or damage. Replace as sets if required.

9 Inspect the differential carrier housing for cracks or other damage. Check the machined thrust washer surfaces inside the differential case.

10 Inspect the yoke for cracks or worn splines. The splines should have a square profile and should not show significant wear on any particular edge. Replace if required.

11 Inspect the drive pinion bearing shim pack for broken or damaged shims. If necessary, replace during the adjustment of the pinion bearing preload.

*Scrape the gasket surfaces on the housing and the cover. Remove all gasket material.*

12 Inspect the axle shaft C-clip lock (if used) for signs of cracks or wear. Replace if required.

13 Scrape the carrier gasket surface and the cover to remove gasket material and sealer.

## Dana Carrier-Tube Assembly

In the following process, I focus on the Dana 60, or 9¾-inch, axle, but the Dana 44 is similar to the 60 so the assembly process is similar, but many of the torque specs for the Dana 44 are different.

1 Using an inch-pound torque wrench, measure the pinion bearing preload by rotating the pinion flange slowly with a torque wrench and record the maximum torque reading.

2 Always verify that you have received the correct parts by counting the teeth on the ring gear and pinion. The ratio can be checked by dividing the number of ring gear teeth by the number of pinion teeth. For example, if the ring gear teeth count is 43 and the pinion gear teeth count is 11, the ratio is 3.91:1 (43 ÷ 11 = 3.91).

Use ratios in the range of 2.5 to 3.5:1 for street use, use ratios in the range of 3.5 to 4.1:1 for dual-purpose applications, and use ratios of 4.10:1 and higher (numerically lower) for drag racing. Overdrive transmissions and/or add-on units change these basic numbers.

3 Use mineral spirits to clean all parts thoroughly. Then blow dry and inspect. Check all new parts for damage or manufacturing imperfections.

4 Use rear axle grease to lubricate all components. Wear Nitrile gloves and pack the wheel bearings with grease.

5 Remember that the factory marked the main caps at disassembly with line-up letters on the cap and the case. Main caps must be reinstalled in their original locations.

**6** The adjustments to be made are to pinion depth, pinion bearing pre-load, backlash, and carrier bearing preload.

**7** While most of these differentials are one-piece units, on two-piece differentials (limited-slips), which included some open units, the two halves were marked at disassembly. Reassemble them in the same relationship. Torque the differential case bolts to 45 ft-lbs. Note that while the 1970-and-newer production limited-slip assemblies are two-piece units, they are serviced as assemblies. There are no clutches or discs inside the newer units similar to the clutches in the older units. Aftermarket limited-slips or lockers may be one- or two-piece units and tend to come fully assembled, ready to install. (See Chapter 7 for more information on limited-slip-differentials.)

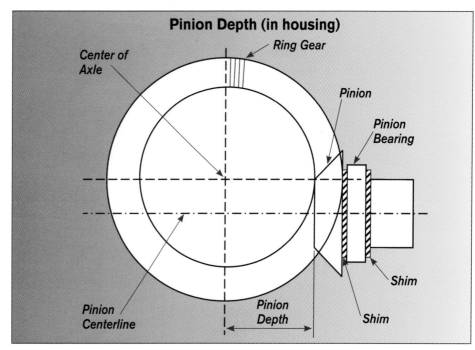

*There is more than one way to set the pinion depth, which is based on the plus/minus numbers that are found on old and new pinions. This approach is fine if you are using a good, original axle. However, if you have a brand-new axle housing or one that was broken or severely damaged, you must go through a more detailed measuring process. That process must also be used if one or both of the pinions don't have the plus/minus numbers. I will leave the more detailed process steps in for reference and added insurance.*

## Dana Differential

Dana 44 and 60 axles use a one-piece, limited-slip differential similar to the Chrysler axles. (See Chapter 7.) The standard differential (called an open differential) is also a one-piece design.

There are several two-piece differentials, which include some limited-slip units and most lockers; the two halves should be marked at disassembly. Reassemble them in the same relationship, so the alignment marks match up. Torque the differential case bolts to 45 ft-lbs (always check manufacturer guidelines). Aftermarket limited-slips or lockers may be one- or two-piece units and tend to come fully assembled, ready to install.

| Axle Torque Specifications: Dana Carrier-Tube | | | |
|---|---|---|---|
| **Axle** | **Dana 30** | **Dana 35** | **Dana 44** |
| Differential Bearing Cap Bolts | 45 ft-lbs | 57 ft-lbs | 80 ft-lbs |
| Ring Gear to Differential Case Bolts | 70–90 ft-lbs | 55 ft-lbs | 55 ft-lbs |
| Drive Pinion flange Nut | 175 ft-lbs | | |
| Carrier Cover Bolts | 30 ft-lbs | 35 ft-lbs | 35 ft-lbs |
| Brake Support Plate Retaining Nuts | 32 ft-lbs | 32 ft-lbs | |
| Driveshaft Bolts (Rear) | | | |
| Spring Clip (U-bolt) Nuts | | 90 ft-lbs | 90 ft-lbs |
| Wheel Stud Nuts | | 75 ft-lbs | 80 ft-lbs |
| Shock Absorber Stud Nuts (Lower) | | 44 ft-lbs | 45 ft-lbs |
| **Axle** | | **Dana 60** | |
| Differential Bearing Cap Bolts | | 70–90 ft-lbs | |
| Ring Gear to Differential Case Bolts | | 100–120 ft-lbs | |
| Differential Case Half Retaining Bolts | | 35–45 ft-lbs | |
| Drive Pinion flange Nut | | 250–270 ft-lbs | |
| Carrier Cover Bolts | | 15–25 ft-lbs | |
| Axle Shaft Retainer Nuts | | 30–35 ft-lbs | |
| Driveshaft Bolts (Rear) | | 15 ft-lbs | |
| Spring Clip (U-bolt) Nuts | | 45 ft-lbs | |
| Wheel Stud Nuts | | 65 ft-lbs | |
| Shock Absorber Stud Nuts (Lower) | | 50 ft-lbs | |

*This chart contains the torque specifications for the major components of the Dana 30, 35, 44, and 60 series axle assemblies.*

(See Chapter 7 for more information on limited-slips). The majority of production Dana differentials are one-piece units in both open and limited-slip configurations.

The following process focuses on the open differential. (See Chapter 7 for information on limited-slips.) Set out all the parts next to the case. This includes pinions, side gears, cross-shaft, washers, and differential bearings.

*The early style, limited-slip differential used in the passenger car Dana axles was a two-piece design. It was replaced by the cone-clutch unit. However, the regular Dana used a one-piece limited-slip unit (clutch-disc style). There are two styles of discs and both with two tabs.*

## Dana Carrier-Tube Differential Assembly

1 Install the thrust washers on the differential side gears and position the gears in the counterbores inside the differential case.

2 Position the thrust washers on both differential pinion gears and mesh the pinion gears with the side gears, keeping the two pinion gears exactly 180 degrees apart. Note: To mesh the pinion gears, rotate the side gears inside the differential.

*A typical cross-shaft and its lock pin looks like this. Most Dana lock pins are pressed in. Some of the newer ones have a small screw in the pin that is removed by using a small wrench.*

*A hammer and brass punch/drift can be used to tap out the cross-shaft in the differential. Be sure to remove the locking pin first.*

3 Rotate the side gear and washer assembly so that the pinion gears align with the differential pinion shaft holes in the case. The pinion and washer is meshed with the two side gears already in the case. The side gear must be rotated to take the pinion out of the window and to the opposite side. Then the second pinion can be meshed with the side gears. The side gear is rotated to move both pinion to line-up with the cross-shaft holes.

If the side gears do not rotate easily, try inserting the end of an axle shaft into the side gear and rotate the gear using the shaft. Use the slot in the bottom of the cross-shaft and a large flat-blade screwdriver to fine-tune. As the cross-shaft gets close to position, use a pin to help alignment.

You need to install the pinion shaft and the lock screw (from the ring gear

*See later section on Checking and Adjustment. You should have checked the ring gear flange runout with a dial indicator at disassembly. The reading should be .003 inch or less. If this step was skipped, it needs to be done before reassembly.*

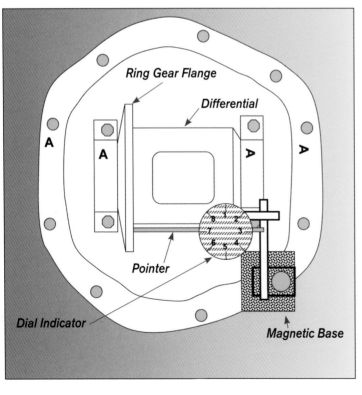

Ring Gear Flange / Differential / A A A A / Pointer / Dial Indicator / Magnetic Base

side) after the axle shafts and C-clips are installed (if used).

4 Examine the ring gear mounting surface for nicks and burrs. De-burr as required. Remove the sharp edge on the chamfer on the inside diameter of the (new) ring gear by using an Arkansas stone or a large, round file.

*Install the ring gear on the differential case pilot, aligning the threaded attaching holes in the ring gear with the machined holes in the differential case flange. Using new ring gear screws (right-hand threads) insert screws through the case flange and into the ring gear. Tighten each screw to 100–120 ft-lbs (on the 9¾-inch axle) using an alternating tightening pattern. Tip: When fitting a new ring gear to a diff. case, torque down bolts in a cross-over pattern, using new bolts, torquing in increments of 25 ft-lbs (try steps of 25, 50, 75, and 100 ft-lbs as required) at a time to the final torque setting. This will allow the ring gear to sit correctly on the case and will prevent cocking the ring gear.*

5 Install the ring gear on the differential case pilot, aligning the threaded attaching holes in the ring gear with the machined holes in the differential case flange.

6 Insert the new ring gear screws (right-hand threads) through the case flange and into the ring gear.

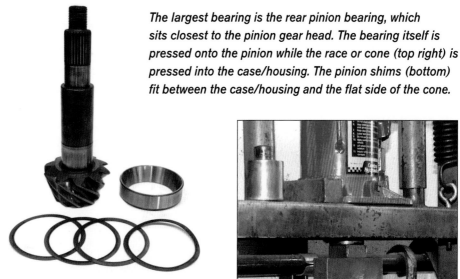

*The largest bearing is the rear pinion bearing, which sits closest to the pinion gear head. The bearing itself is pressed onto the pinion while the race or cone (top right) is pressed into the case/housing. The pinion shims (bottom) fit between the case/housing and the flat side of the cone.*

7 Tighten each screw on the 9¾-inch axle to 100 to 120 ft-lbs using an alternating tightening pattern.

8 When fitting a new ring gear to a differential case, torque down the bolts in a criscross pattern, using new bolts, torquing in increments of 25 ft-lbs at a time to the final torque setting. This allows the ring gear to sit correctly on the case and prevents cocking the ring gear.

9 Position each new differential bearing cone on the hub of the differential case. (The cone taper faces away from the ring gear and no shims are used.) Carefully press on the bearing cones. (An arbor press with a bearing installation tool may be used.) Bearing cones can be pressed onto the differential case one at a time. The case sits vertically in the press. The shim goes on first. You can use a bearing installer and a hammer to seat the bearing cone if a press isn't available.

Refer to the Pinion Depth illustration on page 71. Check the original pinion for its number and check the new matched ring-and-pinion set for their number(s). Record all numbers on your build sheet. The key number for reassembly is the one marked on the pinion gear face. It is a zero (0), minus 1 (−1), plus 2 (+2). You

*Position each new differential bearing cone on the hub of the differential case. (Cone taper faces away from the ring gear and no shims are used.) Carefully press on the bearing cones. An arbor press may be used with the bearing installation tool.*

combine these numbers with the existing shim numbers to find the proper shim thickness.

In most cases you have shim thickness numbers, both on the the new gear set and the old gear set. If this is the case, you can skip to the marking pattern step.

However, if you have no numbers (old gear can't read), any number is not available, you have a brand-new housing, or you have a broken housing (welded on to repair, etc.), you need to refer to sidebar "How to Set Pinion Gear Depth" on page 49.

## Dana Carrier-Tube Differential Case Shims

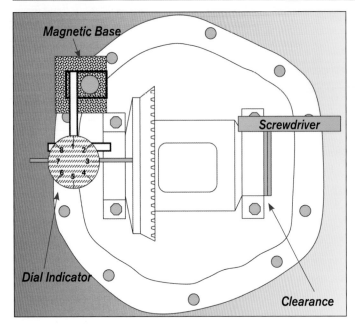

Magnetic Base

Screwdriver

Dial Indicator

Clearance

*Insert a screwdriver blade between the bearing cup and the housing and pry the case assembly as far as possible to one side of the housing. Adjust the dial indicator to zero. Using the screwdriver, pry the case over to the opposite side of the carrier housing and record the reading.*

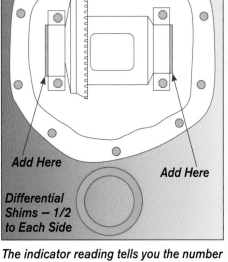

Add Here

Add Here

*Differential Shims – 1/2 to Each Side*

*The indicator reading tells you the number of shims needed to take up the clearance between the differential bearing cups and the case. The shim pack thickness to be placed on the bearing hub between the bearing cone and the differential case will be calculated after the installation of the drive pinion and depth of mesh setting. Half of the total shim goes to each side.*

1 Check the basic setup of the ring and pinion and differential case by positioning the differential bearing cups on their respective cones and pressing them into position. Gently place the differential case in the carrier housing and take care not to drop it.

2 Install the bearing caps in their correct/original positions according to the letter marking by the factory (alignment noted at disassembly) and tighten the bearing cap bolts finger tight.

3 Install a dial indicator with the end contacting the back face of the ring gear. (See "Dial Indicator Use" on page 23.)

4 Insert a screwdriver blade between the bearing cup and the housing and pry the case assembly as far as possible to one side of the housing. Adjust the dial indicator to zero. Using the screwdriver, pry the case to the opposite side of the carrier housing and record the reading.

5 Remove the dial indicator by loosening the mounting screw and loosen

the bearing cap bolts. Remove the bearing cap bolts and bearing caps.

6 Remove the differential case assembly from the carrier housing.

## Preparing to Set Pinion Depth

*A pinion shim pack is made up of several individual shims (bottom). They are installed on the flat side to the bearing cone (top) and then pressed/installed into the case/housing.*

1 Note the numbers etched, stamped, or painted on the head (end) of the drive pinion. One group of numbers (usually two or three digits) is found on both the pinion and the ring gear and indicates that it is a matched set.

Directly opposite this group of numbers is a single digit with a plus (+) or a minus (–) sign before it. If there is no plus or minus sign, consider it to be 0. This number and its sign must be positively identified before continuing. Refer to page 49 for details.

Midway between the two sets of numbers are numbers and letters located to the left and right of center. These were etched for manufacturing purposes only.

2 Install the rear drive pinion bearing cup and shim pack in the carrier. The starting shim pack that goes between the rear cup and the carrier can be determined from the shims removed and the etched marking on the pinion. The + or – number indicates the variation from the nominal distance between the front and the pinion and the centerline of the carrier.

For example, if the pinion that is marked +2 was originally installed with a shim pack with a thickness of .035 inch and the new pinion is marked –1, the shim pack must be increased .003 inch to bring the new pinion to its correct position, .038 inch. This is the approximate setting of the pinion.

Use a pinion depth gauge to measure the final setting of the pinion. Shims are available in .003-, .005-, and .010-inch thicknesses.

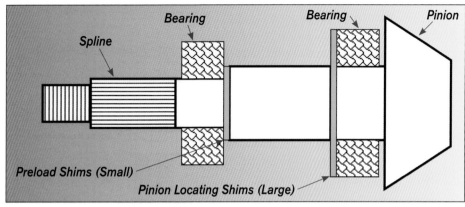

The large shims are called pinion-locating shims or pinion depth shims (for rear bearing). The small shims are called preload shims (for front bearing). Each goes between its bearing and the housing.

The four large shims (bottom right) are rear pinion bearing shims. The five small shims (bottom left) fit at the step in the pinion shaft about halfway up.

3 Install the front pinion bearing cup in the carrier.

4 Lubricate the rear drive pinion bearing cone with axle lube and install the bearing cone on the pinion stem with a bearing tool. Use the bearing tool to press the cone into the case.

5 Position the drive pinion and bearing assembly in the carrier and install the

A gauge arbor (the cross-bar in the photo) has three basic pieces, not counting the dial indicator/measuring hardware. The two metal discs are inserted into the differential case's main bearing bores. (They are sized to fit exactly.) Then the main caps are installed. The disc in the right-side main can be seen here. Then the cross-arbor is slid across between the two discs in the sized holes in their centers. From this basic setup, the gauge block and indicators are used to measure from the across-arbor (the rod) down to the pinion head.

front pinion bearing cone on the pinion stem, without preload shims. Shims are installed later.

In most cases you have shim thickness numbers, both on the the new gear set and the old gear set. If this is the case, you can skip to the marking pattern step.However, if you have no numbers (old gear or can't read), any number is not available, you have a brand-new housing, or you have a broken housing (welded on to repair, etc.), you need to refer to sidebar "How to Set Pinion Gear Depth" on page 49.

When measuring pinion rotating torque, maintain a constant speed as you rotate the torque wrench.

6 The pinion depth gauge tool is a direct-reading micrometer that is mounted in an arbor and calibrated to show the distance from the end of the anvil to the centerline of the gauge set. To check the accuracy of the gauge, install a micrometer and an arbor in the master gauge. Install the checking block and read the micrometer; it should be accurate to within less than .0005 inch.

7 Select the proper adapters from the gauge set that fits your differential bearing cup bores. Install the adapters on the arbor press and position it in the carrier housing. Install the bearing caps and snuggly tighten the cap bolts.

8 Install the step plate clamp assembly on the carrier housing. A step plate is sometimes used to mount the dial indicator/gauge. With some depth measuring tools, a pinion block or gauge block is used with the indicator added on top of the block's flat surface. Position the step plate over the pinion and tighten the step plate screw against the step plate. Make sure the four step plate feet are squarely positioned on the pinion.

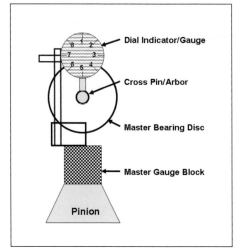

*Measuring setups come in many shapes and configurations. The dial indicator/ gauge can be mounted to a gauge block as shown or a step-plate. The master gauge block fits directly onto the pinion head. The master bearing discs (2) and the cross-arbor help define the center of the axle.*

9 Adjust the micrometer so it is directly above and at a 90-degree angle to the step plate or gauge block/arbor. Tighten the micrometer until the anvil contacts the top of the step plate. Read the micrometer and make a note of the reading. The step plate should measure .400 inch thick. Therefore, add the .400-inch-thick step plate thickness to the micrometer reading.

The nominal pinion-setting dimension from the end of the pinion to the centerline of the axle is 3.125 inches for a "0" pinion. Pinions with a + or – marking require a different setting. For example, if a pinion marked +2 is being installed, add the +2 to the pinion setting dimension 3.125 inches, which becomes the corrected dimension of 3.127 inches.

If the pinion setting is between –.001 and +.003 inch, the pinion position can be assumed to be correct. If the setting is outside these limits, it should be corrected by adding or removing the proper thickness shim behind the rear pinion bearing cup.

10 Remove the drive pinion depth gauge and the drive pinion.

11 If a shim adjustment is required, remove the drive pinion rear bearing cup and add or remove shims as appropriate. Measure each shim separately with a micrometer.

12 Reinstall the drive pinion rear bearing cup and shims and recheck the pinion depth measurement.

## Setting Pinion Depth

For this procedure, you need a rear axle setting gauge. It installs the drive pinion bearing cups and determines pinion depth of mesh. In common axles, the use of this tool is optional.

1 Start both drive pinion bearing cups into the carrier housing.

2 Lubricate the drive pinion bearing cone with axle lube.

3 Position the front pinion bearing cone in its proper bore in the carrier.

4 To install the pinion bearing cup, use a bearing installer and hammer. (See page 107 at top right.)

5 Select a new installer and repeat the procedure for the front pinion bearing race.

6 Install the gauge block part of the tool on the main tool and securely tighten the screw with an Allen wrench.

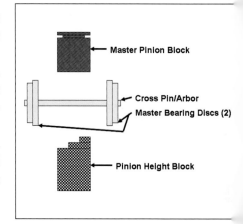

*The axle depth measuring tools tend to have several parts. The master pinion block, the pinion height block, the two master bearing discs and the cross-arbor are typical of the Dana tools. The final piece is the dial indicator/gauge that makes the actual measurement.*

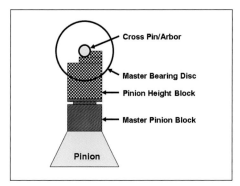

*The typical tool is assembled as shown. The master pinion block sets directly onto the pinion head. The pinion height block fits onto the pinion block and under the cross-arbor. The two steps are designed for different Dana axles. The master bearing discs fit into the main cap bores. In some cases, the discs have two diameters to fit different axles. The cross-arbor fits between the two discs. The dial indicator or gauge sits on the step of the height block to the left.*

**7** Position the crossbore arbor in the axle housing differential bearing seat. Center the arbor so that an approximate equal distance is maintained at both ends. Correctly position the differential bearing caps, insert the bolts, and tighten to 10 ft-lbs.

**8** Using a feeler gauge, select the proper thickness of shims that snugly fit between the arbor and the gauge block. This fit must be snug but not too tight (similar to the pull of a feeler gauge). This measurement is then used in determining the shim pack with the correct thickness for installation behind the rear pinion bearing cup and carrier casting.

**9** To select a shim pack for installation, read the markings on the end of the pinion head (–0, –1, –2, +1, +2 etc.). When the marking is - (minus) add that amount to the thickness of the shim pack selected in step 3 of "Carrier Tube Assembly" on page 49. When the marking is + (plus), subtract that amount. Treat other pinion markings in a similar manner. Shims are available in .003-, .005-, and .010-inch thicknesses.

**10** Remove the tool arbor and tool from the axle housing.

**11** Use a brass drift and hammer to drive the rear pinion bearing cup from the casting/carrier.

**12** Position the correct shim pack in the axle housing cup bore and install the rear bearing cup. (See Step 5.) When the cup is properly seated, remove the tool and pinion bearing cones.

**13** Spread lubricant over the rear drive pinion bearing cone with axle lube and install the bearing cone on the pinion stem using the special tool and an arbor press.

**14** Install the drive pinion and bearing assembly in the carrier and install the original front pinion bearing shim pack followed by the bearing cone (no oil seal yet). The rear bearing has been pressed onto the pinion, with the calculated shims. (See "How to Set Pinion Gear Depth" on page 49.) Using two hands, pass the yoke end of the pinion through the rear bearing cup from the rear of the carrier carefully until your other hand can grip the pinion splines. Install the yoke on the drive pinion. Use a plastic mallet to tap on the U-joint flange (yoke), washer, and nut onto the pinion splines. Use a torque wrench to tighten the nut to 250 to 270 ft-lbs. Once installed, rotate the pinion several complete revolutions to seat the bearing rollers. Hold using a yoke holder.

**15** Attach an inch-pound torque wrench to the nut that retains the U-joint. Rotate the pinion with the handle of the wrench floating and examine the scale on the wrench as it measures the pinion bearing preload. Take readings while the handle is moving through several complete revolutions. Accurate readings can be made only with the nose of the axle in the upright position. The correct preload is 10 to 20 inch-pounds. Add shims to decrease preload and subtract shims to increase preload. Shims are available in thicknesses of .003, .005, .010, and .030 inch.

**16** After correct pinion bearing preload has been established, use a socket and ratchet to remove the nut that retains the U-joint. Then remove the U-joint flange and washer.

**17** Install the oil slinger and gasket. Using a pinion seal installation tool, install the drive pinion oil seal. In most cases, any flat metal object, sized to the bearing seal will serve to tap the seal into place. Many mechanics use an appropriately sized socket and tap the seal into position.

**18** Install the universal joint flange washer and nut. Tighten the nut to 250 to 270 ft-lbs.

## Dana Carrier-Tube Pinion Bearing Preload

**1** Install the front pinion bearing shim pack followed by the bearing cone (no oil seal yet).

**2** Install the yoke, washer, nut, and front pinion bearing cone. The bearing slips down over the splines and into the front bearing cup. If the bearing is reversed, it does not seat properly in the cup. Cup or bearing race was previously installed.

3 Install the yoke holding tool and torque the pinion nut to 250 to 270 ft-lbs. Rotate the pinion several full revolutions. Rotate the pinion using an inch-pound torque wrench and measure the pinion bearing preload.

The correct bearing preload specifications are 10 to 20 inch-pounds for a 9¾-inch axle with new bearings.

4 Install an inch-pound torque wrench on the end of the pinion. Rotate the pinion with the handle of the wrench floating and measure the pinion bearing preload. Take a reading while the handle is moving through several complete revolutions. Accurate readings can be made only with the nose of the axle in the vertical position.

5 The correct bearing preload is 10 to 20 inch-pounds. Add shims to decrease preload and subtract shims to increase preload. Shims are available in thicknesses of .003, .005, .010, and .030 inch.

6 After the correct bearing preload has been established, the pinion depth setting should be rechecked. (See sidebar "How to Set Pinion Gear Depth" on page 49.)

7 Use a ratchet and socket to remove the universal joint flange, washer, and nut.

8 Remove the oil slinger and gasket. Install the drive pinion oil seal using a special tool.

9 Install the universal joint flange, washer, and nut. Hold the yoke with the holding tool and tighten the pinion nut to 250 to 270 ft-lbs. Recheck the pinion bearing preload.

## Dana Carrier-Tube Differential Bearing Preload and Ring Gear Backlash

Two precautions must be observed when adjusting differential bearing preload and ring gear backlash. First, the permissible backlash variation is .003 inch. For example, if the backlash is .006 inch at the minimum point, it may be .009 inch at the maximum point. This variation is permissible runout. It is therefore important to index the gears so that the same teeth are engaged during all backlash measurements.

Second, it is important to maintain the specified adjuster torque to obtain accurate differential bearing preload and ring gear backlash settings. Excessive torque introduces high bearing load and causes premature bearing failures. Inadequate torque does not support the ring gear properly and may lead to free play of the differential assembly and excessive gear noise.

Note that the differential bearing cups do not always move directly with the adjusters; therefore, to ensure accurate adjustment changes and to maintain gear mesh index, seat the bearings by oscillating the drive pinion a half turn in each direction 5 to 10 times each time the adjusters are moved.

1 With the drive pinion and bearings installed and the bearing preload set, install the differential case and ring gear assembly, with their respective bearing cups. Install the bearing caps in their proper positions, align the identification marks, and finger tighten the cap bolts.

*Install the dial indicator onto the housing and position the indicator point on the drive side of the gear tooth. To find the point of minimum backlash, check the backlash at four positions at approximately 90-degree intervals around the ring gear. Rotate the gear to the position of least backlash. Mark the index, so that all backlash readings are taken with the same teeth in mesh.*

*Refer to the measurement taken previously in an earlier step of Installation-Differential Case and Drive Gear. This reading (taken before the drive pinion was installed) represents the clearance between the differential bearing cups and the carrier casting. Perform the following steps to determine the thicknesses of shims required behind each bearing cone to take up the clearance and establish the correct bearing preload and backlash. You can hold the ring gear with your hand to move it back and forth.*

2 Install a dial indicator and position the end against the back face of the ring gear. Move the differential and ring gear assembly tight against the drive pinion, and set the dial indicator on 0 (zero). Move the differential and ring gear assembly in the opposite direction

as far away from the pinion as possible and note the indicator reading.

This reading represents the thickness of the shim pack necessary to take up the clearance between the bearing cup and the case on the ring gear side of the differential assembly. Subtract this reading from the first reading to obtain the number of shims necessary to take up the clearance between the bearing cup and the case at the pinion side of the differential.

3 Remove the differential and ring gear assembly from the carrier.

4 Remove the differential bearing cones from the case. Install the shim pack between the bearing cone and the differential case hub shoulder. Add another .015-inch shim pack to the drive gear side of the differential. (This additional thickness provides the correct bearing preload and backlash.) Reinstall the differential bearing cones.

5 Position a spreader tool on the locating holes in the carrier and finger tighten the screw. Install a dial indicator and spread the carrier .015 to .020 inch. Do not exceed this limit to permit the placing of the differential and ring gear assembly in the carrier.

6 Use a socket and ratchet to install the bearing caps in their respective positions as indicated by identification marks (letters and direction) on the caps and carrier. Directionals point one way on one side while the other side points the other way. Remove the spreader tool. Coat the bearing cap bolt threads with sealing compound, install, and tighten snugly.

7 Use a rawhide (non-metallic) hammer to lightly tap the drive gear to properly seat the differential bearing and cups. Care must be taken in this operation to prevent nicking the teeth of the ring gear and drive pinion as they are meshed together. Tighten the bearing cap bolts to 70 to 90 ft-lbs.

*Attach the dial indicator to the flat surface on the carrier. With the indicator contacting the ring gear tooth, at 90-degrees to tooth surface, measure the backlash between the ring gear and the drive pinion.*

8 Check the backlash at four equally spaced points around the ring gear. Backlash must be held between .004 and .009 inch and cannot vary more than .002 inch among the four positions checked.

9 If the backlash does not fall within these specifications, change the shim pack thickness on both differential bearing hubs to maintain proper bearing preload and backlash.

## Dana Carrier-Tube Gear Tooth Contact Pattern

Establishing the correct contact pattern is a crucial step for properly rebuilding a differential.

The gear tooth contact pattern indicates whether the correct rear pinion bearing mounting shim has been installed and the drive gear backlash set properly—the final setup test.

The correct pattern delivers low noise and long wear.

Running the contact pattern determines the axle has been properly set up. Basically you adjust the depth of the pinion and the left to right location of the differential case. The shape and general location of the contact pattern tells you which way to adjust these components.

To obtain the tooth contact pattern, apply a thin film of yellow oxide of iron on both the drive and coast side of the ring gear teeth. Using a round bar or large screwdriver (between the carrier housing and the differential case flange), apply a load against the backside of the ring gear and rotate the pinion several 360-degree revolutions in both directions. This procedure leaves a distinct contact pattern on both the drive and the coast side of the ring gear teeth.

Maintain backlash between the ring gear and the pinion within the specified limits until the correct pattern is obtained.

Compare your observed contact pattern to the pattern examples shown on pages 21–23 in Chapter 2 to determine if all adjustments have been made properly. The correct contact pattern is very well centered on both the drive and coast sides of the teeth. When the tooth contact patterns are obtained by hand, the actual contact area tends to be small. Under actual operating loads, the contact area increases while centered on the smaller area.

## Dana Carrier-Tube Axle Shaft Assembly and Installation

Once the differential installation is complete, start assembling the rest of the axle. Gather the axles, bearings, and seals that are going to be used and begin prep. Axle grease is very messy and smelly, so you may want to use rubber gloves for these steps.

1 Inspect the axle shaft seal journal for scratches and polish with 600-grade crocus cloth if necessary. If the journal is significantly damaged, you need to replace the axle shaft.

2 Clean the axle housing flange face thoroughly and install a new gasket followed by the brake support plate assembly on the driver's side of the axle housing.

3 Install the new axle shaft oil seals in the axle housing.

4 Install the retainer plate and seal assembly on the axle shaft. The outer retainer clamps the bearing and cup into the housing bore and also clamps the brake support plate to the studs of the housing tube or flange. The axle shaft endplay on the Dana passenger car axles is adjusted by means of a threaded adjuster located in the right axle shaft retainer. Axle shaft endplay must be maintained at .005 to .012 inch. Use a dial indicator to measure it. (See sidebar "Dial Indicator Use" on page 23.)

5 Lubricate the wheel bearings with multi-purpose grease. This tends to get messy; consider wearing rubber gloves.

6 Install the new axle shaft bearing cup, cone, and collar on the shaft.

7 Install a new gasket on the gasket surface of the axle housing. Use a new gasket or RTV to assist in holding the gasket in place. Apply a thin coat of gasket sealer to both sides of the gasket. Install the cover assembly into the axle housing. Tighten the carrier to axle housing screws to 25 ft-lbs. You can install the ratio identification tag on one of the cover attaching screws at this time. Note that the aftermarket services gaskets for the axle covers while the factory often recommends a bead of RTV.

8 Position the brake support plates on the left side of the housing.

9 By hand, carefully slide the axle shafts into the housing and engage the splines in the differential side gear. Be careful not to bang the axle shafts or bearings around in the housing because they could become damaged.

10 Position the retainer plate over the axle housing studs.

11 Repeat Steps 1 through 10 for the right axle.

12 Turn the threaded adjuster counterclockwise on the right axle assembly. This allows you to set the axle's end play. (See Step 4.)

13 Install the retainer nuts and tighten the retainer plate nuts to 35 ft-lbs. Start by tightening the bottom nut.

14 Apply a thin coat of multi-purpose grease to the outside diameter of the bearing cup prior to installation in the bearing bore.

15 Carefully slide the axle shafts into place and engage the splines in the differential side gear.

16 Install foam gaskets on the studs of the axle housing.

17 Lightly tap the end of the axle shaft with a plastic mallet to position the axle shaft bearing in the housing bearing bore.

18 Install the lock screw and tighten to 100 inch-pounds. Most early units use pins; newer units (starting about 20 years ago) use a special hex-head screw.

## Dana Carrier-Tube Carrier Cover

1 Thoroughly clean the gasket surfaces of the cover and the rear axle housing. Use an automotive degreaser.

2 Using a new gasket (or RTV), apply a thin coat of gasket sealer to both sides of the gasket to assist in holding the gasket in place as you install the cover assembly into the axle housing. Tighten the carrier to axle housing nuts to 25 ft-lbs. It's optional to install the ratio identification tag on one of the cover attaching screws. Many owners leave them off. While restorers want to have them, racers who constantly change gear ratios don't install the tags.

Tags are used for production ratios, such as 3.5, 3.9, 4.1. It's a big deal to the resto market but it would help know what's in it years down the road. That's really the reason they were used in the first place. Aftermarket companies service gaskets for the axle covers, while the factory often recommends a bead of RTV.

# Setting Axle Shaft Endplay

The Dana 60 (9¾-inch) axle was installed in Chrysler passenger cars from 1966 through the early 1970s. On these axles, the axle shaft endplay is adjusted at the left wheel. This process is the same as used on the Chrysler 8¾-inch axles. Axles that have C-clips do not use an axle shaft adjuster. Other axles may use different methods for adjusting axle endplay.

Use caution when setting axle shaft endplay. Both rear wheels must be off the ground, otherwise a false endplay setting occurs.

Using a dial indicator mounted on the left brake support, turn the axle adjuster clockwise until both wheel bearings are seated and there is 0 endplay in the axle shafts. Back off the adjuster counterclockwise approximately four notches (notches refer to adjuster lock holes) to establish an axle shaft endplay of .013 to .023 inch.

Lightly tap the end of the left axle shaft with a non-metallic mallet to seat the right wheel bearing cup against the adjuster, and rotate the axle shaft several rotations so that a true endplay reading is indicated.

Remove one retainer plate nut and install the adjuster lock. If the tab on the lock does not mate with the notch in the adjuster, turn the adjuster slightly until it does. Install the nut and tighten to 30 to 35 ft-lbs.

Recheck the axle shaft endplay. Repeat adjustment procedure if it is not within the tolerance of .013 to .023 inch.

Remove the dial indicator and install the brake drum and drum retaining clips.

## Dana Carrier-Tube Driveshaft

1 Install the driveshaft into the transmission (if the driveshaft was removed). Install the rear universal joint of the driveshaft into the saddle of the yoke, aligning the marks made at disassembly and tighten the clamp screws to 15 ft-lbs.

2 Install the brake drums.

3 Fill the unit with oil! Replace the drain plug if removed and tighten. Use recommended lube based on the ring-and-pinion or Sure-Grip manufacturer specifications or recommendations. Use a syringe to fill the axle because typically there is limited room for other oil-fill approaches. A general lube recommendation is as follows: 75W-90 for street, 140W for race. There are also synthetic oils, such as 75-140 synthetic that may offer wider coverage. Replace the oil fill plug.

The unit should now be ready to go. Keep it free from dirt and moisture before fitting. This can lead to failure because it keeps lubrication from critical load areas.

*Fill the unit with oil! Use the lube recommended by the ring-and-pinion manufacturer or the Sure-Grip manufacturer. Use a syringe to fill the axle because typically there is limited room for other oil-fill approaches. General lube recommendations are 90W for street, 140W for race. There are also synthetic oils, such as 75-140, that may offer wider coverage. The early-production Sure-Grip units from the 1960s and 1970s required a special Sure-Grip oil be added to the standard rear axle lube. This special Sure-Grip additive comes in a small can of a pint or less. It should be added at 1/2 full or after 2 pints of standard axle lube. Once the syringe is full of axle lubricant, thread on the front end of the syringe. It may take more than one fill-up of the syringe to fill the axle.*

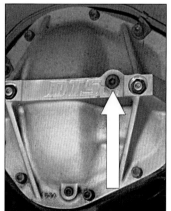

*The fill hole on this rear cover (arrow) is located between structural bolts. The fill hole has been moved up, which means you must measure the amount of lube you are adding and not just fill it to the bottom of the fill hole. The standard fill hole is about 1½ inches lower.*

*If you have a 9¾-inch axle, re-install the drain plug and torque and then remove the fill plug and fill the axle with 5½ pints or until lubricant is between the bottom of the filler plug opening and a point 1/2 inch below the filler plug opening. Replace the fill plug and tighten (if applicable).*

## Break-In Procedure for New Rear Axle Gear Set

On any new ring-and-pinion set with new bearings, especially the higher numerical ratios, excessive heat can build up in the rear end. This over-heating situation can cause durability problems, such as softening, with the gear teeth and bearings. Avoid over-heating by performing the proper break-in procedure. All new axle gear sets require a break-in period.

Be sure that the axle has been filled to the correct fluid level with the proper axle lubricant before driving the vehicle. The oil rating must be GL5 or higher—follow the ring-and-pinion manufacturer's suggestions.

### Street Vehicles

On basic street vehicles, bring the axle to normal operating temperature by driving it (unloaded) for approximately 10 to 20 miles. Do not run full-throttle (heavy) accelerations or create any shock loads (hard launch). Stop and let the vehicle cool completely (about 30 minutes). Repeat this procedure two or three times. As an option, you can also drive gently for 100 to 200 miles with no heavy loads.

### Off-Road and Trail Vehicles

Drive the vehicle (unloaded) off-road or on-trail for approximately 15 minutes. Do not use full-throttle accelerations. Stop and let it cool for about 30 minutes. Repeat this procedure two or three times.

### Circle Track Race Vehicles

Run approximately six to eight laps at slow speed and then let the vehicle cool for 30 minutes. Repeat for six to eight laps, then two or three laps at full speed, and then cool again for 30 minutes.

### Drag Race Vehicles

Perform an initial run-in, such as a one part-throttle run down the drag strip, and then let the vehicle cool for 20 minutes. Drag strip race cars are only driven short distances and heat is not typically a problem with the proper lube and backlash installation.

### Trailer Towing

If trailer towing is intended, an additional break-in of 200 to 300 miles is required without the trailer. This is very important! To properly break in a new gear set, a minimum of 500 miles (general street break-in of 200 miles plus the additional 300 for trailer towing use) of driving is essential before towing. On the first actual trailer tow, drive 15 miles then stop. Repeat two more times for a total of 45 miles to fully break-in the gears.

### Optional Additional Step

It is optional to change oil after first 500 miles (consult your ring gear manufacturer). Remember, there are acceptable noise levels that may vary from manufacturer to manufacturer. Break-in of gears is paramount to gear life. The initial run-in should be at low speeds. This enables gears to run in without overheating.

## Dana Upgrades

The Chrysler 9¾/Dana 60 carrier-tube rear axle has been around for many years.

*Rear axle covers are used on all carrier-tube axles and they can usually be seen installed on the vehicle if you look at the rear of the axle. The location and visibility mean that it is a good place to customize your vehicle. Covers come in all shapes and styling themes from painted stamped steel (stock), to chrome, to cast aluminum and special cast aluminum with logos.*

It was installed in the fastest muscle cars, including the Charger, Challenger, Super Bee, and many other muscle cars of that era. Because the Dana axle was used in so many racing applications, much of the early special hardware and special modifications were based on the 9¾-inch axle. The aftermarket manufacturer's capability has grown from this initial demand.

### Ratios

The one aspect of rear axles that seems to have been a constant is the general availability of ratios. They are available into the 5s. The low numbers, such as 2.5 and 3.0:1 on the other end of the scale, are handled by overdrive ratios or add-ons in the transmission area. Additionally, many of the higher numbered ratios, such as 4.88 and 5.12:1, are offered in a better material for heavy-duty use or drag racing. These super-material gears are called "pro gears."

### Bearings

Rear axles wear out pinion, differential, and axle shaft bearings. Since they are commonly replaced, they maintain their availability along with other service items. While they may not always be available individually, they are readily available in service or repair kits. For rear axles, always replace parts as sets.

### 4-Wheel Disc Brakes

Brakes may not be considered a

*In the Chrysler/Dana rear axle family, Sure-Grips are the most popular name for the special differentials sometimes called Positractions, limited slips or lockers. The clutch-type Sure-Grip has maintained service parts and general availability. The newer cone-type Sure-Grip was only serviced as an assembly because there were no clutches or discs inside the unit to be replaced. These basic cone-style Sure-Grips are still available. There are also a whole group of new Sure-Grips, or lockers. Some function as air lockers, some as electric. There are many different styles and technologies available today. See Chapter 7. Detroit Locker is shown is very popular with the off-road market.*

rear axle part, but they bolt directly to the axle housing, and in many cases must be removed to allow the rear axle to be rebuilt. All original 8¾-inch axles used drum brakes. Many of the 8¼-and 9¼-inch axle also used drum brakes. Starting in the mid 1990s, manufacturers began offering disc-brake conversion kits for these axles. This allows owners of many of these older cars to upgrade their braking systems to 4-wheel disc brake systems. Manufacturers now also offer better drum brakes such as upgrading production 9-inch drums to 10-inch drums.

### Narrowed Housing

The aftermarket rear axle business really started with narrowing Dana 60 (9¾-inch) axles and making the shorter axles that went with the narrower housing. The most readily available units were offered by Chrysler through their performance parts group, called Direct Connec-

tion or Mopar Performance. The original narrowed axle was called the 52½-inch, and the second one was called 44½-inch. After this, the aftermarket took over and offers almost any width desired. The limiting factors tend to be the suspension mounting brackets and spring seats and room for the braking hardware.

### The J8

The J8, a military version of the Jeep Wrangler, is sold for export. That means that they are very difficult to find in the United States and waiting for one to be crashed delays your project too long. These special J8 Wranglers used a special Dana 60, which means they were narrowed to the Wrangler width. They come with a 4.10:1 ratio and Sure-Grip and a 5-on-5½ bolt pattern (wheels). They seem to be popular with off-road builders. The demand convinced Chrysler (Mopar Performance) to offer these J8 Dana 60 axles

(9¾-inch) as complete assemblies, which includes brake assemblies and suspension brackets (mounting points). There are two versions currently available: one for standard JK use and one for leaf spring use.

### Fabricated Housing

Shortly after the narrowed axle demand created the rear axle market, aftermarket manufacturers began fabricating new housings rather than narrowing existing ones. These unique housings are cut and welded together, but look fabricated and not like the original. Unless the unit is painted, plated, or a logo added, aftermarket fabricated units all look similar. These units started in high-end drag racing, but have moved into many other forms of competition, as well as show cars and customs.

The demand for the narrowed axle assembly increased in the faster drag racing categories because racers wanted narrow axles and had higher loads and stresses that created additional demands on the housing. There was so much cutting and welded going on to the existing part that the fully fabricated housing was actually less work and stronger in finished form. Once the aftermarket could make their own axle housings, they branched out to many other axle designs. This technology offered big upgrades to other axles.

These fabricated axle housings look unique and may not be accepted in all racing categories. NHRA Stock and Super Stock classes allow the 9¾- and 8¾-inch narrowed axles in Chrysler race cars but not the fabricated units. The fabricated units are legal in many other classes. Rules vary and are constantly changing and being updated, so always check with your local tech director and sanctioning body for the latest update.

*For the Chrysler/Dana rear axle family, Sure-Grip differentials are the most popular for the special differentials sometimes called limited-slips or lockers. Service parts for the clutch-type Sure-Grip are still available, and the aftermarket offers assemblies. The newer cone-type Sure-Grip was only serviced as an assembly because there were no clutches or discs inside the unit to be replaced. These basic cone-style Sure-Grips are still available.*

# THE DIFFERENTIAL

The first differentials were rudimentary, and modern limited-slip differentials have evolved substantially from these early units. When cars were first manufactured, the ring gear was bolted to the solid axle shaft to make the car go forward, but the differential only operated properly when it traveled in a straight line. Basic geometry states that when a vehicle goes around a corner, the outer wheel must travel farther than the inner wheel.

This basic requirement created the standard, or open, differential. This unit allows the inner and outer wheels of the vehicle to travel at different speeds (distances) as the vehicle goes around a corner. To accomplish this, the solid axle is cut so it isn't solidly attached to the ring gear. Splining two side gears to the ends of the axle shafts connects the axle shafts to the ring gear. Two side gears are then connected together through two pinion gears mounted on a pinion shaft. The whole assembly is mounted inside a solid case called the differential housing or differential case.

This basic set of hardware is called an open differential. This standard differential is sometimes called conventional. It is fitted as standard equipment on most vehicles. It is a very good differential for everyday street driving on paved roads.

## Parts

The basic parts of the typical open differential are: differential case (housing), side gears (two) splined for the axle shafts, pinion gears (typically two, but four may be used) that mate with the side gears, pinion cross-shaft, lock pin, and differential bearings (two).

These parts must be compatible and should be complementary, so they

*The differential case holds the ring gear, but the insides are much more complex than just a metal case with small springs, gears, and clutches inside. The axle shaft is splined into each side gear (left and right). The clutch discs and plates are behind each side gear, between the gear and the case/housing.*

*An open differential has two side gears, two small pinion gears, and one cross-shaft. Some limited-slip assemblies have two side gears and four small pinion gears mounted at 90 degrees on a double cross-shaft. The four-pinion setup is shown.*

can be assembled. The early units were designed to be disassembled easily and also serviced easily. As differential units have become more advanced and offer more technology, it often makes sense to remove the differential and send to the manufacturer for service.

## A Bit of History

Beginning in 1962, Chrysler offered two different Sure-Grip assemblies: the Power-Lok and the Trac-Lok. The Power-Lok was used from 1962 to 1969. In the beginning these special Sure-Grip differentials were used in Chrysler 8¾ inch axles. In 1966 they were added to Dana 60 axles in Chrysler cars. The Trac-Lok was introduced in late 1969 and was used in all Chrysler axles for the next few years. The Chrysler 7¼-inch axle was produced with a Sure-Grip unit only in

the model years 1964–1966 (the basic Power-Lok design).

The early second-generation 8¾-inch Sure-Grip was originally called the Borg-Warner Spin Resistant. As time passed, the two terms (Trac-Lok and Power-Lok) were used by others such as the AMC 20 and Dana axles. The names and the features of these early Chrysler units appear to be somewhat consistent, but these same names used in other models could mean almost anything. Sure-Grip, limited-slip, and Posi-Traction are the general descriptions for these performance differentials; I focus more on their use than on the various marketing names.

## Production Types

Originally there was only the open differential and then the limited-slip was added in the early 1960s. The limited-slip is sometimes called Sure-Grip or Posi-Traction or Posi. Sure-Grip is the Chrysler product name for limited-slip and Posi-Traction is the General Motors product name for limited-slip. Since then, many other versions or designs (such as the locker, manual locking, torque-sensing, and spools) have been made. As a result, so many variations and manufacturers have created a lot of overlap and many

options. Each version has its own characteristics and features and some are easier to explain than others.

### Open

The open or conventional differential is by far the most common. It transmits power from the ring-and-pinion to a set of pinion gears and a set of side gears to the axle shafts. Power is typically applied in equal amounts to both sides. However, if one wheel slips (loses traction), the opposite wheel receives very little power. It spins one of the two rear wheels by itself. It has no slip-limiting capability and is not used in racing or with high-powered engines.

### Limited-Slip

Many names are used for a limited-slip differential in automotive applications. It is often called a Sure-Grip assembly. It is also called a Posi-Traction or Posi. The limited-slip name seems to be the most general and the most descriptive. A limited-slip differential limits the amount of slip of one axle or wheel relative to another. How the differential limits the slippage between the two wheels/axles is what separates them into the following six basic categories: limited-slip disk, limited-slip cone, standard locker,

This Power-Lok limited-slip differential is installed into an early 742 case for a Chrysler 8¾-inch axle. Note the two-piece case with the split just to the right of the ring gear teeth.

*The open differential uses a one-piece case with a big window in its side (actually one toward the top and one on the bottom as shown). You can see the small pinions and the cross-shaft.*

A typical limited-slip differential fills up the inside of the case/housing. In this case, the housing is a two-piece design. The bolts that hold the case together are at the top of the photo. Note that the end of the cross-shaft in the center of the photo fits into a V-slot pointing downward.

Another style of limited-slip uses small coil springs to apply force that allows the unit to function. You can see the vertical cross-shaft and the small pinion gears behind each coil spring.

manual-control locker, torque-sensing, and spool. With so many aftermarket manufacturers offering limited-slip assemblies, there probably should be more categories. Even with only our six groups, there is some overlap.

*Limited-Slip—Disc:* Perhaps the oldest limited-slip design is the style that uses friction discs placed between steel plates. Chrysler called this the Power-Lok differential and used it in production from 1962 through 1969. There are two main types of limited-slip differentials: disc or clutch-pack. The original Chrysler-style unit uses Belleville washers to provide the clutch friction that allows it to work properly as a limited-slip. Yukon makes these rebuildable and very popular units that work well in street conditions and at the racetrack. Yukon currently makes them.

Eaton currently makes the other type of unit, which is called the Eaton Posi, and uses small coil springs to apply the frictional pressure. Clutch packs, both friction discs, and Belleville washers are available to service these units. With this design, the friction discs are splined to the differential side gears and therefore turn with the side gears. The steel plates have tabs that lock into notches in the differential case and therefore turn with the case. All components can be replaced within

The cone-style unit fits in the same space as the clutch-disc unit. However, inside, a tapered cone section, which is added to the back of each green side gear, replaces the clutches. The case is tapered to match. This coil spring system is similar to that of the clutch unit. Note the position of the yellow pinion gears.

The locker is a smaller, lightweight design with a two-piece case construction.

these units, and they provide excellent performance in high-performance street and race track applications.

*Limited-Slip—Cone:* Trac-Lok, the second generation of Chrysler limited-slip differentials (the cone-style), was introduced in late 1969. (The name "Trac-Lok" was also used by Dana and AMC for clutch-disc units.) This limited-slip differential was used on 1969/1970 and newer models up to the mid 1980s when the original company sold its production rights and the names changed. These two production limited-slip differentials (Trac-Lok and Power-Lok) are interchangeable as assemblies. Neither production limited-slip assembly is available from Chrysler today, but similar units are available from the aftermarket such as Yukon (disc) and Auburn (cone).

The cone-style is similar to the disc-style unit because they both use friction to limit the relative movement between the two axles. The method of creating this friction takes completely different paths. The disc-style unit uses a basic flat-plate clutch while the cone-style unit has the backside of each side-gear cut at an angle or tapered and the mating surface in the differential case is cut at a similar taper or angle. Small springs in the center of the case push the angled side gear against the angled case creating friction.

Cone-style units are available for a wide variety of axles. The largest supplier is Auburn Gear. This style of differential is not rebuildable in the field. Chrysler did not offer any service parts and recommended replacing the complete assembly. These cone-style units offer smooth operation on the street and have a trouble-free reputation.

### Locker

The locker design includes a large amount of differential-locking technology and it is used on all positive-locking differentials.

*Standard Locker:* Standard lockers are sometimes called automatic lockers, but

*A manual-control locker is larger than a standard locker or automatic locker. A small compressor supplies the air pressure. When not applied, this unit functions like an open differential.*

*If you could see inside of the torque-sensing differential it would look very complicated. Once assembled, you do not see the gears that are shown here in a cut-away illustration for display purposes. There are no clutches inside, only gears. They offer very smooth operation and can be used in the front position of 4WD applications.*

*Spools are simple units with no moving parts. The inner holes are for lightening only.*

# Differential Case Solutions

One of the problems that differentials must solve is to keep the ring gear and pinion in contact with each other through the full range of gear ratios that are used for that specific axle. As the axle ratio changes from a 3.0 ratio to a 4.0 ratio, the ring gear tends to have more teeth and the pinion tends to have less teeth. As the pinion is designed with less teeth, the result is a smaller diameter. The result of the smaller diameter, if nothing else changed, would be that the ring gear and pinion would no longer be in contact. There are two basic solutions to this problem.

The left-hand drawing below shows a standard ring-and-pinion alignment with the teeth of the ring engaged with the teeth of the large pinion (11 to 14 teeth). The right-hand draw-ing below shows that the ratio has been changed to a lower gear (bigger number) that has a smaller-diameter pinion (7 to 10 teeth). The teeth on the ring gear are no longer in contact with the teeth on the pinion. This condition must be corrected.

The top drawing shows the thicker ring gear solution, which is used in the Chrysler 8¾-inch axle. Material is added to the back of the ring gear so that the distance between the teeth and the mounting face is greater.

The bottom drawing shows a second solution, which is used on many axles. The ring gear mounting flange is moved to hold the standard-thickness ring gear engaged to the small-diameter pinion.

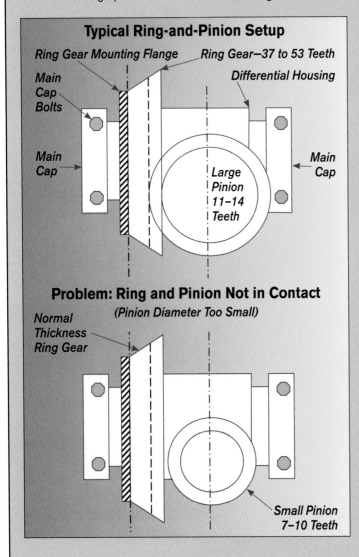

**Typical Ring-and-Pinion Setup**

Ring Gear Mounting Flange — Ring Gear—37 to 53 Teeth

Main Cap Bolts — Differential Housing

Main Cap — Main Cap

Large Pinion 11–14 Teeth

**Problem: Ring and Pinion Not in Contact**
*(Pinion Diameter Too Small)*

Normal Thickness Ring Gear

Small Pinion 7–10 Teeth

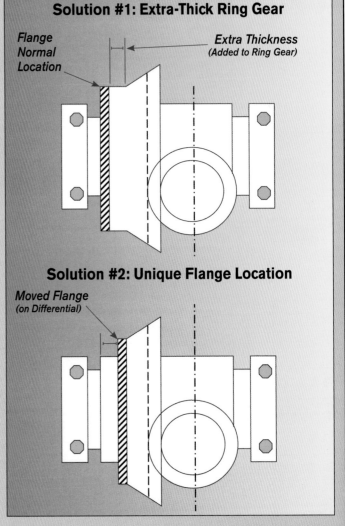

**Solution #1: Extra-Thick Ring Gear**

Flange Normal Location — Extra Thickness *(Added to Ring Gear)*

**Solution #2: Unique Flange Location**

Moved Flange *(on Differential)*

not in the sense of an automatic transmission. They transmit power through a set of dog clutches that lock automatically. These units are extremely strong and durable, but they can be harsh in operation and noisy during cornering. They are popular in off-road applications. The largest supplier and best-known brand is the Detroit Locker.

*Manual-Control Locker:* The manual-control lockers are not that much different than the standard lockers, except for the method of locking the two axles together. Manual-control lockers offer the driver the option of a conventional differential or a fully locked differential. This control is done at the touch of a button or cable. This quick-and-easy option offers versatility for a vehicle that is used in both street and off-road applications or competitions.

This group of lockers could be divided into two groups: air controlled

*This is a ring gear for a low ratio, which is about 4.5. Note thickness between bottom of the teeth and differential flange. It is an 8¾-inch axle.*

# Determine Differential Type

The biggest advantage of the basic Sure-Grip or limited-slip in acceleration situations or racing applications is that it divides the available power/torque between the two rear wheels. This allows more power and/or torque to be put to the ground and used to accelerate the vehicle harder and quicker whether cornering or going in a straight line.

One of the first steps in using a rear-wheel-drive vehicle in acceleration contests or racing is to determine whether it has a Sure-Grip. If it does, the next step is to determine if the Sure-Grip that you have is still good. Sure-Grips do wear out.

The simple test for a Sure-Grip versus limited-slip differential is as follows:

- Jack up the rear end of the car and support it on jack stands. Both wheels must be off the ground. Confirm that the parking brake is off and that the transmission is in neutral.
- Position yourself so you can see both rear wheels/tires at the same time (under the car), near the ground, ahead or behind the tire. The routing of the exhaust pipe has a lot to do with the best location.
- Rotate the left-side tire counterclockwise.
- If the right-side tire rotates in the same direction, this indicates a limited-slip differential.

The following is a more detailed test for the correct installation and function of the standard-type limited-slip differential. Remember that this procedure may not work for lockers and spools.

*Jack up the rear of the car and support it on jack stands. With the engine off, and the parking brake off, try to rotate the wheels. Use both hands.*

- Raise the rear axle off the floor, so that both tires are completely off the ground. Support the rear on jack-stands. Double-check that the parking brake is off.
- With engine off, place the transmission in park (automatic) or first gear (manual).
- Grip the tire with both hands and try to rotate the tire/wheel (in either direction). Consider using gloves.
- If you find that it is extremely difficult or impossible to manually turn either wheel, the limited-slip differential is operating properly.
- If you find that it is relatively easy to continuously turn either wheel, it means the differential is not performing properly and should be removed, replaced, or rebuilt.

*This is a ring gear for a high-ratio differential, which is about a 3.0. Note the thickness between the teeth and the differential flange.*

*This is the differential case for Dana 60 axles. The one on the right has the higher mounting flange, compared to the flat surface they are sitting on. The one on the right is designed for 4.56 and higher ratios (bigger numbers) and the one on the left is for 4.10 ratios and lower (smaller numbers).*

and electric controlled. The air-controlled units have been around the longest while the electric-controlled units are quite new. The air-locker style has a small air compressor as part of the kit and the air pressure is what locks the axles together. In electrically controlled units, electrics and wires replace the air pressure. With the air or electrical off, the differential acts as an open differential, which is ideal for street use.

ARB makes the air-controlled unit, which is older and more popular. This style of manual-control locker gives the driver total control over the differential's lock-up point. The electric designs are new and expanding in applications and features.

### Torque-Sensing

These units, about the same size as the standard limited-slip differentials, are the most difficult to define because the case/housing is full of little gears, which makes it look very complicated. There are no clutches inside. Engine torque moves the side gears, and the rest of the gears are designed to lock the axles together when this movement occurs.

Torsen and others make these differentials that have a reputation for excellent slip-limiting performance and smooth operation. These are used in some military applications, such as Hummers. They are a good unit for FWD applications, such as on the front of 4WD or all-wheel-drive units.

### Spool

The spool locks both axles together at all times so there is no differential action. This means that both rear wheels always turn at the same speed, therefore these vehicles do not corner well. Therefore, spools are not recommended for street use. Spools also require the use of racing axle shafts for safety reasons. They are very lightweight and simple—no moving parts. They are popular in drag racing and faster racing categories, not dual-purpose or street-strip vehicles.

## Special Case 1

Some axle designs show a special differential case required with certain axle ratios. This situation is caused by the size (diameter) of the pinion head. As the axle ratio becomes higher (numerically smaller such as 2.76 or 2.45:1) the pinion ends up with more teeth. The actual axle ratio is the number of teeth on the ring gear divided by the number of teeth on the pinion, so the number of teeth on

the ring gear is somewhat limited by the diameter of the ring. Therefore, if it were any larger, it wouldn't fit into the existing axle housing.

These resulting high (numerically low) ratios use more teeth in the pinion, which increases its diameter. The ring gear must mate-up to the pinion head, so the ring gear-mounting flange has to be moved away from the axle centerline to allow a large diameter pinion head. As the axle ratio becomes lower (numerically larger such as 3.55 or 3.91:1) the pinion has fewer teeth and therefore becomes smaller in diameter. To get this new, smaller pinion to mate-up to the ring, the ring mounting flange must be moved over to align with the smaller pinion. The other solution is to make the ring gear thicker, as done in the Chrysler 8¾-inch.

Only two axles do not have a carrier break: the Chrysler 9¼-inch and the Chrysler 8-inch. Both the 7¼- and 8¼-inch axles have the split in the 2.4 changing to 2.5/2.7:1. Any ratio in the 2.2 or 2.4:1 area is only used in production and not available in the aftermarket.

Aftermarket manufacturers tend to focus on the lower (numerically higher ratios, such as 3.5 and 3.9:1. So as long as you don't have a 2.4:1 ratio now, you should be okay. The AMC 20 axle and all Dana axles put the break in the 3.0 to 4.0 area, so you must be much more careful

Differentials for the lower (numerically higher) ratios are available from the aftermarket.

With the exception of the Dana axles, this dual-differential situation is solved for the limited-slip or Sure-Grip axles because the Sure-Grip/limited-slip is only offered with higher axle ratios. For example, with a Dana 60, you must have a Sure-Grip case designed for a 3.9 or 4.1:1 ratio if that is the ratio to be used and it (the Sure-Grip case) must change if you switch to a 4.56:1 ratio. The AMC 20, Chrysler 7¼- and 8¼-inch axles that offer limited-slip options limit this option to lower (bigger number) ratios such as 3.10/3.20:1 and lower (numerically higher numbers such as 3.5 and 3.9:1).

### Special Case 2

On cars built after the mid 1980s that feature some form of anti-lock brakes, you may find that the differential case has teeth that ring a flywheel's ring-gear or the flexplate/torque converter's ring gear. The case may be unique, or it may be the same case machined to accept the steel ring gear. In these cases, a sensor mounted in the housing/carrier lines up with the ring so it can see the teeth on the ring gear. It should not affect the differential's rebuilding process.

*This special case uses some form of locking brakes. Note the small ring gear (bottom) pressed onto the outside of the ring gear-mounting flange. A sensor is also mounted in the housing.*

## Open Differential

The open (or conventional) differential is the most common type of differential, and it's a one-piece unit. It is a good street differential, but can allow one wheel to spin independently of the wheel on the opposite side.

*This 9¾-inch open differential has a large window in the side and one-piece case construction. Once the cross-shaft has been removed, you can lift, by hand, the gears, both side gears, and the pinion gears through this window in the differential housing.*

## Open Differential Disassembly

In general with an open rear axle (non-limited-slip) the cross-shaft must be removed first. A pin holds it in. Some pins are pressed-in and some are threaded in, with a small hex-head on the special screw.

1 If C-clips are retaining the axle shafts, remove the lock pin and remove the pinion cross-shaft. Use a long, thin punch or brass drift and hammer to tap out the lock pin and then a brass drift and hammer to drive out the cross-shaft. The Chrysler carrier-tube axles such as the 8¼-inch use a special screw for the lock pin and it must be unthreaded to

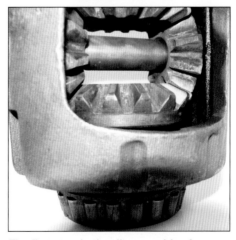

*The first step in the disassembly of an open differential is to remove the (horizontal here) cross-shaft.*

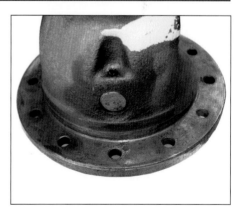

*To remove the cross-shaft, you must remove the pin, which is located just above the round end of the cross-shaft and is pressed into the housing. Some designs use a screw for a lock pin.*

remove. Then the axle shafts can be pushed inward, one at a time, and the C-clips removed. Then the axle shafts can be removed. At this point, the pinion cross-shaft and lock pin may be reinstalled or they may be set aside.

2 Rotate the differential case by hand until you have access to the lock pin. Use the pinion if the differential is still in the housing. Typically, this requires less than half a turn but it could be as much as three-quarters of a turn. Remove the lock pin. Then remove the pinion cross-shaft. Tap the pinion with a non-metallic hammer and brass drift. Most axles have the lock pin pressed in, but Chrysler carrier-tube axles use a screw. Use a long, thin punch and hammer to tap the pin out. Once removed, use a larger brass drift and hammer to tap out the cross-shaft. This is most easily done

once the differential is removed from the housing/carrier.

3 Rotate the case or side gear by hand until one of the pinions appears in the access window in the side of the case. Once the pinion and its thrust washer are located in the window, lift them out by hand.

4 Rotate the case or side gear by hand until the second pinion appears in

*Once the pin has been removed, tap out the cross-shaft. Then you can remove the pinion gears (left and right). Once the pinions have been removed, take out the two side gears (top and bottom). The thrust block is in the center. It can be removed once the cross-shaft has been removed.*

the access window. You can turn the gear by reaching in through the axle splines, but it is easier to use your finger inserted through the access window onto the side gear teeth. Remove the second pinion gear and washer.

5 Remove the two side gears and the thrust washers that are behind them.

6 Clean all parts with mineral spirits and inspect the parts for obvious signs of wear and damage. This includes cracks, chips, and deformations.

## Open Differential Assembly

Once cleaned and inspected, arrange the parts on your work bench, with the differential case in the center. You have two side gears (the bigger ones) and two pinion gears (the smaller ones) plus the cross-shaft and its retaining pin.

1 Lubricate all parts with rear axle lubricant. Lubricate all the clutches, discs, bearings, gear and surfaces that rub or slide. This can be messy, so use rubber gloves. Spread the oil with your finger over entire wear surface.

2 Install the thrust washers on the two differential side gears. Position the side gears and washers on each side of the case.

3 One at a time, place the thrust washers on the pinions and insert them through the large window in the case.

Mesh the pinion gears with the side gears and rotate the side gear or case to bring each pinion gear inside the case. The teeth are large, so you can easily see that the two gears teeth are meshed. You can also feel it if you rotate the pinion gear in both directions (clockwise and then counterclockwise). Align the pinion gears so that they are exactly 180 degrees opposite each other.

4 Rotate the side gears 90 degrees to align the pinion gears and washers with the pinion shaft holes in the case. The easiest way to rotate the side gears is to use one finger on each hand inserted through the two access windows, rotating the tips of the teeth on the side gears. To move the pinions, rotate the side gears in opposite directions.

5 Rotate the case so the pinion cross-shaft pin lock is closest to you.

Insert the slotted end of the pinion shaft through the case, the conical thrust washer, and just one of the pinion gears. Use a large screwdriver to help align the hole in the shaft with the one in the case once the shaft is at the proper height.

6 Install the thrust block (if used) through the side gear hub, so that the slot is centered between the side gears.

7 Keeping all of the parts mentioned in proper alignment, push the pinion shaft into the case until the locking pin hole in the pinion shaft is in exact alignment with the respective hole in the case.

8 Install the pinion shaft lock pin through the hole in the case. Do not insert the pin from the ring gear side of the flange.

## Production Limited-Slip

Within the group of axles covered in this book, several differentials fit into the production category. Limited-slip differential seems to be the most common term for these special axles that try to equally divide the power between both rear wheels or limit the slip of one wheel to the other. Chrysler has used the term Sure-Grip for their limited-slip differentials. All three groups have used limited-slip, and Posi-Traction (or just posi) are also popular.

*The Power-Lok Chrysler 8¾-inch axle limited-slip assembly has a clutch-type unit with a two-piece case. The eight bolts are left-hand thread and visible at the top of the case.*

This section covers three styles of production limited-slip differentials: the 1969 and earlier Chrysler Power-Loc Sure-Grip, the 1969 and newer Chrysler Trac-Lok, and the one-piece AMC 20 and Dana Trac-Lok.

## Power-Loc Sure-Grip

The 1962–1969 Chrysler Power-Loc (Sure-Grip) uses a two-piece case and clutches behind each side gear. It is easily rebuildable and service parts are readily available. It is a very good street and strip unit.

## Power-Loc Sure-Grip Disassembly

Clear enough space around the differential so you have enough room for the parts being removed. You might consider placing them in small zip-lock bags to keep them organized.

The differential and ring gear assembly have been removed from the case.

**1** Remove the ring gear screws and remove the ring gear. Use shop towels to catch the ring gear to avoid damaging it.

**2** Before taking the two halves of the differential case apart, scribe marks on both halves to aid in aligning the case when reassembling.

**3** Rotate the case until you locate the pinion cross-shaft. It sits in a V-slot pointing downward with a large, round-top opening. Two of them reside in the case and are oriented 180 degrees apart.

**4** Rotate the case 90 degrees from the pinion slot pointing downward, and you find one that points upward with the large, round-top opening below it.

**5** Remove the case cap-attaching bolts from the end opposite the ring gear flange.

**6** As you remove the case cap, lift it as straight as possible.

**7** Remove the five clutch plates that are stacked together. Clutch is in hand, and the side gear retainer is left on top.

**8** Remove the side gear retainer, which is splined on its inner diameter. Check it closely because a clutch disc or two may stick to it. Use your hands to pull apart the case halves, but don't hurry because you want to study each individual part. You will want to put it back together in the same manner.

**9** Once retainer is lifted off, the side gear just sits on top. Remove it.

**10** Remove the pinion shafts and the pinion gears. Be careful that the four pinions mounted on the pinion shafts do not fall off.

**11** Remove the remaining side gear by reaching inside the case, which looks like a tower. Watch out for sharp edges.

**12** Remove the remaining side gear retainer. The clutch discs and plates sometimes stick together and stick to the retainer. Just remove any discs or plates from the retainer and place them with the rest of the clutch parts.

**13** Remove the opposite-side clutch plates. They also tend to stick together so be sure that you have them all. The last one may stick to the bottom of the case; may have to use a thin screwdriver to convince it to leave.

**14** Remove the four pinions from the cross-shafts. They fall off easily so the trick is to keep them from hitting the floor.

**15** Press out the lock pin and remove the axle shaft thrust spacer. The

thrust spacer also holds the two cross-shafts together. Place the assembly on a large 1/2-drive socket to protect it and use a small punch and hammer to tap out the lock pin.

**16** A small pin holds the two cross-shafts together. Use a hammer and a punch to gently tap the two sections apart. When the pin's two pieces have been divided, this allows the cross-shaft to be divided. Note that the ends of the cross-shafts have flats machined to form a V.

**17** Thoroughly clean and inspect all parts. Dirt is the enemy of any moving part. Cleaning allows you to see cracks, especially small cracks in your hardware. It also allows you to observe the surface for scuffing and any discoloration.

**18** There are two styles of clutch discs. Some have four tabs or ears while others are smooth on the outside diameter but have teeth on the inside diameter. Each style can be flat or Belleville shaped.

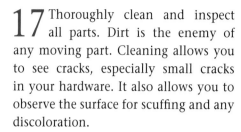

**19** For the 8¾- and 9¾-inch axle, the plate and disc arrangement uses the side gear ring or retainer as a baseline. Notice the dish orientation.

## Power-Loc Sure-Grip Assembly

Once cleaned and inspected, with new clutch parts, arrange the parts on your work bench with the two sections of the differential at the center.

**1** Position each half of the case on a workbench with the clutch well down, next to the bench surface.

**2** Place the clutch plates and discs in their proper sequence and orientation in each half of the case.

*Place the two halves of the case side by side and pile the clutches and discs in front of each half. Each clutch pile should be the same. Then install each clutch pile into half of the case.*

3 Place the side gears into their side gear retainers.

*Place the side gear retainer on top of the clutch pack. Be sure that the teeth of both parts are mated properly.*

4 Insert the splines on the back side of the side gear retainers through the splines of the clutch discs.

5 Locate the aligning pin through one axle shaft thrust spacer. Assemble the pinion cross-shafts on the aligning pin. Install the axle shaft thrust spacer on the lock pin and pinion shaft and tap it into place.

6 Install the four pinion gears onto the cross-shafts.

*Install the four pinion gears onto the cross-shaft.*

7 Install pinion shaft and pinion assembly into the ring gear half of the case.

*Place the cross-shaft assembly on top of the side gear and mesh the teeth of the two parts.*

*The pinion gear assembly has been installed onto the lower half's side gear and clutch assembly. Now the upper side gear built up on top before the second half is flipped over. The upper clutch is built up in the top half similar to the lower half, before the flip.*

8 Slide the cap half of the case over the edge of the workbench and insert one finger up through the assembly to hold it together. Turn the cap assembly over, holding everything in place. Place the cap assembly on the ring gear half, lining up the scribe marks made at disassembly.

*The two halves must mate-up. The V-notch in the case and the downward V-shaft (on right) need to match while the upward V-notch in the case and the upward V-shaft (on left) should also match.*

*Before inserting any screws, the pinion assembly cross has to be installed in the proper V-slot and the scribed marks must line up.*

9 Make sure the scribe marks on each differential case half are aligned. Install the differential case bolts and turn it in several full revolutions.

10 Insert the axle shafts from the vehicle to align the splines inside the differential. Make sure the axle shafts engage the side gear splines.

11 With the axle shafts installed, center the cross-shafts between the two ramp surfaces in the differential case. Tighten the differential case bolts evenly by alternately turning the opposite bolts until all are tightened to 45 ft-lbs. To keep the splines of the side gear and clutch plates in exact alignment during the tightening process, move the axle shafts back and forth as the bolts are being tightened. After assembly, slight misalignments of the splines can be corrected by moving the axle shafts back and forth until free. Remove the axle shafts.

## Two-Piece Trac-Lok Sure-Grip

The 1969-and-up Trac-Lok Sure-Grip differential and its internal parts are serviced as an assembly only. This Trac-Lok was used to the mid-1980s when the original supplier sold its manufacturing arm. Similar units are now built by the aftermarket company Auburn Gear. The Sure-Grip design is a cone-style design, and the case is a two-piece construction. The window in the side of the case allows you to see two small coil springs inside the unit (it looks somewhat like an Eaton disc-style Sure-Grip). The unique feature is the direction of the bolts that hold the case together.

The disc-clutch style of unit discussed above uses a two-piece case with the bolt heads on the opposite end of the case from the ring gear flange. On this

*The differential case for the 1969 and newer limited-slip assemblies is also a two-piece unit. However, the attaching bolts go in the opposite direction. The ring gear bolts and the differential case bolts are both on the same side. The ring of differential bolts is inside the ring gear bolts.*

cone-style unit, the bolt-heads are on the same side as the ring gear bolts. On this style of differential case, the ring gear flange has two circles of bolts: the outer one for the actual ring gear bolts and the inner one for the differential case bolts.

## One-Piece Dana and AMC 20 Limited-Slip

The limited-slip Trac-Lok differential in both Dana axles and the AMC 20 axle is a disc-clutch design similar to the Chrysler Sure-Grip. However, this unit uses a one-piece differential case. The window in the side of the case is larger than usual to allow access to the hardware inside the case.

The marketing names for these various production units can be confusing, such as Trac-Lok used on two of them, Power-Lok used on one and referred to by the more general name of Sure-Grip or limited-slip. I am referring to this unit as the one-piece design to separate it from the others, which are two-piece units.

*This is a Dana 9¾-inch axle Trac-Lok. Note that its name is cast into the top surface.*

## One-Piece Dana and AMC 20 Limited-Slip Disassembly

1 Remove the ring gear and differential assembly from the carrier housing.

2 Install one axle shaft in a soft-jaw vise. The splined end needs to face upward and tighten the vise. The axle shaft's end

should stick up 2¾ inches above the top of the vise, so the axle shaft does not enter the side gear and interfere with the special tool or spacer block. Use caution that the jaws of the vise do not grip on the axle splines.

*The ring gear has been removed with the heads of the screws pointing upward. The secondary ring gear is still on.*

*In disassembling the one-piece differential cases, it can be advantageous to place an axle shaft in a vise vertically and place the differential assembly on it. Here the end of the shaft can just be seen inside the differential opening.*

**3** Set the differential case on the axle shaft with the ring gear bolt-heads up. The case should slip part way over the splines on the axle shaft.

*Once the ring gear has been removed with the case in this position, flip the assembly over. Remember that the pinions, side gears, and clutch (if used) all come out though this window in the side of the case.*

**4** Place shop towels under the ring gear to protect the ring gear when it is removed, if not done earlier. Remove the ring gear bolts with a wrench or socket and discard.

**5** Remove the ring gear from the differential case using a rawhide (non-metallic) hammer.

**6** There are a few differences between the Dana and AMC Trac-Lok differentials. On the Dana version, drive out the lock pin using a long, thin drift.

*Locate the cross-shaft pin hole, which is drilled all the way through. Drive the pin out with a small punch.*

*The end of the cross-shaft is seen in the lower center of the photo. The end of the pin is sticking up directly above the cross-shaft hole.*

On the AMC version, turn the differential case over (ring gear flange facing downward) and re-mount it on the axle shaft. Using two screwdrivers, disengage and remove the snap rings from the pinion cross-shaft. Use caution because snap rings like to jump. Wear safety glasses to prevent eye injury.

**7** Remove the differential case from the axle shaft and remove the ring gear. Re-mount the case in the opposite position on the axle shaft, ring gear flange facing downward.

**8** Remove the pinion cross-shaft using a hammer and brass drift. Sometimes the cross-shaft slides out easily but often requires a firmer use of the hammer.

*Once the pin is removed, drive out the (horizontal) cross-shaft.*

**9** The Dana Trac-Lok differentials are identified with numbers stamped on the barrel of the case. The date of manufacture is stamped as month, day, and year. Above the manufacture date is the complete assembly part number. Record these numbers.

**10** To remove the two pinion gears, a special tool is required. Both Dana

*Once the chisels are removed, turn the side gear to bring the pinion into the window so it can be removed. In some cases, you can re-insert the cross-shaft into its bore (case only) and use it for leverage to turn the case which rolls the pinion into the window.*

*In a one-piece limited-slip differential, such as the Dana and AMC 20 units, the Belleville washer in each clutch pack keeps too much pressure on the pinions to allow removal. You can use a fancy compressor tool, but you can do the same job using two chisels, one inserted from each direction. The side gears are oriented top and bottom. The two chisels have to be thicker than the distance between the two side gears. Once compressed, tap the thrust washers out from behind the pinion gears. Then remove the chisels.*

and AMC axles use this special tool on their limited-slip assemblies. They both call it a "forcing screw" tool. It reaches in through the axle shaft access hole on the differential case and the side gear and has two plates that push on the side gears with the threaded adjuster, turned by a socket wrench. This tool pushes the side gears apart by compressing the Bellville washers in the limited-slip clutch pack.

The special tool can be expensive and hard to find. You can accomplish the

same thing using two chisels by inserting one from each side. They need to be slightly thicker than the opening or gap between the two side gears.

Once compressed, remove the pinion gear thrust washers. Push out using .030-inch shim stock. Using a long heavy-duty bar, rotate the side gears or case until the pinion gears appear in the case's window. Remove the pinion gears as they appear. Lift them out (one at a time) by hand through the access window. It may be necessary to adjust the tension on the Belleville washers using the special tool before the gears/case can be rotated.

Rotate the side gear to move the pinions into position. If required, insert an axle shaft into the side gear and use it to turn the gear itself. You only need to turn one side gear to get the pinion gears to move into position. In some cases, you can use the cross-shaft inserted back into its bore, only in the case itself, to gain

leverage to move the case, which turns the gear (just the upper one, because the axle shaft stays fixed).

**11** Hold the upper clutch pack and side gear with one hand and remove the special tool.

**12** Remove the upper side gear and its clutch pack. Keep the clutch pack stack of plates and discs intact and in exactly the same position while they are being removed.

**13** Remove the differential case from the axle shaft. Invert the case with the ring gear flange up and remove the lower side gear and its clutch pack from the case.

**14** Remove the retainer clips from each clutch pack to allow the separation of the plates and discs.

# One-Piece Dana and AMC 20 Limited-Slip Inspection

**1** If any member of either clutch pack shows evidence of excessive wear or scoring, the complete clutch pack must be replaced on both sides. There are two types of pieces to the clutch pack: the radial-groove clutch plate, which has two tabs, and the concentric groove disc, which has no tabs. One Belleville washer goes next to the side gear.

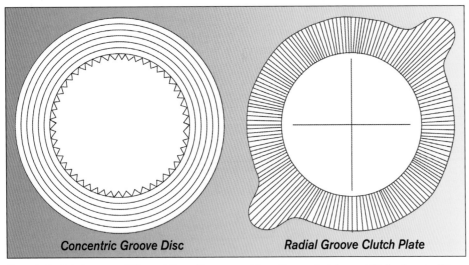

Concentric Groove Disc · Radial Groove Clutch Plate

*Trac-Lok clutches are different from those used in a Power-Lok in an 8¾-inch axle. The plate has two tabs instead of four, plus radial grooves. The disc is similar, except that the Dana units use concentric grooves in the face. The AMC unit is the same as the Dana unit.*

*Many limited-slip differentials use a spring and plate mechanism to apply the frictional pressure in the unit. These springs and plate can be seen in the window and the case is a one-piece unit. A Yukon unit is shown.*

*On this style of unit, you can use a spring compressor, but it is easier to tap them out with a hammer. They come out through the big window, so tap on them from the opposite side. You should also cover the exit side of the differential with shop towels so the springs don't fly away as they exit the case. They are re-assembled using channel locks to compress the springs. Stock-rate springs, such as 200, and high-rate springs, such as 400 and 800, are available. The high-rate springs are more difficult to compress and install.*

*Two styles of discs are in the clutch unit. One is round (top left) and one has two ears (top right). A Belleville washer (bottom) provides the force to make the frictional clutch work.*

*Use a caliper micrometer to measure the thickness of the clutch plates/discs. Measure each of the clutch plates individually. Write in your notebook the thickness of the old ones being replaced and new ones being installed.*

*Once you measure them individually, then measure them as a clutch pack. Record in notebook.*

2 Check the gear teeth for extreme wear or cracks. If one gear is required to be replaced due to wear, both side gears, both pinion gears, and the washers should all be replaced.

3 If excessive wear is noted on the cross-shaft, replace it.

4 If wear is evident on any retainer clip, replace all four clips.

5 Replace the differential case if scoring, wear, or metal pickup is evident on the machined surfaces.

## One-Piece Dana and AMC 20 Limited-Slip Assembly

1 Lubricate all differential components with the specified (by manufacturer) axle lubricant (limited-slip rated).

2 Install the replacement or original clutch pack components in the same position/order as removed. Alternate plate and disc, starting with a plate (with tabs). The Belleville washer (dished) goes next to the side gear, dish away from the teeth. This unit has only one Belleville washer per side. A Belleville washer is dished; it does not lay flat on a flat surface. Placed on a flat surface, the outer part (large diameter) is elevated. In this configuration, the small diameter goes toward the gear teeth and the large diameter goes away from the teeth.

3 Install the clutch retainer clips on the tabs (ears) of the clutch plates. Push by hand on the two clips (because there are two ears on the plates) per clutch pack. Be careful that some plates or discs do not slip and misalign. Be sure that the retainer clips are completely assembled and seated on the tabs of the plates (two per pack).

4 Install the clutch packs onto the side gear splines and install the lower assembly into the case. With the differential sitting on end insert the clutch pack through the access window. Keep the clutch pack assembled on the side gear splines and keep the retainer clips completely seated in the differential case pockets. To prevent the clutch pack from falling out of the case, hold them in place with your hand while mounting the case on the axle shaft. The lower clutch pack is easy to install but the upper one must be held securely in place; it may take a practice run or two to be successful.

Caution: When installing the differential case onto the axle shaft, be sure that the splines of the side gears are aligned with those of the axle shaft. The clutch pack must still be properly assembled in the differential case after installing the case onto the axle shaft.

5 Mount the case assembly on the axle shaft. Note that the axle shaft is mounted in the soft-jaw vise vertically at same height as at disassembly.

6 Install the special gear installation tool on top of the lower side gear. Install the remaining (upper) clutch pack and side gear.

7 Install the rest of the tool while holding the upper side gear assembly in place by hand. Install both pinion gears into the case. Hold the pinion gears in place by hand.

8 Tighten the tool to compress the Belleville washers and provide clearance between the pinion gear teeth and the side gears. Using a heavy-duty bar or tool handle, rotate the side gears or case to rotate the pinion gears into their proper location.

9 Align the shaft bore holes in both pinion gears with the bores in the differential case. Lubricate both sides of the pinion gear thrust washers with axle lube and install the thrust washers. Use a small, thin, straight-blade screwdriver to push the washers into place. Tighten or loosen the tool to permit thrust washer installation. The holes in the thrust washers and the pinion gears must line up exactly with the holes in the case.

**10** Remove the tool.

**11** Lubricate the pinion cross-shaft. Install the cross-shaft with a hammer and brass drift (if required). For Dana axles, use a thin, long punch at disassembly and measure 1¾ inches from the end of the punch. Wrap a piece of tape around the punch. Install the lock pin (ring gear flange facing downward) and hit with hammer and punch until the tape on the punch is lined up with the case.

For the AMC 20, install the two snap rings onto the cross-shaft inside the differential case.

**12** Remove the case assembly from the axle shaft and install the ring gear onto the case using new ring gear bolts. Never reuse the original ring gear bolts.

## Aftermarket Choices

Whether the differential is called a limited-slip, or Sure-Grip or locking differential, the aftermarket makes unit that fits that description. It could be based on clutches and discs or cones clutches or any number of styles of lockers from manual to electric and more seem to be introduced on a regular basis.

### Limited-Slip

Aftermarket manufacturers offer a large variety of limited-slip differentials. While many of these units are similar to some of the production designs discussed above, the parts are unique as individual components but they can be swapped-in as complete assemblies. These units are sent back to the manufacturer to be serviced/rebuilt. The obvious exception is units that use clutch discs.

The aftermarket does not offer an open or conventional type because this style of differential can spin one wheel and isn't used in performance applications. Earlier in this chapter, these differentials were divided into six general categories: limited-slip cone, limited-slip disc, standard locker, manual-control locker, torque-sensing, and spool. To them we need to add two sub-categories: mini-spool and conversion locker. Each unit offers a different approach to limiting the slip between one axle and the other, or how they divide the torque between the two wheels.

Along with the differences in function, there are differences in cost and ease of installation. Production units are no longer available as assemblies from OEM outlets, so you may need a similar unit from the aftermarket. For the rebuildable production units, service parts are still readily available from your local auto parts dealer or speed shop. Many different types of limited-slip differentials are currently offered. One type is limited-slip disc units, which are based on a friction clutch (discs and plates) similar to the 1962–1969 Chrysler Sure-Grip (two-piece) and the AMC 20 and Dana limited-slip (one-piece) units.

Strange Engineering and US Gear offer limited-slip differentials under the Torq-Line brand. They are designed as direct replacements for open or limited-slip differentials. The housings are cast

The basic limited-slip differential is typically used on the street or street/strip cars. In these situations, the clutch units are the most popular.

*The limited-slip differential prevents wheel slip by transferring almost 50 percent of the torque from the slipping wheel to the wheel with good traction. Carbon-fiber clutch packs and heavy-duty springs help redirect the torque to the wheel receiving traction. This unit is fully rebuildable and chatter free, but applications are limited relative to the axles in this book.*

*These Powr-Lok by Yukon units are designed to replace the 1960s clutch-type limited-slip units, such as the Chrysler 8¾-inch axle. Yukon units have a two-piece housing and makes these units for other applications. Belleville washers provide the main static force.*

*This Dura-Grip by Yukon is a four-spring, clutch-style limited-slip. The units are known for their reliability and their rebuild-ability. They use heavy-duty, chrome-moly spider gears and composite clutches. Four small coil springs are visible here in the case's side window. These provide the main static force.*

*This is the new clutch-style unit from Richmond Gear called Powertrax Grip. It uses a large S-shaped spring rather than the smaller coiled springs.*

*This Auburn Gear unit is very similar to the 1969-and-newer Chrysler Sure-Grip, which features a cone-clutch design. Small coil springs provide the friction force. It is engineered to provide smooth torque-sensing operation. The innovative cone-clutch design transfers power to the high-traction wheel for quick acceleration and tight cornering. This Auburn Gear Pro Series features polished cones and a tighter spring pressure (more friction force) for a quicker lockup. This unit is more suitable for drag racing applications than the standard unit.*

from nodular steel and the side gears and pinions are made from nickel steel. They are completely rebuildable. At the time of this writing, applications are limited relative to the Dana 30 and 44, but the company is starting to offer other axles.

These limited-slip cone differential units are based on a cone-style friction unit similar to the 1969 and newer Chrysler Sure-Grip. The main static force is provided by small coil springs.

Strange Engineering offers standard cone-type limited-slips that are ideal as direct replacements for production units. Applications may be limited.

Richmond Gear has recently introduced a new line of clutch limited-slip differentials called Grip by Powertrax. These have a forged steel case and carbon clutch discs. In the center, between the two side gears, is a large S-shaped spring.

### Locker

A locker does not use traditional frictional clutches, disc or cone. The locker works through a set of locking dog clutches. The locked aspect keeps both axles locked together except while cornering when the dog clutch unlocks to allow normal speed differentiation.

*Without the cut-away section used for display purposes, the assembled cone-style Auburn unit looks pretty much like other spring-powered limited-slip units.*

*The Detroit Locker is a two-piece unit and bolts together using eight screws, threaded from the opposite side from the ring gear. It maximizes traction by delivering 100 percent of the torque and power to both driving wheels. The Detroit Locker is designed to keep both wheels in a constant drive mode and has the ability to automatically allow wheel speed differentiation when required (cornering). It has a great reputation for durability and is maintenance free.*

*The Yukon Grizzly Locker is a mechanical positive-locking differential. It features a case made of 8620 high-strength steel with its internal hardware made of forged 8620 steel. The inner clutch teeth have an improved design with a large base radius, which improves strength. Larger teeth help avoid breakage from shock loading. They are used in drag, circle track, and off-road racing.*

*Strange Engineering's Strange Trac is a newer design that's mainly for racing applications. At this time, applications are limited relative to the axles in this book.*

For many years, this group consisted of just units that were air operated. However, a few years ago, units were added that were operated electrically, so the category was split in two.

*Conversion-Style Locker:* These units are much smaller than standard lockers,

*The ARB is an air-operated locking differential that's manually controlled. The advantage of the ARB Air Locker is that it has a pneumatically operated locking system inside the differential. It combines the straight-line traction benefits of lockers and spools with the street driveability of an open differential. An onboard air compressor, supplied by ARB and matched for this application, supplies the air pressure to the differential to power the system.*

and designed to fit inside a standard open differential. Ease of installation and low cost are the basic features of this group.

*Manual-Control Locker—Air:* The slip limiting function of these lockers is similar to that of regular lockers. But the difference is in the way that the locking function is activated. While regular lockers lock up automatically, this group is controlled manually, at the switch of a button.

*Manual-Control Locker—Electric:* This group is very similar to air-operated lockers except that they replace the air operated function and the associated compressor with an electric operation. It is by far the newest category in limited slip differentials and seems to be the most active at this time.

The Yukon Zip Locker is an air-operated locking differential designed for extreme off-road use. It features a case made of 8620 steel with internal hardware made of 4320 high-strength steel to provide maximum strength against failure. Each unit comes with small parts for installation and operation, such as air line and fittings, seal housing, operation switch with cover(s), etc. A variety of air sources can be used for operating this locker.

The Auburn Gear ECTED (Electronically Controlled Traction Enhancing Differential) offers the ability to go from a limited-slip differential to a locker on demand (flip a switch). The device can be applied at any road speed. It can be used in front-axle applications.

The Detroit Electrac functions as a heavy-duty limited-slip differential and a driver-activated fully locked performance differential. This is a fairly new product so applications may be somewhat limited at first.

### Torque-Sensing

These units are often called torque biasing designs. They are gear-driven and very complicated looking. These designs do not have clutches (standard or dog-style) or other couplers. They should be sent back to the manufacturer to be serviced or repaired. They offer very smooth operation and excellent differential action.

### Spool

The spool design solidly locks both axles together all the time, so there is no differential function and both rear wheels always turn at the same speed. Spools are typically made of steel, lightweight steel or aluminum. Lightweight steel is similar to regular steel, except that the outside diameter is scalloped (by machine) and many lightening holes are drilled inside the ring gear index. Strong heavy-duty axles are highly recommended. Most axle and differential manufacturers make spools, but no single company makes spools for all axles.

The mini-spool is similar to a full spool, but it is designed to fit into a standard open differential case. This is a relative new spool category and there are currently limited applications.

## Cross-Shaft Hardware

The cross-shaft is in the center of the differential, and it is part of open differentials and Sure-Grip/limited-slip differentials. The cross-shaft supports the two pinion gears, one on each end. In some limited-slip differentials, two cross-shafts

The Torsen units were some of the first torque-sensing differentials. The original unit was called the Type 1 and the company has now introduced the Type 2. Both make very good units in the front position of 4WD or FWD vehicles.

*The cross-shaft (or pinion shaft) is a solid rod with a slot across one end, which helps align the shaft as you install it. A lock pin is placed in a small through hole on the opposite end to keep the shaft in place. Note the flats on the top and bottom ends of the shaft for oiling purposes.*

*The Dana/AMC 20 style clutch discs/plates; one is round and the other has two ears. The 4 clips at the bottom clip over the outside of the clutch pack to help align the discs and keep it together. The clips snap into place.*

*A small, two-piece pin holds the dual cross-shaft together. The 1969-and-earlier Sure-Grip assembly uses this dual cross-shaft, which has four pinion gears. Notice that the two cross-shafts are the same but one assembly, the machined V-shape on the end of the shaft points up on the end to the lower right but points down on the one to the lower left (not visible in photo).*

are set in the shape of an X while the double cross-shaft has four pinions. Whether two or four pinions, they mate with the side gears, left and right. The cross-shaft (single) is typically held in place by a pin. Not all lockers have a cross-shaft.

*The side gear (left) is larger than the pinion gear (right). In this case, the side gear has 16 teeth while the pinion gear has 11 teeth. The side gear is splined to accept the axle shaft while the pinion gear is not.*

### Pinions and Side Gears

The pinions (two or four), must mate with the differential's side gears; one to the right, and one to the left. These parts should be checked for wear, cracks, or chipping. If there is a problem, the pinions and side gears should be replaced as a set or team. This is every bit as important on an open rear end as it is on a limited-slip differential.

### Clutches and Discs

Not all differentials use clutches; however, clutch-style units based on clutch discs are the most popular. In each style, there may be flat ones and dished ones. These units are rebuildable. The friction surfaces (discs) do wear out and will require service.

### Cross-Shafts

The cross-shaft is in the center of the differential. If the axles use C-clips, the cross-shaft is one of the first parts removed. Similar to the pinion and side gears, these parts should be checked for wear, cracks, or scuffing. If the cross-shaft is worn excessively or damaged it should be replaced.

Cross-shafts are used in C-clip axles, such as the Chrysler 8¼- and 9¼-inch

axles with a low gears. The situation doesn't occur on a 3.55 or 3.91:1, but it does apply on the 4.56 or 4.88:1. When the ring gear is thick, the cross-shaft does not come out of the differential. When the overall ratio is low (numerically high number), the ratio set uses a small-diameter pinion gear that has fewer teeth and therefore a smaller diameter. To mate-up with the small pinion gear, the ring on these ratios must be thicker. Ratios in the 4s have teeth on the ring gear that actually block the cross-shaft hole in the case.

One solution to this situation is a special cross-shaft which has a notch in it. Rotate the notch toward the axle shaft

*The double cross-shaft is actually two identical cross-shafts.*

*One-piece housings typically use a single cross-shaft and two pinions. A two-piece housing (shown) can have dual cross-shafts, four pinions, and two side gears.*

*A large hex-head bolt-style pin replaces the small pressed-in pin on the new limited-slip unit.*

end and push the axle end into the notch and remove the C-clip. Then repeat the process with the notch turned the other way for the opposite axle shaft. This allows the C-clips to be removed and installed in these big number ratios. The trick is that this special cross-shaft must be installed before the ring gear or you will have problems.

Aftermarket ring gear manufacturers know this and include a special cross-shaft with the ring gear set. The trick is that it must be installed into the case before the ring gear is installed. The cross-shaft is typically installed after the

*The ring gear bolts tend to be large and short. They use fine threads. In general, they should not be re-used. Discard at removal. Note the Chrysler axles use left-hand threaded bolts. Note the large "L" on the head.*

*The two-piece Chrysler Sure-Grip differentials also used left-hand thread bolts. The L for "left-hand" is below the LE, which is the supplier ID.*

*Ring gear bolts are large and short. They use fine threads. In general, they should not be re-used. Discard at removal. The Chrysler 8¾-inch axles use left-hand ring gear bolts. Notice the large "L" raised on the head of the bolt.*

ring gear. If you currently have a low gear ratio for one of these C-clip axles, and you swap it for a high-ratio gear set (better economy or less engine speed on the freeway), remember to keep this special cross-shaft with the gear set.

### Pins

A pin (or lock) holds the single cross-shaft in place. The pin must be removed before the cross-shaft. In some cases, the pin is pressed in and must be tapped out with a hammer and brass drift. In some cases, the pin is actually a screw threaded into the case. The double cross-shaft is removed by taking the two halves of the Sure-Grip differential case apart and removing parts in sequence down to the pinion cross-shaft assembly.

### Bolts

Short ring gear screws and long differential screws are two types of screws that go into the differential. The short ring gear screws hold the ring gear to the differential flange. They should not be re-used. Always replace ring-gear screws when the ring gear is replaced.

The differential screws are only used on two-piece differential cases. (The open differential is a one-piece unit so they are not used.) Many Sure-Grip/limited-slip assemblies are based on a two-piece case. In these two-piece applications, the differential screws are quite long.

In some locker designs, there may be more than two pieces to the differential case. On the conversion-style lockers and the mini-spools designed to fit inside the one-piece open differential, this simple definition for differential screws may not apply.

*The bolts holding the two-piece differential together are quite long. This Power-Lok from the 8¾-inch axle has bolts that go into the housing from the non-ring gear side/end. The 1969-and-newer Chrysler Trac-Lok used a two-piece housing, but the attaching bolts were threaded-in from the ring gear side. This creates a second bolt circle, inside the ring gear bolt circle.*

# RING-AND-PINION GEARS

The rear axle ring-and-pinion are discussed as a gear ratio—one number. These ratios are numbers such as 4.10, 3.91, 3.73, 3.54, 3.31, etc. Technically speaking, this number is the ratio between the number of teeth on the driven gear or ring and the number of teeth on the drive gear or pinion. For example, if the ring has 41 teeth and the pinion has 10 teeth, the ratio is 4.10:1. When the axle or wheel makes one full revolution the ratio is 4.10:1 and should be listed as 4.10:1, but this is rarely done. What this means is that the driveshaft turns 4.10

times before the wheel or axle makes one full (or complete) revolution. It is easy to mark the wheel and driveshaft and count one full revolution of the tire.

The second aspect of rings and pinions that is generally discussed is the material that they are made from. They are all made of steel but certain performance/racing applications require more strength. The performance manufacturers offer these high-strength gears under the general term of pro-gears and they are made from very high-strength steel called 9310.

*This is a basic ring-and-pinion. The number of teeth on each determines the axle ratio. For example, 41 teeth on the ring gear and 11 teeth on the pinion make for a 3.91:1 ratio (41 ÷ 11 = 3.91). The ring gear has a basic outside diameter, such as 7.25, 8.75, or 9.75 inches, etc., which determines the size of the axle and its load-carrying capacity.*

Ring-and-pinions are always sold in sets and should always be kept together which means the components cannot be mixed or swapped individually. There are many actual gear ratios, but since it is the result of dividing two whole numbers such as 41 and 10, 9, or 11, you end up with numbers such as 4.10, 4.55, or 3.73. Gears ratios tend to range from around 2.20 to 5.0, 6.0, or in some cases even 7.0. One of the oddities in discussing gear ratios is that commonly referred to high gears are numerically low numbers such as 2.20 or 2.50, while commonly referred to low gears are numerically high numbers such as 4.56 or 5.12.

In a typical RWD vehicle, the engine and transmission rotate along the centerline (fore and aft) of the vehicle. To utilize the engine's power to move the vehicle, the direction must be changed from left to right (laterally). Power comes to the rear by the driveshaft and then to the left and right by the axle. The rear axle and the ring-and-pinion change the direction of power 90 degrees so that the rotation of the wheel/tire can be used to move the vehicle.

Because of the mechanical ratio, the ring-and-pinion also increase the amount of torque that is available at the rear wheels.

# Ring-and-Pinion Sources

The basic ring-and-pinion is manufacturered by a special machining process. While most ring-and-pinions are based on OEM (original equipment manufacturer) axle designs, the OEM service outlets (car/truck/Jeep dealers) no longer stock ratios for these axles. Most of these axles were used in production vehicles in the 1960s, 1970s, and 1980s. You could also argue that the production ratios tended toward 2.9 while the desired ratios might be 3.9. In either case, the aftermarket offers new ring-and-pinions in the desired ratios. Current manufacturers include Auburn Gear, Yukon Gear, Motive Gear, US Gear, Richmond Gear, and USA Standard Gear. All these manufacturers don't always make all ratios for all axle designs.

There are many outlets for ring-and-pinions, including the two large catalog centers: Jegs and Summit. There are also large, well-known distribution centers, such as Precision Gear, The Ring and Pinion Shop, Drive Train Specialists (DTS), and Randy's Ring and Pinion. They generally offer ratios from more than one source.

Additionally, the performance aftermarket manufacturers offer high-strength gears in stronger material. These high-strength gears are often called "pro" gears and are generally made of 9310 steel. These gears are made in the same ratios as standard gears except that most of these parts are made in the 4 and 5 ratio numbers rather than in the 3s.

Some aftermarket companies service all the axles discussed in this book. However, they do not service all the same ratios that were used in production units. Performance and racing customers have made the bigger numbers more popular. Production used ratios of 2.2 to 3.9 or 4.1:1 with an average of around 2.9/3.0 average. The aftermarket offers ratios between 3.0 and 5.0:1.

---

To best use this torque increase, drag racers install lower gears (from 3.5 to 4.5:1). This ratio change increases the torque at the tire and causes the tire to spin or accelerate the vehicle harder. On the other end, it also increases the engine speed (RPM) at the finish line (1/8 or 1/4 mile). Going in the opposite direction, from a 3.5 to a 2.5, lowers the amount of torque but also lowers the engine speed at the finish line. The lower RPM helps increase fuel economy and lowers noise levels at highway speeds. Today there are overdrive add-on units and overdrive transmissions that offer a .7 overdrive ratio (some are as high as .65 or .78). These overdrive ratios offer the choice of having a low gear (4.30 or so) at the track or off-road event and the 3.0 ratio for the highway cruise or trip home.

For a variety of reasons, ratios in the mid-4s are popular in racing and off-roading. This means that ratios from 4.10 to 4.88:1 are readily available in the aftermarket, but rarely used in production vehicles. The 3.55 and 3.91:1 are good dual-purpose ratios and are very popular on the street.

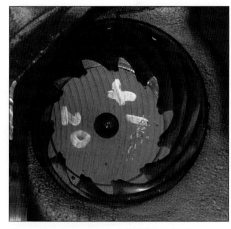

Once the ring gear and differential case have been removed, you can easily see the end of the pinion. You can also count the teeth on the pinion; 11 in this case.

### Gear Teeth

Each rear axle design has certain gear teeth numbers that are popular because the resulting ratio is widely used.

*The ring gear is bolted directly to the differential case. This limited-slip differential has a two-piece case with eight bolts. You can count the number of teeth if there is any question about the actual ratio.*

---

*The pinion gear for a high numerical axle ratio is more than 4. Note the small diameter of the gear head relative to the stem size.*

*The pinion gear size for a low numerical axle ratio is about 3.0. Note the large diameter of the gear head relative to the stem size.*

There's more to the pinion than just the number of teeth; it has 9, 10, or 11. The pinion shaft itself has a diameter that ranges from 1⅜ to 1⅞ inches. The end farthest from the gear teeth is round and has a fine thread that holds the pinion yoke nut. Just before the threads, 26 to 29 splines are cut into the shaft. Make sure you use a pinion yoke that is designed for your axle/pinion.

This aspect only comes into play if you are swapping parts. In addition, the aftermarket makes yokes for almost everything.

Similar to the pinion, the ring gear's identity comes from its number of teeth. Each ring gear has a basic diameter, which is directly related to the axle design's name, such as 8¾- or 9¾-inch. The ring gear is also held onto the

*Add-on overdrive units are becoming popular and readily available for most transmissions, both automatics and manuals (a Gear-Vendors unit is shown). Typically these add-on units replace the existing output shaft and housing, which also hold the overdrive gear set. This arrangement makes the transmission much larger and generally requires the driveshaft to be shortened. A shorter driveshaft can cause problems with higher U-joint angles and that situation might require a rear CV-joint. (See Chapter 10 for details.)*

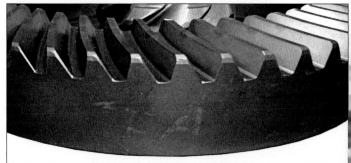

*The ring gear on the left is quite thin from the bottom of the teeth to the back of the ring gear. Therefore, this gear is for a high ratio, perhaps around 3.0, which has a large pinion head diameter. The ring gear on the right is for a low ratio, perhaps over 4.0, and therefore, it has a small pinion head diameter.*

differential by a number of bolts, which can be 8, 10, or 12.

Some applications may need very large axle ratios. In some cases, the gear set for a special ratio can be extremely expensive. A fairly common and inexpensive option is to run the transmission in second or third gear rather than high gear, which is direct, or 1:1.

For example, 6.75:1 ratios are hard to find, but if you have a 4.5:1 ratio, and use the typical second gear transmission ratio of 1.50:1, you have a 6.75:1 final drive. This approach isn't popular in drag racing or off-roading because racers tend to use all of the transmission gears during a race/event.

In the past few years, add-on overdrives have become popular and more available. These add-on units usually replace the transmission's output shaft and housing. The overdrive unit allows the vehicle to have low gears (numerically high number) for the event and yet low engine speeds (RPM) for the drive home. There are also transmissions, both automatic and manual, that have overdrive ratios as the top gear.

In the past few years, perhaps since the early 1990s, many RWD vehicles, both cars and trucks have anti-lock brakes. Part of this braking system is installed into the rear axle. The key part in the rear end is the anti-lock sensor ring, which sits behind the ring gear in the differential.

On newer vehicles that have anti-lock brakes, the speed sensor is mounted on the top of the center carrier offset somewhat to the driver's side. The sensor relays information to the anti-lock brake computer through a wire that feeds into the body's wiring harness.

## Off-Road Ratios

The typical off-road application can almost always use more torque but the main reason for more a smaller gear ratio (bigger number) in off-roading is that bigger tires are used. Many off-road Jeeps and trucks use 33-inch tires and the popular ratio with this setup is a 4.56:1 ratio. In the past couple model years, the Jeep Rubicon comes with a 4.10:1 ratio.

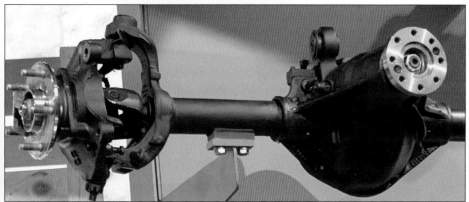

FWD axles are similar to standard rear axles. They are referred to as high-pinion axles, and in some cases, the pinion comes in high as if the axle were upside-down.

## Vehicle Performance

Obviously the gear set ratio is going to affect the vehicle's performance. The vehicle's weight, tire selection, and suspension has a lot to do with how it responds to a gear change. Another player in the performance equation is the engine itself and its torque and power curve. A few years ago, *Car Craft* magazine tested the effects of just a gear ratio

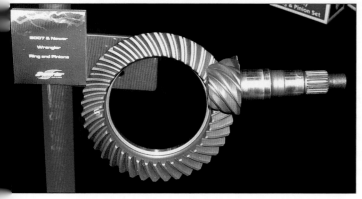

The standard pinion contact point for a typical ring gear is below its centerline. For a high-pinion assembly (shown), the contact point is above the centerline of the ring gear.

*An enlargement of typical RWD rear axle teeth shows that the outside edge of the ring is toward the bottom. As the teeth come down from the inside edge (top) of the ring, they swing toward the left.*

change and found that a change from a 3.0 to a 4.10:1 gained .6 second in quarter-mile ET. Every car is unique and this is just one test but it shows the potential.

## Reverse-Cut Gears

When an axle is installed in the front for a 4WD application, the actual gears are reverse cut. The ratio stays the same. Aftermarket companies label these gears as "reverse cut" gears. (See photo above middle.)

## Heat-Treat and Material

Because of the power that a gear set must transfer, rear axle gear sets have always been made from a good, high-strength steel. Rear axle gears must be strong and also hard to resist wear. Aftermarket gear sets are made from an upgrade in steel over the original.

Once you have defined the material, consider the heat-treat that is applied. All this metallurgy science makes it very hard to compare the mid-level gear sets. However, the best stuff is 9310. Manufacturers save this material for professional gear sets. These high-strength sets are generally called "pro" gears. The high-strength material is more expensive but also stronger for professional drag race applications.

*This enlargement of FWD axle teeth shows the outside edge is also toward the bottom. As the teeth come down from the inside edge (top) of the ring, they swing toward the right. The aftermarket calls these gears reverse-cut; they are only used in FWD applications.*

### Attaching Bolts

The right gear bolts hold the ring to the differential. Chrysler axles use left-hand (LH) threads, while AMCs and Danas use right-hand (RH) threads.

## Cross-Shafts and C-Clips

Cross-shafts are actually part of the differential; they fit inside the ring gear. On some lower ratios (big numbers) the special cross-shaft must be installed first, before the ring is installed.

*Some limited-slip differentials (shown) use a double cross-shaft. The round button in the center holds the two-piece cross-shaft together and also takes the axle's side thrust once assembled. (The standard open differential cross-shaft is a single, straight shaft.)*

*Ring gear bolts should not be re-used.*

The standard (or open) rear axle uses a single cross-shaft while the limited-slip differential (production-based) uses a two-piece or two cross-shafts.

## Special Differential Housings

The ring gear bolts to the differential case. As the gear ratio gets larger in number (going from 2.5 to 3.5 to 4.5, etc.), one major thing tends to happen—the pinion gear gets smaller (fewer teeth). With fewer teeth, the actual diameter gets smaller. To solve this problem, you have two options: the ring can get thicker or the mounting surface on the differential can move closer to the pinion. On all of these axles except the Chrysler 8¾ and the Chrysler 9¼-inch axles, there are two different differential cases. The actual ratio numbers where this switch occurs is unique to each axle design.

*C-clips fit into a groove cut in the end of each axle shaft. They also fit inside the side gear in a machined recess.*

# AXLE SHAFTS AND HOUSINGS

Early hot rodders and custom builders modified axle shafts and housings, and that is how the rear axle market for special products began. These fabricators started projects with salvage units from specific production cars. Some were selected for brute strength, such as the Dana/Chrysler 9¾-inch. Others were selected for specific ratios or limited-slip differentials. As the cars got faster, the tires got bigger.

At first the sanctioning bodies didn't allow modifications to the inside wheel wells, so racers flared the fenders. This made the cars look somewhat coke-bottle shaped. After a couple years, the rules were revised to allow inner wheel well modifications (no fender flares), and this created the need for narrowed axles. Racers started selecting the narrowest axles available, which were typically used on smaller cars with smaller engines (6s mostly, and some small V-8s). These units didn't hold up to the high horsepower of the big muscle car V-8s.

The real problem was the bigger tires. As the tires got bigger, the axle width needed to get narrower. Chrysler Performance Parts (soon to be called Direct Connection, and then Mopar Performance) began solving this problem by offering a narrowed Dana 60 axle, the 52½-inch. (Production widths at this time were 54.9 inches on the 1970 Belvedere/Coronet and 56.5 on the 1970 Barracuda/Challenger). When the new Pro Stock drag racing class was launched, the demand went up for more axles and narrower axles, so the 44-inch was introduced. The aftermarket started making modified versions of these basic narrowed axles and the axle market began to grow.

Measurements are taken over the entire length of the axle tubes. The drag slicks typical of high-horsepower cars in Super Stock at this time were about 12 inches wide; with Pro Stock they became more than 14 inches wide. The axle had to get narrower to allow for these bigger tires.

The axle housing primarily dictates the width of the axle, and as such, it gets modified in all narrowed axles. As the axle housing is narrowed, the axle shaft must also be narrowed (shortened).

In the past the axle housing wasn't given enough credit for the important job that it performs. It is a key player in transferring the engine's power from the ring gear and differential out to the wheels and tires, which move the vehicle. Even with this critical job, axle shafts are often overlooked or forgotten.

In the past 10 to 20 years, all this has changed and there are now many more options available for any car, truck, or Jeep for on-road performance or off-road competition.

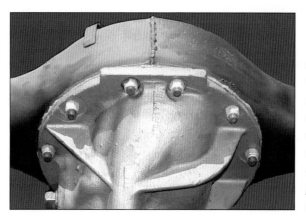

*The center section of the banjo-style axle removes toward the front (shown at bottom of photo). With a banjo-style axle, the ring-and-pinion are part of this assembly. The main housing (top of photo) is called the banjo and is a one-piece unit with no separate tubes pressed into the center.*

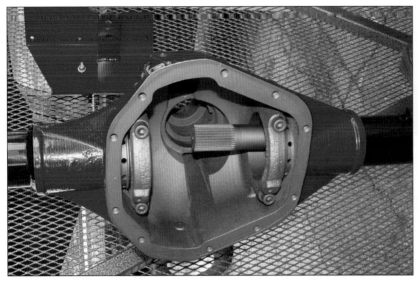

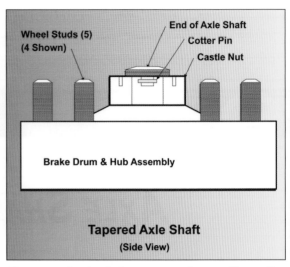

The axle's ring and pinion are removed from the rear on a carrier-tube axle. The cover bolts on the rear of the center housing. The axle shafts fit into the center housing. One two-bolt bearing cap on each side holds the differential and housing.

The tapered axle shaft uses a castle nut with a cotter pin on the end of the axle shaft. This is an old AMC 20 axle.

The typical axle shaft has splines on one end (to the right) and a large, round disc or flange on the other end (to the left). The flange has a five-bolt attaching pattern that matches the wheel's bolt circle. The straps toward each end are for display purposes only.

The AMC 20 rear axle uses tapered axle shafts. A large castle nut with a cotter pin hold the hub onto the axle shaft. Typically, a dust cover goes over the nut.

## Production Axle Shafts

There are two basic styles of production axle shafts: tapered and flanged. The flanged-style shaft is the more common and also very popular in racing and competitive events. Most production-based axle shafts are slightly under-cut just outboard from the splines. The typical performance/racing axle shaft has one constant diameter, which makes it somewhat stronger and stiffer.

### Tapered Axle Shafts

The steel axle shafts have a certain length and diameter. Splines are found on one end and a large disc on the other, which is typically called the flange. The AMC 20 and the early model Chrysler 8¾-inch axle (1964 and earlier) are a different design. These two axles have tapered axle shafts, which means that there is a large nut of the end of the shaft. The tapered axle shaft uses a hub. At this point, the two axles are no longer share a common design. The hub on the AMC 20 is splined to the tapered axle shaft while the 1964 and earlier Chrysler 8¾-inch uses a keyway to locate the hub on the tapered axle shaft.

The AMC 20s splined axle shafts seem to work fine, but the tapered axle

The flanged axle is the most popular style of axle. It has five studs pressed in, which matches the wheel's bolt circle. The pilot diameter in the center properly locates the wheel onto the axle.

*The axle shaft flange comes in many shapes. Some have 5 large holes spaced around five smaller holes (left). The smaller holes are for the wheel studs and the larger holes are for lightening. Some have larger lightening holes (right).*

shaft version of the Chrysler 8¾-inch axle is difficult to work on and is typically upgraded to the 1965 flanged Chrysler 8¾-inch axle—correct width, correct bolt circle, and it bolts to the suspension.

All of the rest of the Chrysler, Dana axles are flanged units. A very few of the newer AMC 20 axles also had a flange, but they are had to find.

### Flanged Axle Shafts

All of the 1965 and newer Chrysler 8¾-inch axles used flanged axle shafts as did all of the Chrysler 7¼-, 8¼- and 9¼-inch axles. The Dana axles also use flanged axle shafts. They are easy to identify because there is no large nut in the center of the axle shaft's bolt circle. Rather than a nut, the center of the flanged axle shaft has a 2- to 3-inch centering pilot.

### Splines

On the other end of the axle shaft from the flange are the splines. The number of splines, a key issue on this end of the shaft, is not a constant over-all of the axles, but varies with a specific axle design and basic shaft diameter. For example, the AMC 20 has 29 teeth. The Chrysler 8¾-inch has 30 teeth while the Dana 60 may have 35 teeth. Keep in

*The flange (right) on the axle shaft sits outboard of the axle shaft bearing, retainer, and seal. The bearing fits inside the axle tube end and the retainer and seal bolt up to the axle tube's flange (left).*

*The axle shaft has splines on one end (left). The number of splines is important because it must match the internal splines on the side gears in the differential. You can tell that this is a production axle because it is undercut to the right of the splines and it gets larger in diameter toward the right end. (A race axle shaft is straight; with the same diameter all the way across.)*

*Some carrier-tube axles use the C-clip method of axle shaft retention. The C-clip fits in the notch cut in the end of the shaft (right). C-clips are used on Chrysler 8¼- and 9¼-inch axles. Some Dana axles also use C-clips.*

mind that these are very general statements and there are exceptions.

There are Dana 60 axles with 30-teeth splines. The splines on the end of the axle shaft must match with the splines in the side gears inside the axle's differential. Typically, the aftermarket manufacturer knows the number of splines on your axle by the make of axle (AMC, Chrysler, Dana), and the year it was produced.

With the standard axle spline, the larger the number of splines, the larger the spline diameter is. This larger diameter would allow the axle shaft to be stronger. Big axles, such as the Dana 60, have 35 splines. However, larger shafts and slightly smaller axles have slightly smaller splines and therefore smaller diameter axle shafts.

### Wheel Studs

You never think much about wheel studs until you try to put the wheel on the axle and it doesn't fit. The most common problem is length. Production wheel studs are designed for production steel wheels. Many aluminum wheels and racing wheels are thicker in the center and require longer studs. To change studs, the old ones must be pressed out and the new ones pressed in.

If new axles are being used, you can install the correct longer studs before assembly into the axle. Some of the longer studs have a special rounded end. This feature tends to help with wheel nut installation.

### Four-Wheel Drives

The axle that is used is the front of the 4WD system is similar to the rear axle, but they may not be the same. The most common front axle usage is a Dana. The Dana 44 is very popular, but the smaller Danas, such as the 30 and 35 are also used. The Chrysler 8¼-inch axle is used in some front applications and the Dana 60 is sometimes used.

It is not uncommon to have the front axle be one size smaller than the rear axle, such as the Dana 44 front and a Dana 60 rear. The AMC 20 and the Chrysler 8¾-inch axles are not used in front locations. Axles that are used in the front have the gears reverse cut. The aftermarket

Wheels studs come in all sizes and shapes. Increasing wheel width to get a larger tire contact patch is the most common change for performance applications. The wide wheels made of aluminum have thick center sections and tend to use long-shouldered nuts. The end of the stud should protrude past the top of the nut, which makes longer wheel studs very popular. The end of the stud is sometimes rounded and the beginning of the stud has no threads. This helps install the nuts.

The fabricated axle housing is the end of the road. Once a manufacturer can build a fabricated housing, it they can build any axle design. The appearance of fabricated axle housings is unique. They are not legal in all racing classes. Moser made this 8¾-inch Chrysler axle housing.

The housing for a FWD axle in a 4WD system looks unusual because of its steering knuckles (ends) and shorter length of the axle tubes; also many use a high pinion.

lists these special gear sets, same ratio, that are called reverse cut. Other than the special gears sets, the front axles rebuild the same as the same design rear axle.

Some builders turn the front axle upside-down in certain off-road applications. These unique front axles are called high-pinion axles and is done to gain clearance to the ground. This is only done is the front position.

### Narrowed Axles

The most obvious feature of an axle shaft is its length from the end of the splines to the face of the flange. Any given set of production axle shafts are designed for the specific width of that axle shaft housing. If the production housing is narrowed, the axle shafts must be shortened.

In the late 1960s and early 1970s, some production axles were actually shortened, but since then, it is much easier to make all-new axle shafts to the desired specifications. Many manufacturers offer axle shortening service. The reason for narrowing the axle housing is to gain tire clearance. Narrowed axle assemblies come with shorter axles than the production version.

### Axle Flanges

On the outer end of the axle, the large disc is part of the axle is called the flange. Typically, five studs are pressed into the flange. The bolt circle diameter of the studs in the flange dictates the wheel's bolt circle. That means that the wheel's bolt circle must match the bolt circle of the studs in the flange of the axle. In turn, the flange must match the brake drums or rotors. This is not usually an issue. Most AMC and Chrysler cars use the 5-on-4½-inch bolt circle. Many Jeep and Dodge trucks use this same bolt pattern. However, there are Jeeps and trucks that have larger bolt patterns such as 5-on-5-inch and even six or eight bolts.

The main exception to the 4½-inch bolt circle car group is the 1960–1972 A-Body Chrysler products (Valiant, Dart, early Barracuda, Duster, Demon, etc.). All of these cars had a 5-on-4-inch bolt circle, which required 4-inch bolt circle wheels. Wheels with this small bolt circle are hard to find for special projects like racing, customs or oversized wheel applications. The 4½-inch bolt circle is desired for racing and other custom projects. Moser, Strange, Mark Williams, or another aftermarket axle maker could make custom axle shafts for this application.

A second approach is to swap axles. In 1973, the 4½-inch bolt circle was introduced on the A-Body cars. This axle also used disc brakes on the rear. These 1973 and newer 8¼-inch axle shafts do not fit the older 8¾-inch axles. However, the complete 8¼-inch axle assembly from the 1973–1976 Chrysler A-Body cars can be swapped into the earlier 1967–1972 cars. They have the same width and suspension mounts, but you may have difficulty with the parking brake cables.

## High-Performance Aftermarket Axles

Racing is the outlet for aftermarket products, and in the early days of aftermarket differentials, many racing applications needed narrowed axle shafts. As axle shaft technology improved, the sanctioning bodies began allowing spools in more and more classes/categories. The spool demands better axle shafts and the aftermarket met this demand. The aftermarket got to where they could make anything. Once manufacturers had the technology and basic tooling, they could make anything.

The typical production axle shaft has splines on one end, and a flange on the other end. In between, there tends to be steps or areas in which the axle shaft diameter is different than the spline diameter. There can be undercut sections or forged area reductions. The first heavy-duty axle shafts offered improved machining—no undercuts, and big, full radii where the shaft transitions from one area to another, such as shaft to flange. These axles were also built with better steel and better, deeper heat-treats. Through racing, the strength and performance of axle assemblies greatly improved, and now that technology has been carried over to the aftermarket. Products that were developed on the race track are offered for high-performance street vehicles. The high-tech axle shafts of today offer many advantages over the production units, not just the shorter length required by a narrowed axle. Manufacturers also offer almost any length and any bolt circle desired.

### Material

The typical production axle shaft is made of SAE 1055 or 1541 steel. The axle shafts are forged and then machined. The super-high-strength steel used in racing axle shafts is somewhat of a closely guarded secret, but is probably made of one of the chrome-moly-nickel high-strength steel alloys, such as 4343 and 300M. Heat treat specifics are also closely guarded, but they cover 100 percent of the shaft and extend deeper into the steel.

## Axle Housing

The axle housing is the largest single piece of the rear axle, and its job is to hold everything together. As has been mentioned earlier, the banjo and the carrier-tube are the two kinds of axle housings. The one-piece banjo housing looks like a banjo with the center section removed.

Carrier-tube axles include the AMC 20, the Danas, the Chrysler 7¼-, 8¼-, and the 9¼-inch. The carrier tube axle housing is actually three separate pieces,

*This Chrysler 8¾-inch banjo axle housing has a center section that removes toward the front of the vehicle. The round center section at the rear is part of the housing and does not remove. The spring seats are welded-on, on each housing tube toward each end, and the axle shaft flanges mark the end of the assembly.*

*Carrier-tube axles are constructed of three pieces: the center section or carrier axle tube (left), and the axle tube (right). This Dana axle has a coil-spring suspension with the spring seat welded on top of each axle tube.*

*The Chrysler 8¾-inch banjo axle removes toward the front by removing 10 nuts. It is the only one of the axles discussed in this book that removes toward the front.*

which includes the central carrier, and two axle tubes pressed-in from each side and spot-welded. This type of carrier-tube construction lends itself to being narrowed, so it is only fitting that the Dana 60 was the one that started the trend toward narrowed axles.

The standard (or production) banjo axle housing has the same width, and also has brackets welded on for the rear

suspension to attach or locate the axle. The wheels actually attach to the axle shaft flange. Removing the axle shafts reveals the backing plate bolted to the end of the axle tube. There are typically four or five bolts, and the pattern is unique to the axle design.

While there are many patterns, only a few relate directly to the Chrysler/Dana axles. Perhaps the most popular Chrysler axle pattern is the five-bolt Mopar pattern from the Dana 60 and Chrysler 8¾-inch. (It is the only five-bolt pattern while the rest are four-bolt patterns.) The 8¼- and 9¼-inch Chrysler axles use a smaller four-bolt pattern. Strange Engineering offers a large Mopar tube pattern. Moser, Strange, Mark Williams, and Lamb each offer a symmetrical four-bolt pattern (3 inches square).

Almost all of the axles use the basic 3-inch tubes. Smaller axles use smaller axle tubes. For example, the Chrysler 7¼-inch axle uses 2½-inch tubes. This isn't really an issue until you try to attach the rear suspension brackets to the tubes in an axle swap (new car construction).

Some aftermarket fabricators offer brackets with the smaller (or bigger) radii. However, on the newer versions of the 7¼-inch axles, the axle tubes are swedged, which means that they change diameters. The end that presses into the center section stays the same size, but the

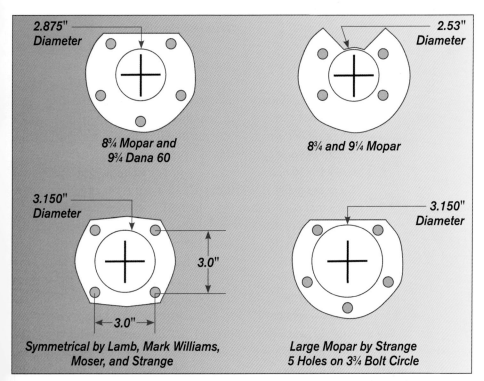

8¾ Mopar and 9¾ Dana 60 — 2.875" Diameter

8¾ and 9¼ Mopar — 2.53" Diameter

Symmetrical by Lamb, Mark Williams, Moser, and Strange — 3.150" Diameter, 3.0", 3.0"

Large Mopar by Strange 5 Holes on 3¾ Bolt Circle — 3.150" Diameter

*On the end of each axle tube, the axle housing flange has a four- or five-bolt pattern, which matches the retainer and it's used to hold the braking system to the axle housing. The 8¾- and 9¾-inch Chrysler/Dana axles use a five-bolt pattern. The 8¼- and 9¼-inch Chrysler axles use a four-bolt pattern with a large V-notch at the top.*

*Strange Engineering offers a large tube diameter, five-bolt pattern for Mopar axles. Most performance aftermarket axle manufacturers use a symmetrical, 3-inch, four-bolt pattern.*

*The center section case of an 8¾-inch banjo axle removes toward the front. The ring and pinion remain in the housing or case until disassembly on the workbench. Note the casting number toward the lower left, which is used for identification; 489 are the last 3 digits.*

*This Chrysler five-bolt unit has an axle tube flange at the end of the axle tube. Note that the studs are pressed in. The leaf-spring seat (toward the right) is welded on close to the end.*

### Housing Flanges

On the end of each axle tube near the spring seat and brake assembly, there is a small flange that is part of the tube itself. This flange has four or five bolts (studs in most cases). It holds the brake assembly onto the axle housing assembly.

### Center Housings/Cases

On the banjo axle (Chrysler 8¾-inch), the center section removes toward the front of the vehicle and the main part of this center section is the housing or case.

The last three digits of the casting number identify these cases: the 741 is the small-stem pinion and not used in racing competition; the 742 is the large-stem pinion and is very popular in racing; and the 489 is the tapered pinion and also popular in racing. Mopar Performance sells an aluminum version of the 742 case, which is much lighter and has added ribs for increased strength and stiffness. A nodular iron reproduction of the 489 case is also available.

### Center Carriers

The center part of all carrier-tube axles is called the carrier or carrier housing. The two tubes are pressed into the center housing and welded to make the assembly.

outer ends have a 3-inch diameter so that all suspension brackets from other larger axles fit.

The large bolt pattern on the center of the housing is unique for this group of axles. The banjo axle (the Chrysler 8¾-inch) has a ten-bolt pattern on the front of the housing. The Dana 44 and 60 patterns are on the rear. Both have ten-bolt patterns but the Dana 60 is about 1 inch wider than the Dana 44. The 8¼-inch Chrysler is also a ten-bolt cover and it is on the rear but its shape is round. At the big end of the list is the twelve-bolt Chrysler 9¼-inch axle and the almost-round AMC 20, which has twelve bolts also. No two of these patterns are the same.

*The Chrysler/Dana 60 9¾-inch carrier-tube axle removes toward the rear by removing 10 nuts. There are many axles that remove in the same direction and also have 10 attaching bolts.*

*Strange Engineering has introduced its own version of the 9¾-inch 60 axle. They are brand new. Strange has added the side adjusters inside the case. The adjuster fits between the main cap and the carrier housing (in the photo, to the left and to the right). On each side there is a lock screw attached to the main cap that fits into the adjuster to keep it in position.*

### Narrowed Housings

The basic narrowed housing is an axle based on a production version. Let's assume that it was a 1970 Challenger axle (one of the widest Dana axles used in passenger cars, at 56.5 inches) and it was narrowed 3 inches per side. While this is correct, it doesn't tell you what you've got. For example, the 1970 Road Runner had a narrower production axle (54.9 inches) than the Challenger. Other body styles are even narrower than the Road Runner.

Big Jeeps, such as the Cherokee, have wider axles than smaller Jeeps, such as the Wrangler. In the early days of narrowed axles, Chrysler found that it was helpful for the customer to know the width of the axle (such as 52½ inches) rather than how much it was narrowed. So the first narrowed axles (Dana 60s) were called 52½-inch axles (Super Stock) and the second version (Pro Stock) was a 44.0-inch axle. Both of these axles were complete assemblies.

After a rush for these factory-offered, brand-new axles in the early to mid 1970s, they faded away and haven't been offered for many years. Custom axles, which have many more features, from many aftermarket manufacturers

*Narrowed rear axles tend to look somewhat short or stubby. The shocks or springs tend to get close together and often sit much more vertical (straight up and down) than the production system.*

*Many Jeep axles are currently available for the J8 Dana 60 and several versions of the Rubicon are available from Mopar Performance.*

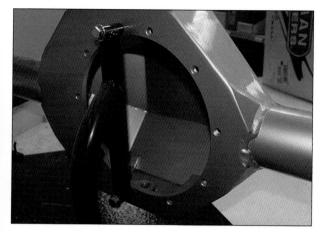

*The flat face of this flange doesn't have the attaching studs pressed in yet. The 8¾-inch center section bolts to this face. (The vertical bar is not part of the axle housing and is used for display purposes only.)*

replaced these special axles. However, as of this writing, the Dana crate axles are on the horizon, but whether they can get to these numbers (widths) hasn't been published yet.

*Jeep Specials:* A special axle was installed on some Jeep models based on needs or requirements for the vehicles. In some cases, it was just a special ratio or a special limited-slip or locker, or bigger/better brakes. The Rubicon received one of the special axles. Currently, the J8 seems to be the most popular of these special axles or models. Perhaps its popularity is related to the difficulty of finding them.

The J8 is a military Jeep Wrangler with 5-on-5½-inch bolt circle wheels and features a Dana 60 axle with a 4.10:1 ratio and limited-slip differential. The J8 military Jeep was built for export only, and that makes it hard to find in the United States. However, Mopar Performance currently sells special J8 axles (Dana 60s) in two configurations: leaf and coil springs. They also carry the special Rubicon axle and several others. These axles are complete assemblies, such as brakes, brackets, yoke and cover, ready to install.

### Fabricated Housings

Other than ratios and limited-slips, almost everything in racing rear axles started with the 9¾-inch Dana 60 axle. As muscle car engines made more power

and torque and tires got better, the cars went faster and axles were in jeopardy of breaking. Bigger, stronger axles were needed and the Dana 60 was the answer for this application.

*Braces:* The next step in axle technology was adding braces to the housing to help reduce axle deflections, which were causing axle failures.

The added bracing approach was used on the banjo/8¾-inch axles. The braces ran from simple and short to long and large. It usually ran from left to right along the back of the axle tubes and across the center housing, with consideration for getting the ring gear and differential out (in order to service it). These

braces were welded to the existing axles.

*Cover Stiffeners:* The stiff rear cover may have evolved from other bracing attempts on carrier-tube axles, but they seem to be a straightforward approach. The cast cover (aluminum) is thicker and has stiffening ribs to help spread the load. The ten-plus bolts attach it to the housing. To this basic approach, manufacturers add a bridge across the rear and tie it into the main caps for added stiffness.

*Fabricated 8¾:* Next came the fabricated housing, which incorporated the rear brace in its construction, so it didn't need to be added at a later date. The housings are very strong and stiff. While the Dana 9¾-inch was one of the first housings, the fabricated units are now hard to find. It always seemed as though once you could build a 9¾-inch axle or a 9-inch axle, then you could built anything, but it took a few years to happen. Moser offers a fabricated 8¾-inch axle that looks like other fabricated axles and offers similar advantages. It is a banjo axle and incorporates the 8¾-inch removable center sections.

*Stamped Banjo 8¾:* Moser offers a complete stamped-steel banjo housing for the Chrysler 8¾-inch axle. The

*The leaf-spring spring seat is pretty straight forward, but some rear suspensions require many additional welded-on brackets. For the leaf-spring suspension, a spring seat welds to the axle.*

*Coil springs need a spring seat too, but they also need brackets for the links or controls arms, brackets for the track bars, and perhaps brackets for the shocks depending on the design. If the vehicle, suspension, and axle housing stay the same, it is not a concern when swapping axles or axle housings. Note that the upper control arm of the suspension is attached to the top of the housing.*

This modified four-link rear suspension has the bracket (arrow) holding the pivots to the axle tube. The coil-over shock is behind the four-link bracket.

This typical four-link, drag race suspension has multiple holes in the upper bracket (toward the upper left) and the lower link (below the four-bolt flange, lower left) are desired for four-link adjustment. The basic housing is a fabricated unit.

These spring seats are welded to the axle tubes and are designed for a leaf-spring suspension. They have a 3-inch tube radius. Do not try to cut off the old spring seats intending to re-use them. Just use new ones. The head of the leaf spring center bolt pilots in the round hold in the center of the flat part of the spring seat.

complete housing is the largest part of an axle. Carrier-tube axles can be broken down into two axle tubes and the center housing, but the housing is a solid one-piece unit in a banjo-style axle. The banjo-style housing allows rear stiffeners to be welded-on to increase the axle stiffness. This straightforward approach is not as easily done on carrier-tube axles because the rear cover must remain accessible.

## Brackets

Brackets are most often welded onto the axle where they are used to locate the axle on the rear suspension. One bracket is used on either side for a typical leaf-spring suspension car. Coil-sprung cars use many brackets, which often includes two for the coils and two or more for the various control arms and track bars.

The type of rear suspension and the body model of the vehicle typically determines the specific brackets required. Aftermarket companies offer axle housings and complete assemblies with the brackets already welded on, in the proper location, which can be very helpful and

saves you a tremendous amount of time. Note that the Jeep CJ and YJ both use leaf springs on all four corners. The Jeep TJ uses coil springs on all four corners.

One feature of many brackets is that they are designed for mounting directly to the axle tube. This means that the diameter of the axle tube is a major concern. The most common tube diameter is 3 inches. Some of the smaller axles,

such as the Chrysler 7¼-inch axle, have 2½-inch tubes. The newer 7¼-inch model uses swedged tubes which means that the outer ends are 3 inches, but the center is 2½ inches.

Some axles have brackets mounted to the center part of the axle, rather than the outer ends. This location is dictated by the rear suspension design. These bracket designs aren't concerned with the 3-inch diameter. Instead, height, compound angle(s), and location are very important to proper suspension operation. Aftermarket manufacturers offer axles with these brackets already installed.

The spring seat is welded on the bottom side of the tube. The suspension bracket is bolted onto the tube using two large U-bolts. If a leaf spring is used, it fits between the spring seat and the bracket; two U-bolts hold it in place.

*Two of these pinion snubbers (top) are special performance units. The other two are basic production units with the rubber bumper at the bottom.*

*This adjustable pinion snubber is typically used in drag racing. Vertical square tubing (one piece inside the other) replaced the original rubber bumper. The bumper is now raised at the top. The pin at the center adjusts the snubber.*

### Spring Seats

Spring seats are the most common brackets, and are welded to the axle tubes. In a leaf-spring suspension, the spring seat is located the axle in the vehicle and holds the axle to the suspension. In a coil-spring suspension, the spring seat is welded to the top of the axle tube and more (separate) brackets are used to locate the axle in the chassis.

### Pinion Snubbers

The pinion snubber is actually part of the suspension system, but bolts to the top of the axle housing in the center, so it is also technically a bracket. Two or three threaded holes on the top of the axle housing are used to mount the pinion snubber. The pinion snubber comes in several sizes with various features, but the production design is a steel bracket that bolts to the axle and a square rubber bumper mounted on the front end with attaching bolts at the rear of the bracket.

## Upgrades and Swapping

Axle shafts and special housings were the first axle parts after the ring-and-pinion to be modified. Once the aftermarket manufacturers started making fabricated housings, any upgrade tended to end at the fabricated housing. Moser released the fabricated 8¾-inch axle, which is probably the most difficult to make, because it is a banjo axle.

Fabricated axles are more expensive than stock axles, so consider if buying such an axle is necessary. Can you afford it and is it legal in your class or category (if the vehicle is used in competition)? Another thing to consider is appearance. Fabricated axles do not look like production axles.

*This 8¾-inch Chrysler banjo axle has a stiffening brace added to the rear of the housing. It extends almost from one spring seat to the other spring seat. These braces can be purchased separately for the 8¾-inch axle. They are welded to the housing.*

*This DTS axle cover is a cast-aluminum design but has added ribs and stiffeners to help strengthen a carrier-tube axle. This one is for a 12-bolt, 9¼-inch axle.*

Many key items from the muscle car era are no longer available. Most of the engines are no longer produced—the 426 Hemi ended in 1971, the 440 in 1978, the 383/400 in 1978, The 360 in 1992, the 340 in 1973. Many of the axles discussed in this book were used in the muscle car era and are now gone (the Chrysler 8¾-inch ended production in 1973). The AMC 20 stopped in 1986. On the flipside, Dana axles, such as the 44 and 60, date back to the muscle car era and are still available today—brand new!

### Covers

All carrier-tube axles use a bolt-on cover on the rear of the housing. The number of bolts in this cover and the shape of the bolt pattern are used in axle identification. The banjo axles do not use a rear cover. Typical production covers are stamped-steel and painted. The first upgrade was to a chrome-plated unit. Since then, rear covers now come in all sizes and shapes, many with special logos.

### Braces

Adding braces to standard production axles may be what lead to the creation of the fabricated axle. Adding braces to a banjo axle (the Chrysler 8¾-inch axle) is reasonably easy because it can go straight across the rear of the tubes and housing. The ring and pinion in the center section go out the front so they do not need to be considered in this application.

In carrier-tube axles, braces added to the rear allow for the fact that the rear cover has to be removed and the ring gear and differential must be removed to the rear. In some cases this means that the rear cover is often designed into the overall brace/stiffener system (bosses, ribs and extra bolts).

### Crate Axles

In 2012, Dana introduced a new axle program called crate axles. These are fully assembled axles (to the studs in the axle shafts). Dana currently has axle ratios of 3.73 through 4.56:1, with 4.88 and 5.13:1 available soon. It is offering both the Dana 44 and Dana 60 versions. Additionally, Dana offers axles for both the front and rear locations.

### Gaskets

On banjo axles, there is a large gasket between the center section and the main housing. On carrier-tube axles, there is a rear cover sealed with RTV or a gasket that bolts to the center housing. Aftermarket units seem to prefer the use of a gasket, while production units lean toward the use of RTV.

### Banjos

The Chrysler 8¾-inch banjo axle uses a gasket and has ten studs mounted in the flange face. These studs hold the gasket in place while the center section is installed over the studs. If you want the gasket to sit flat against the face, spray it with gasket sealer to help the gasket to stick.

### Carrier-Tubes

RTV is recommended for most production carrier-tube axles. However, aftermarket companies service actual gaskets for these same carrier-tube axles. In most cases, if you upgrade to a special rear cover, such as chrome, aluminum or heavy-duty/special, the manufacturer often provides a gasket for use with the cover. Axle rebuild kits also lean toward gaskets. Gasket are easily damaged and should not be re-used. If you only need the axle gasket, they are serviced separately by Mr. Gasket and Fel-Pro or they are available from one of the distributors listed in sidebars "Rebuild Kit Sources" on page 29 and "Ring-and-Pinion Sources" on page 151.

With the carrier-tube axle, screws (not studs) hold on the cover. If you spray the gasket with gasket sealer, it tends to stay in place while you grab the cover and get it into position to install the screws.

*Dana is offering crate axles that come as complete assemblies. These are based on the Dana 44 and Dana 60 axles, plus a couple more. There are both front and rear versions. The initial ratios are 3.73, 4.10, and 4.56, with 4.88 and 5.13 due to be added later.*

# AXLE HARDWARE

The rear axle rebuilding process is mainly concerned with the rear axle itself, the differential, the axle shafts, ring and pinion, housings, and parts that directly affect these parts. Similar to almost every part or assembly in a four-wheel vehicle, the axle is an area of concern.

The main concerns for the rear axle are basic upgrades and repairs. Twenty-five years ago, axle ratio selection and the addition of a production limited-slip were about the only changes made in the axle area. Everything else fit into the repair/service category. Today, the changes and upgrades are almost without limit.

## Yokes

The yoke is splined to the front of the pinion and a large nut holds it on. The screws/nuts that hold the driveshaft to the yoke are the first fasteners to be removed during an axle rebuild. The yoke's internal spline must match the pinion's splines. While various axles are similar, the specific splines tend to be unique to the axle design. Perhaps the one exception to this rule is the Chrysler 8¾-inch axle, which has two different splines: 10 (coarse) and 29 (fine).

The second aspect of the yoke is the size and style of U-joint that is being used. The Chrysler 7290 U-joint is about 1/2 inch wider than the 7260 version. Being larger also means that it is stronger, but the yoke must match the U-joint. U-joint retention of the yoke is done by either a small U-bolt and nuts or a strap and two screws.

*The large ring at the bottom of the yoke is a dust shield that helps protect the pinion seal. The height (length) of the yoke is important and tends to be unique to each axle design.*

*Most production yokes are made of cast iron. The splined-hole in the center slides onto the pinion, and a large nut and washer hold it on. Four screws or two small U-bolts (one at each corner) fasten the driveshaft to the yoke.*

*The U-bolt method of attaching the driveshaft to the yoke uses two small U-bolts that go across the top of the U-joint itself, one per side. Two nuts per U-bolt are attached on the back side.*

The strap and two bolt method of attaching the driveshaft to the yoke uses a metal strap across the top and two screws that attach each strap to the yoke. In OEM axles, production straps are by far the most popular.

Most production yokes were made of cast iron (cast or forged). Today, the aftermarket offers various versions of all these original yokes, and these plus steel and aluminum (7075-T6 versions) are CNC-machined from billets.

## U-Joints

The typical production vehicle has one U-joint on each end of the driveshaft. With any axle, U-joints come in two or three sizes—small and large. The U-joint must also be designed for the style of driveshaft retention strap or U-bolt. In passenger cars, the strap and two screws is by far the most popular system.

The cross length is one factor in the size and strength of the U-joint. The diameter of the bearing cap is another factor. The style of U-joint varies between attaching methods (straps and U-bolts).

The U-joint sits in the saddle of the yoke. Two screws or a strap on each side retain the U-joint. The small tab at the bottom of the saddle keeps the bearing cap in place. (The bearing cap has been removed from the opposite side for display purposes.)

The straps or U-bolts are only used in the rear U-joint.

The 1310, 1330, and 1350 numbers are from Spicer. The 1330 U-joint was used in the big-block, high-horsepower engines with manual transmissions (426 Hemi and 440 cars). The 7260 (small) and 7290 (large) are from Chrysler.

In many cases, serious drag race and many off-road 4WD vehicles upgrade to the U-bolt system. This requires the U-joint and the yoke to change.

A CV joint is a special type of U-joint. A common adapter joins the two U-joints. These are very important in vehicles that have high driveshaft angles. High driveshaft angles are more common in vehicles with shorter wheelbases. Note that these U-joints are held in by a snap-ring. The Spicer unit is shown.

This style of driveshaft retention has a small U-bolt on each side of the U-joint. The U-bolt goes across the top of the U-joint and the two nuts are attached on the underside of the yoke saddles. The bearing caps or cups on the ends of the cross are not in the saddle of the yoke. When the driveshaft is removed from the yoke, the cross looks like this, which holds the caps/cups on. I recommend running tape around the cross to keep them in place.

In many high-performance and racing applications, customers choose to upgrade the rear U-joint by using U-bolts rather than straps and screws. This conversion requires a new yoke (readily available for all axles), the U-bolts and nuts, and the new joint.

Aftermarket companies offer U-joints that can adapt various driveshafts to various rear axles by having two styles of U-joint in the same part. The two vertical caps are one style, and the two horizontal caps are another. For example, if you have a 7290 Chrysler yoke and a driveshaft with a 7260 U-joint, there are special U-joints to mate them.

Another popular upgrade, especially in Jeeps and off-road applications, is the CV ("CV" stands for "constant velocity) joint. This joint is actually a double U-joint, one right next to the other. CV joints are highly recommended for vehicles with high driveshaft angles. This high-angle situation is particularly important with short-wheelbase vehicles, such as Jeep Wranglers.

### Driveshafts

The driveshaft delivers all the torque to the rear axle. It connects to the rear axle through the yoke and U-joint. The yoke must match the U-joint, and on the other end of the driveshaft, the weld-cap must match the U-joint. Chrysler sold a 3¼-inch HP driveshaft kit for many years but the most popular one today seems to be a 3-inch diameter tube. Many production tube diameters were smaller in the 2½- and 2¾-inch area. Another aspect of driveshafts is that the HP aftermarket tubes tend to be straight, one size/diameter all the way, while many production tubes were swedged, meaning the diameter was reduced at one end or both.

Today most aftermarket driveshaft tubes are made of chrome-moly steel. The 3-inch diameter is the most common, but larger ones are used in certain racing applications. Lightweight versions are made of 6061 aluminum.

### Pinion Snubbers

A pinion snubber is actually a rear suspension part, but it bolts to the top of the axle housing center section. Pinion snubbers were used on all high-performance Chrysler cars in the muscle car era. They bolt to a flat pad on the top of the center section of the axle housing. All Chrysler 8¾-inch axles have this pad. Most other Chrysler axles used in passenger cars also have the pad. The tricky one is the Dana 60 (9¾-inch) axle. Dana 60 axles were used in the 1966–1971 big-block cars, 426 Hemi and 440s. For a long time, the Chrysler version of the Dana 60 was the most popular and most readily available version of this axle. All the racers used it because it was the only axle that could withstand the abuse from high-horsepower, manual-transmission drag cars.

Today Dana makes many other versions that are more readily available and most of these do not have the pinion snubber pad machined. The basic pinion snubber helps keep manual transmissions from breaking driveshafts and U-joints if a mistake is made. In street cars, you can use the pinion snubber to help the car hook-up in acceleration conditions.

*Pinion snubber attaches above the yoke and bolts directly to the center housing of the axle. Pinion snubbers are commonly used on passenger cars. In production, it is used mainly as a safety device but in racing it is additionally used to help in acceleration situations. In this aspect, the snubber needs to be adjustable–the height can be increased. Note the two bolts toward the bottom of photo that hold snubber in place, The pin goes through the square bracket and the retaining clip can be seen on the left side. Removing the clip and pin allow the height of the snubber/bumper to be adjusted. Axle carrier is toward the top of the photo.*

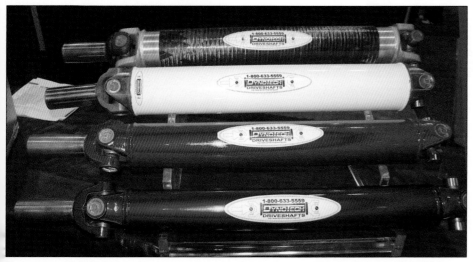

*The black driveshaft (top) is a composite. It's the strongest and the most expensive. Typical aftermarket driveshaft tubes are made of chrome-moly steel (red and blue), which is stronger than the original material. Aluminum driveshaft tubes (second from top) are lighter and made from a special alloy selected for the driveshaft application. Note that the ears on each end of the driveshaft are in line. This alignment should always exist. The second one from the top is a 4-inch tube; the third one from the top is a 3½-inch tube; and the bottom one is a 3-inch tube.*

*The production-style Chrysler pinion snubber for the 8¾-inch banjo axle is not adjustable and sits right above the axle's yoke. It is bolted to the top of the carrier housing. To the right, the rubber bumper is fitted into the bracket.*

All production pinion snubbers were fixed at a given height. Aftermarket companies offer adjustable units for performance applications. The standard adjustable unit adjusts with a pin, meaning there are only a few height settings available. Newer snubbers have a threaded adjustment for unlimited height settings.

## Brakes

Brake assemblies bolt to the ends of the axle tubes, and are not directly involved in an axle rebuild. If the axle is left in the vehicle, once the brake drum or rotor is removed from the system, the axles can be removed and the brakes set aside until reassembly.

Many early passenger cars were built with 9-inch drum brakes. There were also 10- and 11-inch rear drum brakes. When most passenger cars and trucks went to disc brakes, production companies maintained drum brakes on the rear. In the past few years, disc brake conversions for these production axles have become very common.

The bolt pattern in the end flange at the end of each axle tube is the point where the two systems are brought together. Each axle design has its own bolt pattern. (See Chapter 9 for more detail on axle housings.) Brake kit manufacturers offer a wide range of kits.

Off-road Jeeps have a similar problem because big tires are often installed. Big tires require better brakes. Most Jeeps have had front disc brakes since 1980,

*The drum brake mechanism is more complicated than you might think. With the actual brake drum removed, you can see the front shoe (left) and part of the right shoe (right). Typical rear drum brakes come in three basic sizes: 9, 10, and 11 inches. This brake drum assembly bolts to the axle tube ends by four or five bolts. The axle design determines the number of bolts and the pattern. The large pilot hole in the center of the assembly has four small holes in it. Only two are used to hold the assembly to the display board.*

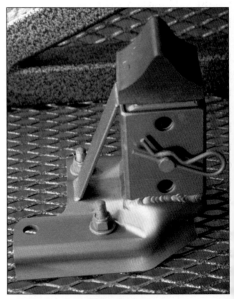

*This is an adjustable pinion snubber. The pin and the retaining clip can be removed so the snubber can be moved up. In positions higher than stock, the snubber contacts the body sooner and affects the rear suspension actions, especially in hard acceleration from low speeds or a standing start.*

*Rear disc brakes aren't very common on many muscle cars. Recently, aftermarket manufacturers offer kits to upgrade rear drum brakes to disc brakes. The disc brake rotor (large round part in the center) is the easy part. It fits over the studs in the axle shaft, so the bolt pattern is important. This rotor is drilled for two different five-bolt patterns. The caliper (large part that sits over the rotor in the upper right) actually mounts to a bracket that bolts to the end of the axle tubes.*

*The disc brake caliper attaches to a bracket that is attached to the axle tube. The disc brake pads are located inside the caliper and rub directly on the rotor. The brake line attaches to the backside of the caliper.*

*All carrier-tube axles have a cover on the rear side of the center section. The cover has a unique shape and a specific number of bolts holding it on, which help to identify the axle. In production, these covers are typically painted black. The aftermarket offers chrome-steel and cast-aluminum units. The factory often recommended using RTV as the cover gasket while the aftermarket offers actual gaskets.*

but the rears can use an upgrade. Jeeps use the rear disc brakes from the larger Grand Cherokee, which have the same pattern on the tube ends.

Disc brakes provide far better performance than drums, so if that option is available, they are preferred because they offer better fade resistance. There are advantages and disadvantages to both. Typically the performance drum rear brake is heavier than the equivalent disc brake package. Disc brakes also tend to operate better in adverse conditions, such as water or mud.

Most production vehicles use a reinforced rubber brake line from the body to the axle. Because these lines must operate in a pretty hostile environment, consider upgrading to braided steel brake lines.

## Rear Covers

Most production rear covers on carrier-tube axle designs use a stamped-steel cover. The typical first upgrade is to a chrome steel cover. Chrome covers are readily available from the aftermarket.

The next step is a cast-aluminum cover, which are also readily available in the aftermarket and come in many styles. Some special cast-aluminum covers have braces on the rear side and thicker sections for more rigidity. These covers offer added strength and stiffness to the axle.

Many production carrier-tube axles recommend using RTV to seal the cover to the housing based on factory information. Most aftermarket units use an actual gasket.

## Axle Lubes

The last thing to do in an axle rebuild is to fill the axle assembly with oil. The first question to ask before you pour any oil into the housing is: Do you have a limited-slip differential? The reason this is important is because open differentials use a standard rear axle lube. Production-style limited-slip (Sure-Grip) differentials use a special axle fluid. The factories did this with a 4-ounce can of special Sure-Grip additive added to the standard axle lube. Fill the axle half full with the Sure-Grip additive, and then top it off with standard rear axle lube.

The general lubricant recommendation is an API-grade GL5 hypoid gear lubricant, graded SAE 75W-90. For trailer towing and racing, consider upgrading to a synthetic graded at 80W. The tricky part is that many synthetic gear lubri-

cants are good for both open and limited-slip differentials. Double-check with the gear and differential manufacturers for specific recommendations. This is especially true concerning the various gear and locker differentials.

Be aware that most rear axle lubricates have a very strong odor; and, always wear rubber gloves.

It is not easy to pour the oil directly from the bottle/can into the axle. In most cases, you need to fill an oil syringe with the oil. With the syringe's tube inserted through the fill hole, squeeze the oil into the axle.

*The last step in the rebuild process is to add oil to the axle. Rear axle fluid such as this 75W-90, is special. Some rear axle fluids are offered as synthetic (shown). Lucas Oil offers a wide range of gear oils from standard to synthetic. They also come in many viscosities.*

## Axle Specification Chart

A lot of basic specifications relate to the various axles discussed in this book and it can be handy if all of these general specifications are located in one place, such as the chart below. Remember, the Chrysler 8¾-inch is the only banjo axle, which removes the pinion OTF (out the front). All the rest of the axles are basic carrier-tube axles that remove the pinion OTB (out the back).

| Axle | Chrysler 7.25 | Chrysler 8.25, 8.375 | Chrysler 9.25 | Chrysler 8-3/4 |
|---|---|---|---|---|
| Production Years | 1960–1985, 9 bolt | 1971–1988 in cars | 1970–1985 in cars | 741 case, 1957–1968 |
| | 1986–1997, 10 bolt | 1966–present in trucks | 1966-present in trucks | 742 case, 1957–1968 |
| | | | | 489 case, 1969–1974 |
| Style | Carrier-tube | Carrier-tube | Carrier-tube | Banjo |
| Ring Gear Diameter (inches) | 7.250 | 8.250, 8.375 | 9.250 | 8.750 |
| Ring Gear Attaching Bolts | 8 | 10 | 12 | 12 |
| Thread Size | 3/8 x 24 LH | 3/8 x 24 LH | 7/16 x 20 LH | 3/8 x 24 LH |
| Cover Bolts | 9 or 10 | 10 | 12 | None |
| Third-Member Bolts | | | | 10 |
| Carrier Breaks | 2.47/2.76 | 2.45/2.56 and up | None | None |
| Pinion Spline (inches/teeth) | 1.375/27 | 1.625/27 | 1.875/29 | 1.750 x 10 |
| | | | 1.875 x 29 | (742 case, straight pin |
| | | | | (489 case, tapered pin |
| Housing Attaching Bolts | | | | 10 |
| Side Gear Teeth | | 27 | 31 | 30 |

| AMC 20 | Dana 30 | Dana 35 | Dana 44 | Dana 60 |
|---|---|---|---|---|
| 1968–1986 | 1967–present | 1984–present | 1960–present<br>1966–1973 in cars | 1963–present (all) |
| Carrier-tube | Carrier-tube | Carrier-tube | Carrier-tube | Carrier-tube |
| 8.875 | 7.200 | 7.562 | 8.500 | 9.750 |
| 8 | 10 | 8 | 10 | 12 |
| 7/16 x 20 RH | 3/8 x 24 RH | 3/8 x 24 RH | 3/8 x 24 RH | 1/2 x 20 RH |
| 12 | 10 | 10 | 10 | 10 |
| 2.76/3.07 & up | 3.54/3.73 | 3.31/3.55 | 3.73/3.92 | 4.10/4.56 |
| 1.625/28 | 1.375/26 | 1.375/26 | 1.375/26 | 1.625/29 |
| 29 | 27 | 27 | 19 or 30 | 30 or 35 |

# Source Guide

Advance Adapters
4320 Aerotech Center Way
Paso Robles, CA 93446
www.gotatlas.com

ARB 4 X 4 Accessories
720 S.W. 34th St.
Renton, WA 98057
www.arbusa.com

Auburn Gear
400 E. Auburn Dr.
Auburn, IN 46706
www.auburndiffs.com

Autotech Driveline
29 Journey
Aliso Viejo, CA 92656
www.wavetrac.net

Bickell RaceCars
141 Raceway Park Dr.
Moscow Mills, MO 63362
www.jerrybickel.com

Bicknell Racing Products
1733 Maryland Ave.
Niagara Falls, NY 14305
www.bicknellracingproducts.com

Chassis Engineering
1500 Ave. R
Riviera Beach, FL 33404
www.chassisengineering.com

Chassis Shop
1931 N. 24th Ave.
Mears, MI 49436
www.chassisshop.com

Chassisworks
8661 Younger Creek Dr.
Sacramento, CA 95828
www.cachassisworks.com

Currie Enterprises, Inc
1480 N. Tustin Ave.
Anaheim, CA 92807
www.currieenterprises.com

Dana Holding Corp.
6201 Trust Dr.
Holland, OH 43528
www.dana.com

DTS Drivetrain Specialists
26400 Groesbeck Hwy.
Warren, MI 48089
www.drivetrainspecialists.com

Dynotech Driveshafts
1731 Thorncroft
Troy, MI 48084
www.dynotecheng.com

Eaton Performance Products
26101 Northwestern Hwy.
Southfield, MI 48076
www.eatonperformance.com

ExxonMobil
3225 Gallows Rd.
Fairfax, VA 22037
www.exxonmobil.com

G2 Axle & Gear
400 W. Artesia Blvd.
Compton, CA 90220
www.G2axle.com

Gear Vendors Overdrive
1717 N. Magnolia Ave.
El Cajon, CA 92020
www.gearvendors.com

Inland Empire Driveline
1540 Commerce St.
Corona, CA 92882
www.iedis.com

Jegs
101 Jegs Place
Delaware, OH 43015
www.jegs.com

Jerico Racing Transmission
443 Pitts School Rd. NW
Concord, NC 28027
www.jericoperformance.com

Jerry Bickel Race Cars
141 Raceway Park Dr.
Moscow Mills, MO 63362
www.jerrybickel.com

Keisler Overdrive
2250 Stock Creek Blvd.
Rockford, TN 37853-3043
www.keislerauto.com

Lamb Components
1259 W. 9th St.
Upland, CA 91786
www.lambcomponents.com

Liberty's High Performance Products
6390 Pelham Rd.
Taylor, MI 48180
www.libertygears.com

Lucas Oil Products
302 North Sheridan St.
Corona, CA 92880
www.lucasoil.com

Mancini Racing
P.O. Box 239
Roseville, MI 48066
www.manciniracing.com

Mark Williams Enterprises
765 S. Pierce Ave.
Louisville, CO 80027
www.markwilliams.com

Mopar Performance Parts
www.mopar.com

Moser Engineering
102 Performance Dr.
Portland, IN 47371
www.moserengineering.com

MotiveGear Performance
1001 W. Exchange Ave.
Chicago, IL 60609
www.midwesttruck.com

Passon Performance
309 Turkey Path
Sugarloaf, PA 18249
www.passonperformance.com

Precision Gear
460 Horizon Dr., Ste. 400
Suwanee, GA 30024
www.precisiongear.com

Randy's Ring & Pinion
10411 Airport Rd. SE
Everett, WA 98204
www.ringpinion.com

Ratech
11110 Adwood Dr.
Cincinnati, OH 45240
www.ratechmfg.com

Richmond
1208 Old Norris Rd.
Liberty, SC 29657
www.richmondgear.com

Ring & Pinion Shop
36180 Grosbeck Hwy.
Clinton Twp., MI 48035
586-792-2560

Rockland Standard Gear Inc.
150 Route 17
Sloatsburg, NY 10974
www.rsgear.com

Rugged Ridge
460 Horizon Dr., Ste. 400
Suwanee, GA 30024
www.ruggedridgeoffroad.com

S & W Race Cars
11 Mennonite Church Rd.
Spring City, PA 19475
www.swracecars.com

SMR Transmissions
3030 Concession 8
Bradford, ONT Canada L3Z 2A5
www.smrtrans.com

Spicer
6201 Trust Dr.
Holland, OH 43528
www.dana.com

Stainless Steel Brakes Corp.
11470 Main Rd.
Clarence, NY 14031
www.ssbrakes.com

Strange Engineering
8300 N. Austin Ave.
Morton Grove, IL 60053
www.strangeengineering.net

Summit Racing Equipment
P.O. Box 909
Akron, OH 44309
www.summitracing.com

Superior Axle & Gear
6895 Speedway Blvd., Unit 101
Las Vegas, NV 89115
www.superioraxle.com

The Timken Company
1835 Dueber Ave. S.
canton, OH 44706
www.timken.com

Torsen
Two Jetview Dr.
Rochester, NY 14624
www.torsen.com

Trans-Dapt Performance Products
12438 Putnam St.
Whittier, CA 90602
www.tdperformance.com

US Gear Corp.
9420 Stony Island Ave.
Chicago, IL 60617
www.usgear.com

USA Standard Gear
10411 Airport Rd.
Everett, WA 98204
www.usastandardgear.com

Warren Gear & Axle
3491 Ten Mile
Warren, MI 48091
www.warrengear.comcastbiz.net

Wilwood Disc Brakes
4700 Calle Bolero
Camarillo, CA 93012
www.wilwood.com

Yukon Gear & Axle
10411 Airport Rd.
Everett, WA 98204
www.yukongear.com